# The Fearn Bobby

# Ian McNeish

# THE FEARN BOBBY

## Reflections from a Life in
## Scottish Policing

Ian McNeish

*The Fearn Bobby: Reflections from a Life in Scottish Policing* by Ian McNeish.

First published in Great Britain in 2018 by Extremis Publishing Ltd.,
Suite 218, Castle House, 1 Baker Street, Stirling, FK8 1AL, United Kingdom.
*www.extremispublishing.com*

Extremis Publishing is a Private Limited Company registered in Scotland (SC509983) whose Registered Office is Suite 218, Castle House, 1 Baker Street, Stirling, FK8 1AL, United Kingdom.

A CIP catalogue record for this book is available from the British Library.

ISBN: 978-0-9955897-1-1

Typeset in Goudy Bookletter 1911, designed by The League of Moveable Type.

Printed and bound in Great Britain by IngramSpark, Chapter House, Pitfield, Kiln Farm, Milton Keynes, MK11 3LW, United Kingdom.

Front cover artwork is Copyright © Joceline Hildrey Illustration, all rights reserved. *jocelinehildrey@yahoo.com*
Back cover artwork from Pixabay.
Cover design and book design is Copyright © Thomas A. Christie.
Author images are Copyright © Anne McNeish (internal) and Eddy A. Bryan (cover).
Incidental illustrations by Qubodup at Openclipart.org.

Excerpts from *Coal Not Dole: Memories of the 1984/85 Miners' Strike* by Guthrie Hutton (2005) are reproduced by kind permission of Stenlake Publishing Ltd., all rights reserved.

Internal photographic illustrations are Copyright © Ian McNeish, unless otherwise indicated. While every reasonable effort has been made to contact copyright holders and secure permission for all images reproduced in this work, we offer apologies for any instances in which this was not possible and for any inadvertent omissions.

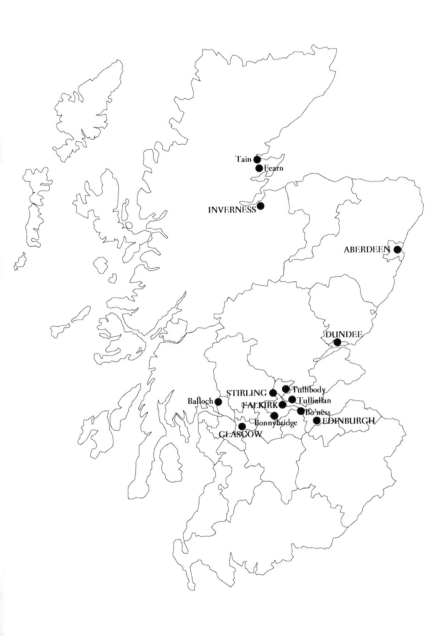

Tain
Fearn

INVERNESS

ABERDEEN

DUNDEE

STIRLING    Tullibody
            Tulliallan
Balloch  FALKIRK
         Bo'ness
         Bonnybridge   EDINBURGH
GLASGOW

# THE FEARN BOBBY

## Reflections from a Life
## in Scottish Policing

Ian McNeish

# INTRODUCTION

I was enjoying my retirement. Cycling, the occasional game of curling, a hill every so often, and a bit of photography. With these and taking in a rugby, or football match every now and then – as well as family connections and coffee shop visits – life was good. Where had I found time to work?

Then along happened Dr Thomas Christie, a thoroughly decent, hard-working and enthusiastic individual. 'I wonder,' quoth he, 'will you write a book for me?'

'Oh? What kind of book?' I tentatively enquired. It was a pointless question as, never having written any kind of book, or even contemplated such a venture, what difference would it make what it was about? It wasn't likely to happen. 'Your policing experience', came the casual, matter-of-fact reply, as if I did this every day.

I managed to blurt out: 'But there are hundreds of books about policing!'

'I know,' he said, 'but yours won't be like the other hundreds'. I did not reject the idea out of hand, and asked for time to consider.

So that is why, in an attempt to find my answer to his question, I found myself stravaiging the country, searching newspaper and Council archives, trying to locate and recall incidents I had been involved in over the years and some other stuff I thought might give the book a touch of gravitas. I found the whole experience cathartic, and a release from some issues that had blocked my mind for years. You will be horrified to know that after a month of searching and deliberating, I reached a decision. I met up with Tom in the ubiquitous coffee shop and gave him my answer. 'Yes, I will give it a go.' To be honest, from the first moment Tom asked the question, I was a bit overawed at the prospect. I just needed time to build some confidence and start believing I could live up to the challenge and not let him down. There would be no ghost writer; I was on my own.

I soon found other motivation to write the book; inspiration, really. It was the many colleagues I had shared so much with over the years. Some horrific experiences, some scary moments. Tragedies. Life and death incidents. Along with their bravery and their simple and meaningful friendship, support and camaraderie. Their ability to keep smiling, when the obvious option was crying and even the moments that we did cry. Their ability to keep getting up and getting on with the next one, whatever that was. And something else; their never-ending capacity to laugh at themselves. I dedicate my efforts in writing this book to every front line officer past and present, but in particular, two officers – friends of mine – who did not come home at the end of their shift. They are Sergeant Harry John Gauld Lawrie, BEM, killed in a helicopter crash during a mountain rescue on Ben More on 1st February 1987, aged 45 years. And Edward James Walton, killed in a road accident while an observer in a patrol vehicle, on 13th May 1989, aged 34 years. I hope I have not let them down.

I was also in mountain rescue and had spent time on the mountain with Harry. On the night he was killed, our team was called out. We mustered in the post at Menstrie, a sad and sombre bunch. As we waited on the order to move to Crianlarich, lying about on the floor of the post, resting on our rucksacks, something happened that none of us will ever forget. One of our team, a folk singer, unearthed his guitar and sung 'The Lion and Albert', made famous by Stanley Holloway. For some bizarre reason (because if you listen to the song, you might wonder why), it seemed to fit our mood and lifted our spirits.

Eddie Walton and I had worked together as constables in Tullibody. In May 1989 I was a Sergeant, working out of the area but resident in Tullibody. Eddie still worked there, and we remained friends. He routinely, on his late shifts, would pop in for some supper. My last memory of Eddie was on one such night in May 1989. My wife was walking backward, in front of him, knocking the crumbs from his uniform as he left the house. We were laughing at the state of his uniform. I never saw him again. He was killed later that week.

I must not forget my mum and dad, for without their love and guidance, I would be nothing. But who, if still alive, would be both baffled and in shock at the thought of me writing a book and – I dare to hope – perhaps a touch proud. As the book develops, the reader will be led thither and yon as I meander through situations and incidents and, occasionally, muse on mysteries, methods and management. It will be obvious why. I just hope you hang on and enjoy the journey.

# CHAPTER 1

IT is the summer of 1976, and my duties are to police the Fearn peninsula in Easter Ross. The police office was a small single room extension, at one end of the house, in the village of Hill of Fearn. It was a single officer station, and I policed the area alone. Just like Hamish Macbeth, really. He was a fictional character in a television drama; a Constable posted to a police office near a rural village, the character was created by M.C. Beaton for a long-running series of novels before being adapted for TV. Sometimes I felt like I was acting in a drama myself. I lived there with my wife and two young sons; a third would follow a year or two later. I was out late patrolling in the Fearn area when my crackling police radio informed me the Tain officers were en route to a serious road accident near Meikle Ferry, just north of the town on the A9. Was I able to assist? It was 20th August 1976; I had barely completed two years police service.

During the 1970s and probably for decades before that, it was the custom – certainly in the north of Scotland – for young people (and some not so young) to follow the weekend dance circuit. It would not be unknown or unusual for some to drive sixty miles or more to reach their destination. Typically these would be quiet village halls from as far afield as Golspie, Evanton, Inver and beyond. Halls that normally hosted the occasional beetle or whist drive, local concerts, as well as a myriad of community-based meetings and events, would – on these weekend nights – be visited by excited hordes of young people intent on listening to and dancing to their favourite local band. I would also guess that some would be travelling the same roads their parents had travelled a generation or so before, and perhaps some would be the result of relationships forged then. It had only taken me a few minutes of blue light driving to get to the scene.

I am soon sitting – sprawled, really – on the driver's door sill of a Sunbeam Rapier that has run out of road and crashed into a stone wall at Ardjackie, beside the A9 just north of Tain, Ross-shire. The car had four occupants, three of whom are out being given first aid and having their injuries assessed by a local doctor, who is also our police surgeon. The driver is laying in my lap with his head on my chest and his feet trapped by the pedals. He isn't moving and he isn't speaking. The doctor, who examined him first, then left me to support and comfort him. On his return a few minutes later, to carry out a second examination, he said, very simply, with no emotion, 'he is dead'. The driver was the son of the car's owner. His journey to the place and time of his death started at a dance in Bonar Bridge. He and his friends were driving to a party in Tain but none made it that night; he never would. The incident passed almost as if I was in a dream. We continued as we were trained to do, with thoroughness, compassion and with professionalism. Nevertheless it was, certainly for me, a humbling and surreal experience. The young man was twenty-one years of age and he died being held by a complete stranger.

I had dealt with death before that point of my career and would again. More often than I care to remember and, even though some did affect me more than others, this was somehow different. Perhaps to some, such an occurrence might not be that unusual, to me it was. Nobody had ever died in my arms before. What right did I have to be the last person holding him when he died? I was a stranger. I did not even know his name at that time. Should one not die in the comforting presence of one's loved ones? It didn't seem fair. But such thoughts, such emotions, are useless, really. They were then, and they are now. It was never about me. William – that was his name, is still his name – would probably have died whatever we did. Selfish or not, I felt remarkably sad, and forty years later as I write this down, I still do. One of my colleagues would have the unenviable task of breaking the terrible news to unsuspecting parents. The ripples caused by the news would wash that shore for a long time and, even if reducing, would never stop. I had feelings of guilt. Could I have done more for William that night on 20$^{th}$ August 1976? My journey to that place had taken me the thirty years of my life, and has taken me most of the rest of my life to try and understand. There is not always an answer.

For thirty years I carried a police Warrant Card. During that time I rose through the ranks from Constable to Chief Inspector. The Warrant Card does not differentiate between ranks and the power it carries is the same, no matter what rank one might achieve. It entrusted me, the holder, with considerable power over my fellow citizens. Given the correct circumstances, I could arrest them, detain and question them, search them, enter their houses without their permission, and more. Some might argue, this card gave the power to affect lives, although I would suggest their own actions were probably what affected their lives; I merely had the power to intervene, enquire and bring those actions to the attention of the appropriate authority. Was I a fit and proper person to wield such power? What was the police service getting when it recruited me? More importantly, what did the various communities I worked in and with get? What did I expect of the police service? Were either of us disappointed? In the pages that follow, I will attempt to explore these questions and perhaps find answers, even if only to myself.

I thought I should include my 'values' at this juncture, but rejected the notion. Values are subjective – as is justice, I suppose. Values are moulded in the environment and customs to which one is exposed. Therefore, as an overarching guide to a person or behaviour, they are perhaps unhelpful and quite meaningless I contend. I am reminded of Carlos Ruiz Zafon's book, *The Angel's Game* (2008), that contained the following: 'Justice is an affectation of perspective, not a universal value'.

I will take you right to the beginning, to where I was born and brought up. What kind of place it was, and how I interacted and immersed myself and allowed it and its people, its history, to infiltrate my very being. I will try to explain the life influences of my parents, and how their experiences percolated to me. What follows, therefore, is an attempt to explain the context of my development – not just within the family setting, but in the community environment where I was raised, including the influence of friends and more. I will also touch on my employment experiences before joining the police service, and when in the police service I will meander through it, covering what I regard as important issues, coupled with actual incidents – sometimes to illustrate points, and sometimes just to tell a story. It is my aim to explain, as best I can, who I am and what made me tick. More importantly, did I serve communities to the best of my ability? Did I handle the power invested in me properly? And lastly, would William's parents – who I never met – have been comforted in some way knowing it was me who held their son when he died?

A person is moulded by many influences: physical, environmental, parents, people met, opportunities afforded, denied, perhaps missed. Decisions, emerging out of that potpourri of circumstance; some not even made by you, all transpiring to shape one's destiny. Psychologists argue that the first eighteen years of one's life is when the most profound changes occur in terms of physical, cognitive and social development. Family, and the social context of the family, is the single most important element in a person's development. I think it a bit more complex than that.

# CHAPTER 2

I AM Ian McNeish, although a look at my birth certificate will show, instead, John McNeish. I am not John McNeish. When my dad registered my birth, he was not allowed to put Ian on the certificate. The Registrar said the Gaelic Ian was not allowed and the English equivalent, John, had to be used. Despite my dad's protest, John it had to be. So I was less than one month old and I had been subjected to a racist act at the hands of the state. I am a 'bulge' baby, born in 1946, just after the Second World War. I was born into a world of Identification Cards, food rationing, and a language quite different in many ways from the language of today; Turf Accountants, The Store, Oddfellows, and other quaint expressions that are largely forgotten. We kept blankets in a cist. There was an explosion of births in the years immediately after the war. Squaddies, getting back to normal, after years of being away from home. My mum was often heard to remark that some babies were born with bruising on their wrist; caused by hanging on until after the wedding. In the USA they referred to the post-War increase in births as 'baby boomers'. In Britain, these post-War births were called 'bulge babies', not 'baby boomers'. Over the years our language has been eclipsed by foreign terms, particularly American terms. Hence 'baby boomers' is now common usage by our 'informed'

media and others. Our own, perfectly acceptable term, 'bulge babies' has been destined to the language dustbin. Similarly hijacked is our Hallowe'en. When children knocked on a neighbour's door in our younger days, dressed up in some costume or other, they politely said, 'please help the guisers', because that is what they were: guisers. The word means to dress fantastically, and is linked to the French word 'mime'. The guiser then performed some act, a song, a trick or even a joke and thus earned an apple or a handful of nuts and maybe, just maybe, a bit of loose change. Now we are faced with the alien 'trick or treat'. Well, not at my house. Why do we surrender our language and customs so easily?

Bulge babies, like myself, were still in the shadow of the war and never far from its influences. People in the village I lived lost loved ones. One of my aunts, married to my mother's brother, lost her seventeen year old brother when the merchant ship he sailed in was torpedoed and sunk off the coast of North Carolina in 1942. We were aware of that. We were also aware that had the American Admiral, Edward Joseph King, supported a convoy system for merchant shipping in the west Atlantic and had the lights on the Eastern seaboard of the United States been dimmed at night, the merchant ships would have had some protection and would not have stood out like beacons, as they sailed along, backlit by the lights on shore, all making the German submarine's job easier. Parents talked. As I grew and developed, went to school and mixed with more and more people – school chums, friends, relatives, neighbours and eventually work colleagues – I became more and more aware of its legacy; certainly in terms of death and loss, but more than that. However, I was a child, growing up. I had never heard of a psychologist and if I had heard the word cognitive I would probably have thought it was something to do with my bike. I had no idea what was important. From birth till I was about eight years old I was raised in Bonnybridge, Stirlingshire. When I reached roughly eight years of age my dad got a job in Alexandria, and we moved to Balloch. During our time in Vale of Leven, mum took very ill and had to go into hospital for a long time. Dad had no way of working and looking after two young children, so my brother and I went back to Bonnybridge to live with our grandad and an uncle. That was perhaps the lowest part of my life. They were kind people. My malaise was not about them.

Bonnybridge was typical of so many small towns across Scotland: industrial and predominantly working class. Just another gritty wee working class enclave. Famous for iron foundries, a cigarette factory, the Forth and Clyde canal, and brick works. My abiding memory of these establishments was the noise. Not just the noise of the working factory or foundry, but the noise of the early morning foundry whistles, piercing the early morning torpor as they invited their respective work forces to 'come on in'. They could be heard all over the village. Each establishment's whistle had its own distinctive note. I think they may have been old ship's whistles. There was also the distinctive smell. Passing the cigarette factory, the aroma of tobacco was overpowering. Then the ever present smell that surrounds all iron foundries, roasting or burning, moulding sand. The moulding temperature of molten cast iron, being about 2,500 degrees, roasted the sand. I am assured the best moulding sand comes from river bed sand. However, I am not in a position to debate that finer point of the moulding trade.

And of course there was the famous shout: 'Dirty Bonnybridge'. A term with alternative views as to its origin. One suggestion was that it had to do with the foundry workers, coming home at night covered in dust and grime. The more popular source emanates from the world of football. I always thought it was a direct reference to the Bonnybridge Juniors football team and their style of 'no nonsense' football. However, that seems to be erroneous. There are a couple of competing, alternative accounts for the term. One suggests it relates to a specific Scottish Cup encounter played in Falkirk between Falkirk and Bonnybridge Grasshoppers, not the Juniors. Grasshoppers existed from 1875 until 1901. The Bonnybridge team being accused of dirty tactics during that game seems to be one source of the term. A totally different suggestion leads back to the early years of the twentieth century. It seems waste from a nearby coal mine was overflowing into the River Bonny, creating a foul smell. However, a more noxious substance was found to be polluting the River Bonny in the early part of that century: human waste from the recently-built sewage works for the town. It was inadequate for the rising population, and in about 1913 the health authorities intervened and ordered remedial work be carried out. The overflow had been going on for a few years, resulting in a foul smell constantly pervading the valley.

So, take your pick: dirty foundry workers, foul smells, or just fouls? Personally I prefer the football version; not because it sounds any more plausible, it just has a bit more whimsy. Anyway, many years after the origin of the term, I was with a friend in Blackpool for the 'Illuminations'. A huge adventure for two young villagers from Bonnybridge. It was September 1962, in the days when coaches departed from towns all over the UK carrying families and young, wide eyed 'adventurers' to Blackpool. In our case, from Falkirk bus station. Whilst there, we went to a football match: Blackpool was playing Tottenham Hotspur in the old English first division, at Bloomfield Road. Midway through the first half, during a quiet phase of the game, the famous Bonnybridge war cry rang out from amongst the orange scarves that thronged the terracing on the opposite side of the ground from our position: 'Durty Bonnybrig'. What more proof does a body need? Has to be fitba' related. By the way, Spurs won the game by two goals to one. I was sixteen years of age then, and so was my friend. We were definitely going to go into a pub in Blackpool, seriously. We got to the door of one or two. We did not enter any. Why? Because we were a product of our time, when respect was still a guide to behaviour, as was doing the right thing. We were not brought up to go into pubs; so despite our intentions and our bravado, we could not bring ourselves to break our code, our upbringing, whatever one would call it.

But, scratch a bit deeper, Bonnybridge – probably like most other towns and villages – has much more to offer. Examples of new Stone Age pottery from the area exists, dating back to about 2,500 years BC. A solid gold bracelet, dating from about 1,800 years BC, offers further evidence of Bronze Age settlement and perhaps trading. The bracelet being similar or even identical to jewellery also found in Ireland from the same period. The bracelet can be seen at the Scottish National Museum in Edinburgh. The remains of a 'dun' and other Iron Age settlements from about 200 BC have also been unearthed. I suppose the 'piece de resistance' has to be the Antonine Wall and the remains of the Roman fort at Rough Castle, just east of High Bonnybridge. Vallum Antonini, a turf and wood construction built on stone foundations that stretched across Scotland from Bo'ness on the River Forth in the east to the River Clyde in the west, a distance of about forty miles. It was, for the most part, about ten feet high and on average about fifteen feet wide. It had a deep trench along its north side. It was built in about 138 AD at the behest of the then-Roman Emperor Antoninus Pius, and took about four years to build. It was only functional as a defensive feature for about twenty years, after which it was abandoned as the Romans headed back behind Hadrian's Wall before eventually heading back home to quaff mulsum and lie about in the Roman sun. The part of the wall at Seabegs is still clearly visible and remarkably preserved: an area we called the Doctor's Wood. That part was nearest where we lived and many a happy hour was spent running up and down it, morphing from Legionnaires to woad-painted savages as we fought to repel the hordes from the north or overwhelm the keepers of the wall. Antonine's Wall in Bonnybridge is a World Heritage site. So even as children we had some knowledge of the Romans. In the centre of the village, the eagle-eyed will spot a plaque on a wall at the 'Radical Pend' that runs under the canal and was once the main route from the village to High Bonnybridge. The Pend is so named to commemorate a workers' uprising in Scotland. In the early nineteenth century, skilled workers' wages dropped by more than a half, leading to serious hardship and poverty. A political solution was difficult, probably impossible, as votes were only available to property owners and to those of 'worth'. In 1820 an estimated 60,000 working men put down tools and went on strike. A group called the Glasgow Radicals had been informed they could get arms and ammunition in Falkirk at Carron Ironworks. As they walked along the towpath on the Forth and Clyde Canal toward Falkirk, government soldiers ambushed them at Bonnybridge. After a short skirmish, most of the Radicals were captured and taken to Stirling Castle for incarceration. They were found guilty of Treason and their leaders, John Baird and Andrew Hardie, were hung, drawn and quartered. The remainder were sent to Australia. A few years later they were all pardoned. Too late, however, for Baird and Hardie. More recently, Bonnybridge achieved some level of fame through the Stone of Destiny. An event within my lifetime. The stone was stolen – released, some may say – from the Houses of Parliament in 1950 by four Scottish Nationalist supporters. It broke in two and, while one part was left in England, the 'captured' half was returned to Scotland and hidden in St Andrew's Works, High Bonnybridge. Time passed, and the two parts of the stone were reunited and returned to Westminster. Some have doubts as to whether or not the reunited pair are actually a match. In 1996, on St Andrew's Day, the stone was returned to Scotland and housed in Edinburgh Castle, where it can be seen to this day. On its return several thousand people lined the Royal Mile in Edinburgh to see it in procession from the Palace of Holyrood to the Castle. My youngest son, Alasdair, then a soldier in the Argyll and Sutherland Highlanders, was one of the escorts that day. Needless to say his mum, brothers and a proud dad were in the crowd. Bonnybridge is not just a gritty wee working class settlement to be passed through without a thought. It has a history; just look and ask.

In terms of language – or to be more accurate, dialect – I lived not for from the isogloss, the dialect 'watershed' of central Scotland. Not far west of Bonnybridge is the village of Banton, near Kelvinhead (the latter hardly a village, just a row of houses). The Bonny Water originates in that area, as does its more famous relative, the River Kelvin. The Kelvin boldly strikes out west, striving to team up with the Clyde and into the more guttural – some might say 'more strident' –

harsher accent of West Central Scotland; the 'hey you, Jimmy' sound. Meanwhile, the more casual Bonny Water flowed east to gently meander through Bonnybridge into the River Carron and then the River Forth, to the more genteel, melodic, 'sing song' lilt of the east of Scotland, the 'you'll have had your tea' sound. That divide is also identifiable by other expressions. On the Kelvin side, any fizzy drink in a bottle – no matter the flavour – may have been called 'ginger'. Meanwhile on the more sedate, Bonny side, the expression – no matter what fizzy drink was in the bottle – would probably be known simply as 'lemonade'. The language about the house was also interesting. To me it was just normal. Looking back, one can connect some of it directly to the War; the expressions and terms that mum and dad used. Dad used to always ask for a cup of char, or a cup of gunfire. Both meaning a cup of tea. Doolally, or Doolally Tap, was used to describe someone with suspect mental health issues. These words and phrases link directly to the military and warfare. The latter from a military transit camp located at Deolali, a town some hundred miles or so north of Bombay (now Mumbai). The camp housed soldiers waiting to be shipped home. Some may well have suffered mental health issues, although some argue it was the boredom of waiting to get home that caused the issues. It has also been described as a Sanatorium. It appears the British soldier had difficulty with the Urdu pronunciation of the town and did what soldiers the world over do, came up with their own. Hence Doolally. Incidently the suffix, Tap, was added by the squaddies. It is the Hindustani word for 'fever', a completely different language. Trust a soldier. Phrases like, 'dinnae fash yersel' – meaning, don't bother. And 'haud yer wheest' – meaning, stop speaking, hold your tongue – are just old Scottish phrases. They are little heard now, as our language is overwhelmed by 'proper' English and American English. We are the poorer for that. We are urged to embrace the vibrancy of other cultures, and that is good. But please do not consign our own to the dustbin in attempts to be welcoming. We have a culture and a language, yes, as vibrant as any other. Stop being ashamed of it.

Years ago, a friend of mine, whilst working at customs somewhere in England, used the 'wheest' phrase I just mentioned, to a customer. He was disciplined for swearing at the man. Pathetic cowardice on the part of the person in judgement. Whilst a serving police officer I was rebuked by the Sheriff at a trial once for answering 'aye' to a question. 'Yes' is the word he wanted to hear. I thought, but did not utter, the following: but 'aye' is preferred to 'yes' in our Parliament, and also when addressing the captain of a ship one may well say 'aye, aye, Captain'. Replying 'yes, yes' might well be regarded as insubordination. 'Aye' is a perfectly proper usage.

Looking back, I honestly think I was lucky in so many ways. Not just our quaint language, but our ability to play outside at innocent games we made up. The lassies played for hours jumping over, under and through skipping ropes and at the same time singing songs they either made up or heard, some not repeatable. But not all. This is part of a skipping song:

> Sweetheart, sweetheart will you marry me?
> Yes Lord, Yes Lord at half past three.
> Ice cake, spice cake, soft parfait and
> We'll have a wedding at half past three.

They used to sing this as bouncing a ball against a wall:

Hard up, tin can,
Tini Black has got a man.


There were more and even more to the wee rhymes
shown. Bottom line, we were active and self-motivated. We
played a lot of football and ran about, usually enacting some
conflict or other. I am not sure the word 'obese' had been invented. I was really lucky in another respect, and that is the
first two houses I was brought up in. I thought every house
was like ours. I probably did not think it quite like that. I was
a bairn and, if any thoughts entered my head, they certainly
were not about what kind of house I lived in. Nonetheless, I
was lucky, and it was not till I was much older and had sam-
pled a variety of dwellings that I might have compared them.
But, you know, I didn't; it is only at this stage of my life with
a bit of reflection, coupled with experience and age and explaining to my grandchildren how lucky they are, that the
differences have even become apparent.

I spent my early years in Thornton Avenue, Bonnybridge, staying with mum and dad at the home of my maternal grandfather, Patrick O'Hara. His wife, my maternal
grandmother, died in childbirth in 1934. She was forty-one
years of age. The house was a substantial, four apartment
semi-detached affair, with a front and a large back garden. It
had a big bathroom and kitchen complete with Rayburn
stove, used to heat the water, always in plentiful supply. The
gardens were big enough for just about all our vegetable
needs.

We moved out to a house of our own not long after my
little brother was born. His birth was the trigger that got
mum and dad a new house all to themselves. It was a prefabricated house – a 'prefab' – in Greenhill on the south-west of

Bonnybridge. These houses were constructed in 'kit' form, in some of the factories that had previously been used for manufacturing military equipment during the War. They were made of concrete panels, with metal windows and internal walls. One luxury; they all came with fully fitted kitchen and bathroom. Once made, the parts were transported to a site; it took about forty hours to have one erected and ready to occupy. There was a huge demand for housing at that time, as military personnel were returning home after the Second World War. The Temporary Prefabricated Housing programme was meant to be a temporary fix, and the 'prefabs' were designed to last ten years, to allow for more substantial houses to be built. So we moved from one 'luxury' post-World War One council house to another style of post-World War Two 'luxury' house. Yes, a lot different, but nonetheless a good, spacious family home. We loved our prefab, even although the windows were a bit twisted and the walls ran with condensation. They were cold in the winter, and getting to bed proved to be a tad 'baltic'. However, our dad's greatcoat flung over us was the cosy solution. Well, that along with a hot water bottle and brotherly cuddles. It was so cold that our breath was visible, and ice formed on the inside of the windows. Even after we moved to our prefab we still spent much of our time in Thornton Avenue, the family headquarters. During the vegetable and rose-growing season, grandad had an important task for me. The local Co-operative had horse-drawn carts that went round the streets with produce for sale. My important task was to run after the cart with a bucket and fill it with fresh, steaming horse manure. Yes, feed for the garden. I did not possess gloves. The fact that horse manure was, still is, a notoriously dangerous substance – as it contains a variety of parasites that can prove fatal if ingested by dogs and other animals – seemed not an issue to grandad. Roses, tatties and onions had a higher order and, anyway, he knew I was not going to eat horse shit. I needn't have worried about my lack of gloves, as the house had ample washing space.

During the First World War, a policy of building quality council housing was developed. It was particularly for members of the armed forces returning home at the conclusion of hostilities. The policy evolved from Part 3 of the 'Housing for the Working Classes Acts of 1890 and 1909'. (That term, working classes, will appear later when I touch on why the police were even invented – or should that be introduced?) Loans were made available to Local Authorities across the country for the purpose. It became better-known as 'Homes Fit for Heroes', a term first used by David Lloyd-George, the then-Prime Minister. Across the Stirling County Council area some six hundred such homes were built. Thornton Avenue in Bonnybridge being one such scheme. My maternal grandmother and grandfather, who saw active service in Europe as a driver in the Royal Field Artillery, were allocated a hero's home, number 8 Thornton Avenue, Bonnybridge. It stayed in the O'Hara family for an uninterrupted eight decades or so, until the last of my uncles died in the 1990s. My early memories of the house involved finding all sort of war relics, First World War medals, a gas mask, an old khaki great coat, a brass cigarette box, and a tin hat. The brass cigarette box was in fact the Princess Mary 1914 Christmas Gift. I see it can fetch anywhere from £40 to £100 on some auction sites these days. I have no idea what happened to my grandad's box.

Another interesting element of life in these post-World War Two days was food rationing. Merchant ships were being attacked and sunk, and certain foodstuffs were becoming scarce. In 1940 the first rationing of food started, and ration books were issued. To use it, one had first to register. Only certain shops could be used. The shopkeeper would keep a record of the food bought. The government encouraged people to use margarine instead of butter, and tried to get people to eat corned beef and powdered eggs. Most staple food was rationed. For example: people were restricted to one egg, two ounces of cheese, four ounces of bacon, and two ounces of tea a week. Other foodstuffs, like bread, were similarly restricted. You were only allowed one pound of jam and twelve ounces of sweets a month. This went on for fourteen years, and came to an end in 1954 when I was eight years old. I well remember being sent to the Co-operative to get food and using the ration book. One treat was getting bread. It was not sliced, and was the good old Scottish loaf wrapped in white greaseproof paper. I used to peel back the edge of the paper and pick the outside of the bread to chew on the way home. There would always be a telling off.

It was not until my dad moved to his job at the Vale of Leven Co-operative Society, and we moved house to Dalvait Road in Balloch, that I got my first experience of a private landlord's house. No bathroom, just a small cubby hole of room for a lavatory. One bedroom, and a recess in the 'main' living room/kitchen area, where a second bed was situated. There was a solid brick-built wash house outside at the foot of the external stair. Four families shared the 'steamy', as it was called. It had a large metal tub inside a brick outer lining. The brick outer had an arched opening that was lined with firebrick. My mum would fetch water in a bucket and fill the metal 'bath'. She then kindled a fire in the opening and waited until the water was boiling before adding soap powder, stirring it with the big wooden ladle and washing the clothing.

There was also a set of long-handled wooden tongs to lift the clothes from the boiling water when they had been washed. A large zinc bath tub hung in the steamy. That was where one bathed, winter and summer. On occasion, if we were lucky, my dad would bring the zinc bath into the house and we would have the luxury of a wash by the fire, usually on a Sunday night. One fill of water for the adults and perhaps a fresh fill for the children, but that was not guaranteed. One needs to understand, the steamy and the zinc bath were communal and shared between the four families on the stair, so there was a rota of use. In other words, a bath was a once-a-week activity, perhaps. There was, certainly in our steamy, an additional factor. One of the 'stair' dwellers, and legitimate partner in the communal steamy, worked as a gamekeeper in a nearby estate. His job involved, naturally enough, trapping vermin. I was always suspicious of the metal cages that were stored in a corner of the wash house. What were they for? Who owned them? I found out. I came home early from school one day and heard a commotion emanating from the steamy. High pitched squealing. I pushed the door open and there was our gamekeeper neighbour with a rat in each cage. The tub was filled to the brim with water and he was immersing the caged rats in the water. He was not washing them. He chased me and I scuttled off, never to venture back when he was around. I used to wonder if he cleaned up the steamy before it was mum's turn to get our washing done.

Let me take you back to my prefab after that short Balloch interlude. Despite their temporary ten year life expectancy, 'prefabs' were still standing – and being lived in – fifty and more years later in some areas. Soon after moving in I was fitted out with a natty leather schoolbag, new shorts and leather shoes. I was off to Greenhill Primary School. I was five, and the school was nearly a mile from the house. I walked, every day. I did not get a lift and neither mum nor dad accompanied me. It was the same for us all. I loved school, certainly in my early schooling years. I remember one teacher called Mrs Thomson. There was another one I really liked whose name might have been Miss Hamilton; I'm not sure. One day when my mum asked me if she would know her, I replied: 'You must know her; she walks down past our house every day and she has two big bones sticking out'. The innocence of a child.

Our 'prefab' overlooked the main road that led from Bonnybridge, through Seabegs, and on to the moorland beyond. Moorland that contained many farms and a few clay drift mines. There was also a very busy live ammunition military firing range, called 'The Targets'. Needless to say, as young boys, we were fascinated by the military presence and took every opportunity to sneak about the clay mines and 'The Targets', particularly the latter. We would search all over the area looking for live bullets. We never found live ammunition, but we did find empty shell cases. They were really no good to us, as we were not allowed to go there and taking empty shell cases home would have resulted in trouble and a sore arse. There were always military vehicles passing the house. Lorries with soldiers sitting in the back under canvas. Most of the time the flap was tied back letting you see the soldiers sitting along each side. We would shout and wave and would be delighted when they waved back.

One of the stranger vehicles to pass the house was something we called a 'duck'. It looked like a boat on wheels. Years later I learned their proper designation was DUKW. (D: designed in 1942, U: utility, K: all wheel drive, and W: dual wheel axles.) They were designed as dual amphibious and land vehicles, and could travel over land and water. There were no big rivers or lochs in the area, so one assumes they were just being used to transport equipment to the firing range. Another vehicle that attracted our interest as young boys was a square metal box that bounced along, making a serious racket as its metal tracks clashed with the tarred road. It was innocent of wheels. I used to look forward to these vehicles. We called it a 'Bren gun carrier', although it was actually an universal carrier, designed to carry all sorts of equipment around off-road battle sites. We could not have cared less about what it was used for; our only interest was the machine gun that was poking out the front. Maybe one day the driver would fire it. He never did. Well, not when we were watching.

Many years later, whilst serving as a police officer, I would be lucky enough to be transported in such a vehicle. Steering, as far as I could see (certainly in the one in which I travelled), was achieved by pulling on one or other of the two brake levers. I think the levers braked or slowed down the relevant chain track on whatever side required, causing it to slew into a shuddering and violent turn to one side or the other. Using that method, my trusty colleague weaved an uncomfortable path up through a steep heather and bracken-covered hillside to the very top. You might wonder why I was taking this trip. It had nothing to do with warfare or transportation of weapons; it was far more mundane. Our job that day was to take a barrel of creosote to the top of the Struie Hill and paint the wooden hut that sits atop the hill. It is no ordinary hut and is, or was, used to house the sophisticated electronics needed to run the radio repeater mast on the hill. In fact, a mast still adorns the summit to this very day. I assume the modern 'mobile', or cell telephone, being the reason.

When our messy task was at an end, we sat beside the newly creosoted hut and ate some sandwiches whilst taking in the breathtaking view over the Dornoch Firth. It was then I heard the sound of chattering voices from somewhere nearby. I thought the voices belonged to a group of hillwalkers ascending the hill. The pitch of the 'voices' made me think they were female. Despite looking all over the hill I saw not a living soul. As the voices got even louder I was beginning to wonder about my eyesight. Then I saw the source of the chattering and laughed at my naïveté. A huge skien of greylag geese to the north was winging up the Firth and lower than my lofty perch. It was a wonderful sound, and still is. I can never hear chattering geese now without recalling that wonderful day on the Struie Hill and also recalling the Bob Dylan song, 'Lay Down Your Weary Tune'. I had another thought: 'I am actually getting paid! What a job this is'.

There was, in the early 1950s, another form of military transport I witnessed. It was an X Class submarine. A mini submarine, passing west along the Forth and Clyde Canal at Bonnybridge, heading for the River Clyde. Two sailors were standing on deck, navigating it through the lock at the canal bridge. These mini submarines would be towed into position by another naval vessel before carrying out their attack. They would then be towed home. I did not know where the one I saw was headed that day. But it stuck in my mind.

So who was my dad? Thomas Barbour McNeish was born into a coal mining family in Lesmahagow in 1919. His coal miner dad moved his family to Denny between the wars, following work to the Herbertshire Pit. They were, probably not unlike many other working class families involved in that line of work at that time, seriously socialist, even Communist. My dad did not follow his own dad into coal seams. He hewed his own career, shewing different seams. He apprenticed as a cobbler and shoemaker with the Co-operative Society in Denny, Stirlingshire. The Co-operative Society, or 'the Store' as we called it, was over a century old in its concept and was basically a co-operation of retail outlets that shared profits with members through a dividend scheme. That was based on the members' purchases, and was called the 'divi'. Each family had a divi number that you gave to the shop assistant whenever a purchase was made. Co-operative Societies were separate organisations. They however co-operated by combining their collective purchasing power. Whatever description one gave the co-operative, it certainly was based on socialism and 'the store' was pretty much the domain of working class families. It was a cradle-to-grave organisation. My dad worked in the Co-operative movement all his working life and, based on his experiences in that organisation and other unconnected experiences, learned to have grave doubts about the socialist movement. One such experience was in 1956, whilst attending a Trade Union meeting. On the agenda was a motion to raise cash to help the Hungarian refugees, who were at that time being oppressed by their Russian 'overlords'. The motion failed, as some argued the Hungarians were fascists and should not be supported by the socialist movement. Dad's argument that they were refugees, with children, fleeing for their lives, fell on deaf ears. He could have been speaking to himself. No collection took place, and Dad got another lesson about people. Political dogma. It takes precedence to humanity, every time. He was angry and I can, even now, recall that anger.

My dad was a gifted scholar, particularly when it came to mathematics. However, at the age of fourteen he had to finish school and find work to help support his family. As mentioned earlier, he became an apprentice cobbler and shoe-maker with the Denny Co-operative Society. He worked hard and always did. Boots and shoes in these days were made of leather and were relatively expensive. People generally had not the money to buy new footwear every time the sole wore through, hence a major part of dad's work involved repairs as soles and heels were replaced. His apprenticeship lasted six years. It entailed repairing footwear and making it from scratch. Also included in his job were shoe deliveries. He pushed a wooden cart all over town meeting people on his travels as he went delivering repaired shoes and boots to customers and collecting others to be repaired. Each pair for delivery was wrapped in brown paper, held together by twine with cardboard name tags. His wooden two-wheeled delivery cart was heavy, with wooden handles and wooden wheel spokes. Not only did he develop muscles, he also learned a lot about customer service and people during these 'apprentice' years.

His apprenticeship was nearing the end, and he was lined up for a job in a shoe factory somewhere nearby. Things did not develop in that direction for dad. World War Two intervened in 1939, and he quickly volunteered for the army. He felt it was his duty. Years later, I am not sure he would have made the same decision. I once asked him, 'why the army'? He could have opted for one of the other services, particularly the Royal Navy. I have never forgotten his answer. 'If I am on a ship, I am at the mercy of the Captain and if he thinks it is time to earn a Victoria Cross, he will take me with him. In the Army, perhaps I will have a choice.' A tongue-in-cheek answer, or perhaps an indication of a person who could think for himself and a person who, as far as he could affect the outcome, would not be restrained by a system. Dad was a clever man and a free thinker. There was perhaps another reason for dad being so keen to 'sign up'. He was suffering in a really difficult family situation. His mum, my paternal grand-mother, had died some years before and his stepmother appeared to resent her new husband's offspring. She regularly kept her stepchildren short of food and once tried to poison dad and one of his brothers by spreading rat poison on their sandwiches. She was not a well woman, and had a few spells in the local mental hospital. The whole experience taught, or perhaps forced, dad to be self-sufficient, and in doing so to take care of his siblings. I have no memory of ever meeting my step-gran, and little memory of my paternal grandfather. I think I only met him four of five times, if that. I regret that omission.

My dad's war experiences had a marked effect on his life. He joined the Seaforth Highlanders and, as part of the 51$^{st}$ Highland Division, headed across the English Channel in early 1940 – as far as I remember – as part of the British Expeditionary Force (BEF). The early part of their war was called the Phoney War, as they reinforced the weaker northern sector of the Maginot Line. During that early period, war was raging in some areas, but not yet where my dad was stationed. The lull was about to change as the German Army surged through Belgium. War was about to start in earnest for him. While he really did not spend a lot of time regaling us with his war exploits, he occasionally would loosen up on that front and here, as best as I can recall, are a few of his memories.

He, like most of the 51$^{st}$ Highland Division, was captured at St Valery en Caux in June 1940. In the few weeks before that he had been involved in several 'skirmishes', and in one particular encounter he had no idea how he escaped unscathed. He used to say that since that day, every day he lived was a bonus. For dad his war was over and his five year fight for survival had just begun.

He used to say that in the theatre of war, the only battlefield that matters is the small one you are in. You have no idea of the big picture; even a mile or so away is out of your 'ken'. Your job is to win your bit. For a while during the brief few days of action just related, dad actually thought they were doing well and because of that actually believed they were winning the war. Obviously that notion was soon crushed. Dad believed the 51$^{st}$ Highland Division was sacrificed. He argued there were two reasons for that. Britain needed the French to keep resisting for as long as possible, something that did not look very likely at one point. Allying the Highland regiments to stay and battle alongside the French was a tactic designed to keep them fighting. The second reason was far more difficult for dad to forgive. Churchill needed to divert the Germans from Dunkirk to allow the evacuation. Some argue that Dunkirk was before St Valery; however, dad was adamant that was not the point. Even if it was before St Valery, the Highlanders fighting to the south alongside the French still created a diversion. Hence the sacrifice of the 51$^{st}$ at St Valery en Caux. Till he died, dad believed that and never forgave them. He was never comfortable regarding the annual celebration surrounding the Dunkirk evacuation. As he said, 'they never came for us at St Valery'. The story is well told in the 2007 book *St Valery: The Impossible Odds*, edited by Bill Innes, even though it differs in some ways from dad's version.

After capture, the remnants of the 51$^{st}$ were marched, barged, trucked and entrained on the long journey to Poland, where they were imprisoned in various camp complexes. Dad was prisoner 14890, Camp 20A, Thorn Podgorz, in mid-north

Poland. The nearest large city was Gdansk to the north on the Baltic Sea. Prisoners were housed in large huts and, dependent on each prisoner's behaviour, they might be in a punishment billet or a working billet. The working prisoners would work on farms, on wood cutting, or even in processing produce, such as beet preparation. Dad found himself in a working party on one farm or another, working the fields. There tended to be two armed guards to each of these working parties. The guards were as bored as the prisoners. Dad found it easy to escape. You simply kept as far from the guards as possible, looked industrious and waited until the guards were concentrating on something else then simply wander off into the forest. Dad managed that a few times. There was little chance of getting home. Lack of Polish or German tongue was usually the telling factor. If lucky, you might stumble into the resistance, but that was not likely and dad never got that lucky. He did try though. Some never did, and seemed content to work and cause no bother to their captors. Dad felt he had to be as difficult as he could. He described that as doing his bit to help the war effort.

Food was a problem, and their captors were not generous in that regard. The Geneva Convention on feeding prisoners was not rigidly adhered to. Most of the time they were starving on rations of one bowl of watery, greasy soup and a fifth of a loaf of black bread a day. After a while Red Cross parcels would arrive at the camp. These usually contained coffee, cigarettes, chocolate, sweets, butter and a variety of vegetables. People being people, the camp and each hut soon sorted out into a hierarchy. Some were at the top and in charge of trading the contents of the Red Cross parcels. The majority just went with the flow. For example, cigarettes were a good source of trade. Dad and Frank, another Scot, from Townhead in Glasgow, became top dogs and controlled trade. In addition, dad had a seam of eggs from a local friendly farmer and he became the egg baron. The importance of Red Cross parcels in supplementing an otherwise under-nourishing diet cannot be overestimated. Dad often remarked that if it were not for these parcels, some would have starved to death. Despite the Red Cross parcels, most lost stones in weight. That is the main reason I continue to support the Red Cross. Experience in these camps and huts convinced dad of the futility of communism, an ideology that was never far from his family when he was a child. People are not all equal, and will naturally form a hierarchy; it is organic and cannot be manufactured. He would try to tell us that nothing changes. Those out of power simply want into power. They constantly complain about their leaders, and some talk about removing them. They will just put in place the leaders that suit them, and it will be someone else who will complain. It will make no difference in the end. Just a constant drip of dissatisfaction. It is human nature, he would say.

In 1974, the year of dad's early death at 54 years of age, the American author Robert Pirsig penned his iconic and revolutionary book, *Zen and the Art of Motorcycle Maintenance: An Inquiry into Values*. In that book he wrote about what dad had spoken of, perhaps with more eloquence. He said that while we may well revolt and destroy a government, if one does not address the rationale – the systematic patterns of thought that produced the government – you will simply create another government that will mirror the one you removed. 'There's so much talk about the system and so little understanding.' When I read it, I immediately thought of dad. He understood.

As the War was drawing to a close, he recalls hearing 'the guns' getting nearer. He could not be sure if they were American or Russian guns, and hoped for the former. However, the Germans had other ideas and in order to avoid the Red Army they emptied many of the camps and herded the prisoners on a horrific trek, on foot and wearing no more than the clothes they were captured in, through serious winter conditions. Hundreds died from the freezing temperatures and starvation. Among them were some of his friends. Dad recalls being in a huge railway siding and, scavenging about, they found a 'brock' bin with old rotten vegetables, potato peelings and a fish head and other discarded unrecognisable organic matter. They put some water in the mix and boiled it. They were in the middle of their feast when interrupted by high flying aeroplanes that began to carpet bomb the whole area, particularly the railway sidings. They headed for cover and never managed to complete the feast they had prepared. Dad said it was delicious. Further along the march he headed into a field to get some turnips to gnaw on. He was intercepted by a big red-headed German guard who beat him with the butt of his rifle. Till the day he died he had the scar on his forehead and his knee, the latter always giving him trouble. Freedom finally came at the hands of American soldiers. I remember when I was young, living in Greenhill, that dad had an American Colt 45 handgun. He would take us onto the moors and would fire it at targets. I wonder who or what he was imagining when he fired. I vividly remember lying on a muddy railway sleeper bridge over a burn in the Greenhill area as dad tried to shoot trout in the burn. Unsuccessfully, I would think. I never saw the gun again, and never heard what happened to it. He got the hand gun the day of his liberation from an American officer who asked dad why he wanted it.

Dad told him he was going to find a particular big red-headed German and kill him. He limped amongst the hordes of German prisoners and searched. He did not find him. Nor did he find the American officer. Hence the gun in Greenhill, complete with bullets.

On returning home after the war, dad worked at Stenhousemuir Co-operative and mended shoes. Dad's early family and work experiences, coupled with his war experience, produced a seriously determined, clear-thinking person. My dad was not impressed and certainly not overawed by status or rank, and respect had to be earned. He was seldom, if ever, judgemental, apart that is from certain systems and organisations. If he left a legacy to my brother and me, it was to listen, seek evidence, question, take no bullshit, do not judge, and learn to stand up for yourself.

T.E. Lawrence, of Arabia, when being quizzed by some prissy officers, replied, 'You handle Arabs, I think, as you handle Englishmen, or Laplanders, or Czechoslovaks: Cautiously at first and kindly always'. Dad understood the sentiment. I think it would be better for us all if more people understood. He was proud of his life as a cobbler and shoe maker. My brother and I thus became the cobbler's bairns.

Back to my childhood in Bonnybridge. One of my school chums, Alex, lived in a 'prefab' near ours. His dad had 'liberated' a Japanese officer's sword during the War. He kept it in a safe place, but not as safe as he probably imagined. Alex was able to 're-liberate' it on the odd occasion. We were in awe of it, and probably a wee bit envious that our dads had not been brave enough to liberate such a treasure. Whether any of our dads had even been in the Far East seemed not a consideration. I never mentioned the fact that my dad had 'liberated' a handgun and bullets from the War. I think Alex would have been impressed. But dad's War had been different from that experienced by Alex's dad.

Then we were on the move again, to live in Balloch. I think I was eight or perhaps nine years old by then. Dad had a job in Vale of Leven Co-operative in Alexandria. He was to become the manager of the footwear department, both selling and repairing shoes. Hence our move to the Dalvait Road apartment I referred to earlier. School for me was Jamestown Primary. My brother Allister went to Haldane Primary School; I don't know why. We settled in, and life was good. There were lots of outdoor adventures. One of my uncles, my mother's brother, was a chemist in the Imperial Chemical Industries (ICI) at Ardeer, the explosive division. He had an important role and, as far as I could tell, was quite well off. Better off than mum and dad, anyway. He bought a boat on Loch Lomond for us all. It was moored in the River Leven and we, certainly in the better weather, spent many weekends up at the loch camping on the islands and swimming in the water. Our school summer holidays were mostly spent in the boat on the loch – yes, for weeks – Inchmoan and Inchtavannach being our usual resting places. Our boat, the *Seahawk*, slept four with comfort. Others could somehow squash into the uncovered stern area, though this was not recommended for adults. Sometimes we would put a tent ashore and the children, Allister and me, would sleep there. Occasional sorties to the village of Luss would be made if we needed to stock up on provisions. We would sail to the top of the loch and call in at various places on the way; Rowardennan, Inversnaid and Ardlui. We had no wish to be anywhere else; it was a great adventure, and we loved every minute of that part of our young lives. Being able to swim was an advantage. No, it was essential. My method of learning to swim was probably not conventional. I was nine or ten years old and staying in Balloch. Like all young scallywags I could not steer clear of danger, or perhaps just adventure. I could hardly swim and, one day after school, a group of us wandered up the road from Balloch to the old pier, intent on going for a dip in the loch. The old pier at that time was out of use and starting to decay. It was a typical old timber construction, a wooden platform supported by vertical and crossed timbers. There were vertical, metal-runged ladders at intervals along the side that reached from the platform into the water. From memory I guess the pier would have been at least twenty feet or so high, from platform to water. Perhaps higher. I thought it looked very high, particularly when standing on the edge plucking up courage to leap into the inky blackness of the loch. The pier was quite long, and entry was forbidden. I think there might have been 'keep off' notices, though I'm not certain. However, what I am sure about is the mass of barbed wire stretched across the entrance. Picking one's way through the barbs was a fearsome enough task, but that would pale into insignificance when trying to explain to parents how one's best school jersey got trashed by barbed wire. Parents who in these days, not long after World War Two, had little enough clothes for their own back. With jersey and skin intact, we breezed along the wooden platform, carefully avoiding the holes. It was an old and decaying structure. I never knew what ship ever used it. Then we are ready for the next stage: stripping off our good jerseys and every other stitch of clothing in order to don our woolly trunks. Speedo had not reached Scotland at this time. Well, if it had, certainly not to this gang. In fact, in these days we might not have felt 'decent' in slinky swimming apparel. That is a discussion for another forum. So, here was my moment of destiny: learning to swim.

I stood on the edge, transfixed by fear. The water, dark grey and foreboding, looked a long way down. 'How deep is it?' I heard myself ask, to no-one in particular. Someone said: 'Aye, it will be fifty feet'. I am not sure what difference that made; I could not swim anyway. To add insult to injury, I was bloody chittering with the cold – frozen, and I was not even in the water. I then asked, 'what do I do?' The reply came: 'Just jump and, when you get in the water, keep your hands under and paddle like a dog. It's easy'. Then I was on my own as the rest did just that. They jumped. Well, I think some dived. Having been suitably briefed, I jumped too. To anyone who has never experienced this, trust me, you get a shock. First there is that feeling when your innards seem to be heading into the back of your throat, and there is the 'sploosh' as you hit the water with a violent impact. I had no idea how deep under the water I went. At first I had no idea where up was, not to mention the water up my nose. My next memory was thrashing my arms about and trying to move up. The impact followed by the thrashing must have been almost instantaneous, although it felt like an eternity. I did have the presence of mind to hold my breath, and that helped. Then my head was above the water and I was paddling like a mad dog. With my 'swimming' pals encouraging me, I paddled over to the pier and grabbed one of the ladders. Safe at last, safe at last. I just held on like a limpet for a few minutes until I got my bearings and my breath back. Then off I went, paddling along to the next ladder. And so it went on for an age. My pals were swimming out a fair distance. I did not envy them. I was more than happy to stay safe by the pier. Swimming under it and climbing out onto the wet timber cross pieces was good fun. Then it was up a ladder and into the water again. We kept that up for what seemed ages, then it was time to get home for our 'tea'. We ran about a bit to dry off before getting our damp bodies into our clothes. Our next adventure was getting back through the barbed wire. Who cares? I could swim! Well, paddle. This turned into a regular adventure, and my confidence grew and nobody drowned. Jumping off the deck of the *Seahawk* into the loch and swimming under it to come out on the other side was now easy.

School was going well, and I passed my eleven plus and headed to Vale of Leven Academy in one of the top streams. An incident during my first week at the academy marked me as a trouble maker. It was so unfair, yet over the years I have witnessed similar scenarios which result in the 'injured' party who responds to the initial aggressor being punished. I was in a group of similarly nervous pupils at the academy. It was our first week up from primary school. We were just trying to find our way around the new experience and the support of the group was important. Some third year boys approached and said something. I did not hear it properly and said nothing. One asked if I was deaf and grabbed me round the neck, pulling me towards him, at the same time grabbing my hair and roughly running knuckles hand through it. I pushed him away and he became quite aggressive, asking if I thought I was a big man? What happened next came straight from my dad's coaching about not being aggressive toward anyone, but – on the other hand – not being pushed about. I stepped into him and punched him in the midriff. He staggered back. I took up the 'boxing' position as taught and, each time he came at me, I hit him again. He never managed to punch me and eventually fell to the ground with me standing over him. I had boxed him to a standstill. I had only hit him in the head once; the rest of the time it was in his stomach. He ran away into the school. He obviously reported the incident, because as all the pupils stood in their class lines waiting to be called into the building in the proper order, whatever that was, there was a delay. The rector appeared at the top of the entrance stairs and looked up and down the lines. One of the teachers pointed to me. The rector said, in a booming voice, 'Will the boy McNeish come with me?'. I walked past the assembled school, red faced and embarrassed, up the stairs and directly to his office. He would not listen to me and told me I was a disgrace. He then administered his punishment. That was the first and not the last time I would feel the sting of the Lochgelly Tawse on my hand. Six times he hit me. I would never forget that day. I did not feel cowed or intimidated, nor did I feel humiliated as he suggested I should. I was furious, yes, even at my tender years. How dare he? I was minding my own business and was picked upon by a bully, yet I got punished. It was a lesson I would never forget, although not the lesson the Rector thought he was giving. My aggressor was not punished.

Apart from that, things went reasonably well. Getting punished at school in these days was easy. Forget the words when reciting a theorem or a poem? Small things like that got you punished. It was often a choice between one hundred lines or two of the belt. I always chose the latter. It hurt but was over quickly. I was developing strategic thinking, even then. It was not all bad in the Vale of Leven. I have good memories of going to the Hall Cinema in Alexandria on a Saturday morning. It cost a tanner to get in. No, not a tenner: a tanner. That was the nickname for the small silver-coloured coin worth six old pennies, pre-decimal. (It is unclear where the name came from, though the most likely reason is that the designer of the coin was called John Sigismund Tanner.) The show was usually two films, in black and white. One might be a serial and the other a comedy, like The Three Stooges: Moe, Larry and Curley. There was usually a cowboy film. That is where I got out of step with everybody else in the cinema. I am related to the Menominee tribe from Wisconsin, near Green Bay. My dad's sister married a full-blooded tribesman. So my American cousins are half Native American Menominee and half Scot. I was the only one cheering the other side. I also support the Green Bay Packers in the NFL. Whatever film was shown, one usually had goodies chasing baddies, and the house was full of loud cheering.

I had another bad experience at school. I played football and had played for Jamestown Primary School. At the secondary school I was in the mix and going to training. The first real game of the season came along and Vale of Leven Academy were playing a home game at the local junior club's pitch. I was told by the PE teacher I was in the team, playing at right half, wearing number four. I was full of expectation when I turned up at the allotted hour, complete with clean boots. Ready to go. My first sense of unease came when I read the team list on the door of the dressing room. My name was not on it. I did not go in; I felt a bit stupid. However, I hung onto the idea they had made a mistake. One of the teachers came out and I asked him about the team sheet and said I had been told I was in the team. He was quite short with me, 'You are not in the team. Who told you that?' I waited about outside for a few minutes before sneaking off. I did not go straight home in case I was asked what I was doing. I never returned to training. It did make me feel a bit foolish.

Then mum took ill and our world changed. It was not disclosed to us children what the illness was. It was breast cancer, something that perhaps was thought of as unattractive then and, because of that, seldom talked about and never in front of the children. She was diagnosed one week and into Vale of Leven Hospital for the operation the next week. Mum was thirty three years of age. Her mother died in 1934, when forty one years old. Mum was fourteen years of age at the time and while she, a brother and an older sister stayed in Bonnybridge, their other siblings were sent to live with relatives on the maternal side of the family. They were many miles away in Aberdeenshire or Kincardineshire. With thoughts of her mother's early death, her mind must have been in a turmoil. This was the late 1950s, when medicine was probably less successful in saving cancer patients than today. Things did not look good. She had a radical mastectomy, losing a breast and attendant lymph systems. She then went on to receive radiation treatment. Allister and I were whisked out of our schools with a day's notice and taken to live with our grandad and an uncle in Bonnybridge. I transferred to Denny High School, and my brother to Bonnybridge Primary School. I was in shock and got really depressed. I must say at the time I did not recognise my situation as being linked to depression; I was just seriously lost and sad. Grandad must have found it really difficult trying to feed and please two young boys. He and my uncle Danny were so kind, and did try their best for us. The runny porridge and the regular breakfast kippers did little to help. I do not criticise: they were staple diet, just not my preferred option. I never complained. My schooling, as I will refer to later, went downhill. I had no desire to go to school. I did go and I put a face on, but my heart was not in it.

Life moved on and visiting mum in hospital became a regular feature of our weekends. It was a big ward in an old Victorian-style hospital. I struggle to remember which infirmary it was. Mum was in hospital for months, and when we were taken to see her it was difficult. She struggled to even hug us. Breast cancer was terribly disfiguring, certainly then. She was not offered prosthesis, no cosmetic surgery. She wore long sleeved and high necked clothes for the rest of her relatively short life. I never heard her complain, not once. No matter how ill she was and became, she shrugged all suggestion of death away with the phrase: 'I need to live for my boys'. She did the best she could, and both Allister and I are forever grateful. She was in the hospital so often for checkups. She looked good for a while; she always looked good, no matter where her health was. She was so full of fun and irreverence. She made us all laugh. She was a determined lady and she lived for her boys. She shaped our lives; in fact, she shaped many lives, and none forgot that fact when her time came. Despite her positive attitude and her endless spirit, she could not keep the cancers at bay; they never properly went away and, although she held on for a few more years – years that saw both Allister and I move onto employment and university – she died at fifty-one years of age.

# CHAPTER 3

MY employment adventure, my early faltering steps into the 'real' world, began in 1961. Carron Iron-works, in Carron near Falkirk, would be the first recipient of my talents. I had tasted and rejected two other employment opportunities that week. Yes, it was before the globalisation and maximising-shareholders-profits era. There were reasonable opportunities for local employment. Drilling holes in cast-iron bogey wheels in a Bo'ness iron foundry or cleaning ambergris (or some other grease) from the inside of wooden barrels at the Co-operative soap works in Grange-mouth did not attract a fifteen year old 'Junior Secondary Certificate' holder. It was less than two months after my fif-teenth birthday and I was free of my formal state sponsored education. What had flickered into a beacon of educational anticipation, after a successful eleven plus examination, died like a spluttering candle in the gutter so few years later. The only existing record of my school endeavours being the certifi-cate just mentioned. I think the term certificate gives the doc-ument in inflated impression of its importance. It was not a record of attainment. It was a document that acknowledged your existence in the educational system; no more than that.

There had been attempts by my secondary school to retain my services a little bit longer. Not out of a desire to develop my Einstein-like qualities, I may add. For another pressing reason: they were obliged to retain me in their system until I reached the legal leaving age. However, there were personal circumstances developing in my young life that outweighed their legal considerations. My relationship with my uncle in Bonnybridge was becoming difficult, and the prospect of residing with him and my grandad was not an option. I packed my bag and headed for Bo'ness to take up residence, after a three year absence, with my parents and younger brother. That took me into another council area and into another educational authority area. Faced with that, coupled with the fact I was so near legal school leaving age, I assume my file was destined for the 'no hope' basket. I heard no more from them, other than receiving my certificate.

My dad had recently moved to Bo'ness from Vale of Leven to take up position as head of the Bo'ness Co-operative Footwear Department. Allister had left me in Bonnybridge at that juncture and returned to live with mum and dad. They lived in a cockroach-infested apartment in an old building with several other cockroach-infested apartments. Shoes and clothes had to be checked every morning, as they had a knack of crawling into all sorts of places. Feeling a wriggly tickle inside your shirt was not a good feeling. The building was two normal storeys high, plus living space in the attic. We were one up. There were no bathrooms in the building. Out the back was a brick-built building with a row of four wooden, ill-fitting doors, no heating, no inside decoration; just the bricks. That was the lavatory block: a cold, draughty corner of this sceptred isle. One lavatory to three families. Using it was a tactical operation involving surveillance and timing. The last

thing one needed when that last minute call of nature beckoned was to rush down the outside stairs from the apartment,
in the pitch black of a sleet-swept winter night, to be foiled by
a locked door and a strategic cough. I had vacated my 'Home
for Heroes' in Bonnybridge for this experience. But none of
that mattered. I was so pleased to be back with my family.
Back home to Mario Lanza, Kenneth McKellar, and plates of
mulligatawny soup. The icing on the cake. A job beckoned.

So this fresh-faced boy turned up for work, nervous and
excited, at the Structural Department of Carron Ironworks,
situated in Mungal Foundry, adjacent to the main foundry. I
arrived too late to be involved in the manufacture of the famous gun, the Carronade; they ceased production a good few
years before I got there, about two hundred or so. Famous or
not, the old Carron-made guns had an inauspicious start to
their life. They were not that good and in fact were not popular with the Board of Ordinance, the organisation responsible
for commissioning guns and cannons for our military. They
preferred English-made guns. Industrial espionage raised its
head, apparently, and soon Carron was able to amend their
designs and mould stronger guns with reduced 'windage',
making them more efficient and more acceptable to Board of
Ordinance. Windage refers to the space between the cannon-
ball and the gun-barrel. (Probably not what you were thinking.) Too much space led to less efficiency and therefore less
power. So achieving a tighter fit was essential. At the Battle
of Trafalgar in 1805, the first salvo to be fired from Nelson's
flagship, HMS *Victory*, was from a Carron-manufactured
gun. Fame had arrived. If you are at all interested in the story
of the Carronade I recommend a great book by Brian Watters,
entitled *Where Iron Runs Like Water!: A New History of
the Carron Iron Works 1759-1982* (2001).

When I got there, Carron had moved on from the arms race and was involved in the communications race. Its main products in that area were cast-iron post (letter) boxes, the smaller 'lamp letter' boxes, telephone kiosks, and 'cross connection cabinets'. The latter being the boxes one can see at the side of the road with telephone engineers kneeling in front them, working on the complicated array of wires housed inside. Many were moulded, cast and assembled at Mungal Foundry, where the pig iron from the blast furnaces at the main Carron works was remelted in cupolas, poured into moulds in wet sand, and set out in the shapes that made up the various products. I could smell Bonnybridge again. My abiding memory of Carron Ironworks was being inside and witnessing the molten iron spewing forth like a river of blinding lava from the main blast furnace as it was disgorged. The night sky was aflame and visible for miles. Inside the foundry was awash with a bright, eye-burning orange light and sky-high cascades of sparks. Moulders and foundry workers were silhouetted against the glare, casting long ghostly shadows. Dante's inferno could not have been any more hellish. Spectacular heckleburnie. A metaphor for the working man. I was in awe. I felt privileged, and I will never forget.

I was an office junior, and assisted clerical staff with responsibility for dispatched orders. A lot of my time was matching orders with locations and posting out keys for the various makes of letter box. Little did I realise how my job would link me to terrorism. Post boxes and lamp letter boxes were the problem. It was the practice to have the insignia of the reigning monarch moulded onto the front door of these products. When Queen Elizabeth was crowned in 1953, the insignia of her father George VI ceased to be used and was replaced by EIIR. On 28 November 1952 the first EIIR post

48

box in Scotland was installed at The Inch, Edinburgh. Nationalists in Scotland were up in arms. She was the first Elizabeth to reign in Scotland, and the insignia should reflect that properly. The Regnal number should not be present: it should be simply ER. They felt it showed disrespect to Scotland. That message seemed to fall on deaf ears, or perhaps the decision-making was taking too long – who knows? Scottish activists, of some persuasion or other, took it unto themselves to make their position felt. Many post boxes were damaged, painted over, and there were explosions at some. The Inch pillar box was blown to bits by a big explosion. The manager of the Structural Department at Mungal Foundry received a death threat in a letter. Part of my joining instructions from that manager was crystal clear: on no account will you allow an EIIR insignia box to leave this foundry headed for a Scottish location. He was not only serious, he was nervous. I do not think I let him down. To bring you up to date, I noticed recently that letter boxes with EIIR are again being placed at Scottish locations. This whole episode in Scotland's history was marked by a few ditties, penned and sung in appropriate watering holes throughout the nation. 'Sky High Joe', 'Billet-Doux' and 'Sky High Pantomime' by Thurso Berwick. His real name was Morris Blythman, and he was a Fifer. 'The Ballad of the Inch' was another of these protest songs. It is not logged who penned it; some say it was anonymous. Here is a snippet, of 'Billet-Doux', sung to the tune 'Corn Rigs':

It fell aboot the time O Valentine,
Whan the GPO's gey busy O.
Wi pillar boxes fou O Billets-Doux,
Thit a high-explosive wan wis sent ti Lizzie O.

Bo'ness had a couple of interesting memories for me. There was a large railway siding area, and dozens of retired steam engines were parked there waiting their fate. After their majestic life they were redundant and soon to be cut up for scrap. I was an avid loco enthusiast, and spent hours amongst these steam icons. I remember lots of people climbing all over them and removing anything that would unscrew, including engine name-plates and shed identification number plates from low down on the front smoke box door. These were small, oval metal discs with a number and a letter thereon, 65F being Grangemouth for example. Tempted though I was, I could not bring myself to take anything; I suppose one could describe it as theft. I notice some are now selling for hundreds of pounds.

My brother had a rough time at Bo'ness Academy, from the senior staff. On his first day he stood in assembly as all the names were called and each pupil was allocated a class. Allister's name was not read out. The Rector told him off for not listening. Allister assured him he had listened and his name had not been called. The Rector would not listen and made him stand, alone, in the assembly hall. Some time later the Rector returned and it became clear Allister's name was not on any list. He was allocated a mid-to-high streamed class, but not the highest as his eleven plus examination results had merited. Allister got on with his studies. The end of term examination results showed him well at the top, about 97%. A few days later a letter arrived at cockroach villas. Parents called to school because son cheated in his examination. The only evidence the Rector had was the 97% mark. Dad had a few choice words for them. My dad was never cowed by anybody and in particular authority figures, not least blustering bullies. The compromise was that Allister would sit another examination, on his own and under supervision. This time he aced 98%. My dad would not accept an apology and asked it be directed at Allister. The Rector refused. Allister was then transferred into the top stream class and, in typical McNeish fashion, refused to be moved and stayed in the class he had been wrongly allocated to in the beginning. My brother, despite his Scottish Education, developed into a world-famous Doctor of Physics and with a colleague went onto invent the Flip Flop laser and much more. Allister thinks that some in the Scottish Education system have an unwarranted high opinion of themselves. George Eliot might well have been thinking about them when he said, 'I've never any pity for conceited people, because I think they carry their comfort about with them'.

Even today, nothing much has changed in terms of the courage of those in the teaching profession. A young person of my acquaint being bullied, badly bullied. Amongst other things, punched in the throat. Yes, assaulted. A police officer attached to the school advised him not make his complaint official. He explained that the gang, the bullies, had been reported so often, his complaint would make no difference and might well result in the bullying getting worse. What training do our modern police officers get? The school are equally supportive. Their answer was to restrict his – yes, the victim – movements at school, and keep him in the school grounds at the lunch break to avoid confrontation with the aggressors. Inside the school, one of the aggressors produced a knife and held it to his face. That incident went unreported. Why? Because the 'innocent' pupil had lost faith in the whole system and could not see the point in complaining. He continues to be bullied.

I cannot recall how long I worked at Carron. Eighteen months, maybe. I was transferred to a new venture within the main factory, Chatelaine Limited. They made commercial catering equipment. Notably, they fitted out the galley of the P&O liner, S.S. *Canberra*. That liner was later to play a prominent part in the Falklands conflict. Dad secured a new job in a bigger Co-operative Society in Musselburgh and Fisherrow. We were on the move, and this time I was part of the plan. It meant me having to leave Carron to start my second employment hunt. One tactic I employed was walking through industrial sites, knocking on doors and simply asking for work. Another involved taking company names from passing vans and lorries, finding their address and then writing to the company, asking for work. The term CV was an alien concept in these days. Even if it wasn't, I would have had precious little to put in one. The first tactic brought success. I got interviews from two companies in the Thornybank Industrial Site, Dalkeith. Letts Diaries and Ferranti. I was offered work at both, and picked the latter. Back working, and globalisation was still a distant cloud. I worked there for a few months. An opportunity arose to switch to their Crewe Toll factory in Edinburgh. I took that opportunity, and moved from office work to technical, on the tools, work. After a month of training I was launched into the world of electronics as a prototype wireman working for the engineers, doctors and other boffins in the Ferranti Laboratory Block. It was very interesting work and hugely satisfying. This was before printed circuit boards. We still had actual transistors, diodes, resisters, capacitors, and all that stuff. The boffins handed us scraps of paper with a rough sketch followed by verbal instruction, and we made up the test bed.

I worked on some innovative and really interesting projects, a couple very secret at the time. I assembled the prototype ballistics box for the P1127 Kestrel Jump Jet. It would develop into the two-seater Harrier Jump Jet. I produced an electronic assembly that was part of the computer system for the new Pilkington float plate glass development. The molten glass was floated on a bath of metal and it cooled into sheets of flawless window glass. Prior to this development, glass was rolled. I also produced a part of the guidance system for Concorde. The idea was I would create an assembly template. It would then be used in the pre-assembly phase to manufacture the other six. One to go in each of the Concorde aircraft built in the UK. After a few weeks I was asked to make them all, as the pre-assembly team could not meet the specification. So every British Concorde had a piece of my work in the cockpit. For a time I worked at Ferranti's outpost at Turnhouse Airport, before it changed to become Edinburgh Airport. They had two hangars there, and some old aircraft used as flying test beds for their various products – for example, radar and moving map display. The two most used planes at that time were the Douglas DC3 Dakota and an English Electric Canberra Bomber. My job involved fitting developing products into the planes; in the case of the latter, into the bomb bay. The planes were then flown and various 'in-flight' tests undertaken. At that time they had a large reflector dish on the east flank of Ben Cleuch in the Ochils, just above Alva, which was used for reflecting signals. The dish was removed in the late 1980s, I think.

My day at Ferranti Crewe Toll was a long and tiring. I lived in Whitecraig near Musselburgh. (A house with a bathroom, in case you are interested.) Clocking on time at Ferranti was thirteen minutes to eight in the morning. Getting there from Whitecraig took a bit of effort. I got up about half-past five and cycled to Musselburgh, parking my bike at the police office. I then got a county SMT bus to the city, then changed to a corporation bus to Crew Toll. Sometimes I had to get two buses. Three nights every week I went to Leith Nautical College, near Easter Road Stadium. I was studying Radio and TV Servicing. After two years I got my certificate. I was leaving the house just before six in the morning and, on three nights of the week – after getting the last bus from Edinburgh to Musselburgh then cycling home – I was not getting to bed until midnight. It was exhausting. I also played rugby, and fitted in training two nights a week.

My studies got me an increase in my weekly wage to just about eleven pounds. My new designation was Prototype Radio Mechanic. With bonus I could make about thirteen pounds a week. The team I worked with was ten strong, and we worked in a wooden shed out the back of the Laboratory Block. The discussion was often about wages, and a common theme was what it would be like to be paid twenty pounds a week. How rich we would be. I was due to get married and, as my fiancé lived in Falkirk and I lived in Whitecraig, the prospect of getting onto the council house list in Edinburgh was between nil and less than nil. By chance I saw an advert for a company in Essex looking for workers in their factory in Harlow, a new town in Essex. I quietly got interviewed, and secured a job and a new town house in Harlow. My weekly wage soared to twenty pounds and ten shillings. I had located a house and, at the same time, increased my wages to the magic twenty pounds. The air was coloured green when I got back to the hut and told them. I was soon heading out of Ferranti and bound for a new life in Essex with Cossar Electronics. Getting on the train in Edinburgh one overcast, wet Sunday afternoon, late in 1968, on my own, heading for my new life in Essex, was a bit daunting. When I hear Eric Bogle singing 'Leaving Nancy', a song about him leaving home and saying goodbye to Nancy, his mum, in 1969 – same station, same platform – it reminds me of my departure. He was going a lot further mind you. Did I have a choice?

In his 2012 book *Free Will*, Sam Harris argues that free will and choice are illusions. The popular conception of free will seems based on two assumptions; the first being that each of us could have behaved differently than we did in the past, the other that we are the conscious source of most of our thoughts and actions in the present. His book points out, with compelling evidence, that both these assumptions are false. Choices are made for one by events in the brain that one cannot inspect or influence. So, perhaps I had no choice.

Choice or not, I arrived at Liverpool Street Station late that Sunday and managed to catch the last train out to Harlow on a dark, misty night. I had no idea where I was going. I got a taxi to the address provided by the company. This was my lodgings, where I would stay until my new house became available. That would be after the wedding. The lodgings were scary – really scary. I was with a single lady and her sixteen year old son. I never did discover the explanation for her singularity. However, I did discover that her son had mental health issues. I was nervous about my new life in England and apprehensive about my new job. However, I was exhausted and despite my spinning head I drifted off to sleep.

I have no idea how long I had been sleeping when I was rudely awakened by a blood curdling scream. I am not sure 'rudely' accurately describes how I was awakened. I sat bolt upright. It was now deathly silent. Had I dreamed it? Probably just my tiredness and my anxiety. Get back to sleep.

Another blood curdling scream, this time accompanied by: 'he's got an axe!'. I thought, 'fuck, what's going on?'. I sat up again. I was not dreaming. Should I investigate? I was unsure what to do. I listened. Silence again. Then I heard a woman's voice whispering, 'it's all right, there's nobody there'. The soothing whispering went on for a while, then silence. I got up and piled everything I could find against the door. I must have got some sleep. Breakfast came and went with not one word about the mystery axe man. Then I was off to my new life.

It was fine; it was a wage, and it would get me a house. I was on an assembly line, fitting and soldering transistors, diodes, resisters and the like onto boards. It was all repetition and speed. It was seriously boring. I was one of three men in a series of assembly lines of women. They were like lightning, and all the time they talked. I was totally out of my depth; useless. The harder I tried, the more rubber fingered I got. It was a nightmare. The women were not only good at their job, they were gems; seriously kind people. They took this Scottish fish out of water to their hearts. They helped me, encouraged me, finished bits of work for me; they were wonderful.

I went back to my lodgings after work, exhausted and dreading going back in to work the next day. However, the lodgings were another trial. All was fine in the evening. Dinner was good and she was really nice. Her son was a pleasant young man and able to converse. Bed was a nightmare. Every night it was axe men, knife men and screaming. I was a nervous wreck. It was like living in a Hitchcock movie. I was developing a nervous twitch. Breakfasts were serene. It was like a parallel world. Then back to the assembly line and the constant chatter. How they could do it? I guess it is a multitasking thing. When I think back to these days, and consider all the changes in harassment laws and in particular sexual harassment of women in the workplace, I have to chuckle. Are you having a laugh? You have no idea what sexual harassment is till you have been a male in a predominantly female environment. It was constant – and I mean constant, not just verbal. If I was asked to apply 'Femfresh' to one, I was asked to apply it to dozens. I wondered if they thought I had been a nurse in a previous life. Until Cossor Electronics (Factory Three, that was the unit I worked in), I had never heard of 'Femfresh' or some of the other stuff I heard. Nor had I seen some of the things I was shown. Talk about a red neck.

The assembly line and the axe man dreams were to come to an abrupt end. In terms of the latter, my landlady was out one night and she asked if I would take her son to the model car racing club. I did; it looked like good fun. He certainly enjoyed it. On the way home some of the club headed for a libation. I joined them with my young charge. I let him drink a half pint of beer. He was allowed one with his dinner, so I thought, what's the harm? The harm was that I finished up looking for a new landlady. She was furious. I got reported to the personnel department, and I got the heave. Exit stage left. He actually was a good young man, and was honestly starting to relax in my company. Never mind; back to uninterrupted sleeps and brilliant new lodgings with the Batten family. Lovely people. In terms of the assembly line, I think they took pity on me, and I was offered the job as boss of the stores. So I was in management and moving on. It was a bit of a poisoned chalice, however. Those who had been there for years knew exactly who their new boss should be, and it certainly was not a young Scottish upstart. I found it a bit awkward for a while, but they slowly melted and it got more bearable, if not quite perfect. My first real exposure to office politics. Then a rare opportunity emerged, as I saw it. Organisation and Methods. I applied, got selected, and headed into the main factory. Training was intense, and involved a lot of classroom work topped up by practical hands-on work on the shop floor. After a month we were sent out to gain final polishing-off experience at outside factories. I headed for Best Products in Felixstowe, Suffolk. They were an American electrical retail outlet, famous for retro-design electrical products like kettles, lamps and more. I was there for a month, working in their industrial engineering department. The work consisted mainly of examining production methods and suggesting improvements in efficiency. It was very interesting, and opened my eyes to different departments working in partnership to improve the product. I stayed in a small hotel during my time there. It was – still is, I suppose – a quaint old English holiday destination, being on the coast. There was a local theatre, The Spa. I went along one night to watch Tommy Trinder, a similarly quaint old English comedian. His catch phrase was, 'You lucky people!' He actually was funny; a consummate professional, perfect timing and not one profanity.

Then my second loan spell, to an old tenement building just off City Road, London, near Moorfields Eye Hospital. I was there for six weeks this time, and commuted from Harlow every day. Early rush hour. It was bad enough in the late 1960s; I can only guess how unbearable it is today. The journey required three trains, then a walk along City Road from Old Street underground before striking off into the Ebenezer Street area to find the building. It was old, and one that was entered by way of an outside metal staircase. The door I wanted was on the third floor. Inside the structure was mostly wood. A well-worn, scrubbed wooden floor with narrow girder-like roof supports, with lights hanging down from them. It was seriously past its best, and was also a serious fire hazard. I am told it had been a rag trade building in the past. Now it was used to assemble electronic bleeper devices. This was circa 1969/70, so it was new technology then. It was a busy environment, and nobody had a minute. Again, like the Cossor factory it was mostly women working the lines. Unlike the Cossor factory, most of these women were black. I have to say, I have never laughed so much at my work. They were brilliant and genuine people. They, like the Cossor female assembly workers, never stopped chattering. They were really interested in my accent and in Scotland. Women can multi-task; they'd proved it twice now. They, however, never indulged in anything smutty, and I was thankful for that. It was a great experience. They worked so hard and never complained about anything. I never got over how welcome they made me, and how they made work fun. I think they were content, happy, and importantly had no ego and 'climbing the ladder' issues. City Road is famous for being in a nursery rhyme:

> Up and Down the City Road,
> In and out The Eagle,
> That's the way the money goes,
> Pop goes the Weasel.

The Eagle was still about in these days, and still is. And yes, you guessed correctly, I did go up and down the City Road and in and out the Eagle. More than once. Ten weeks on loan and back to Harlow to get on with my real job. I found it interesting, and I enjoyed it. I did learn a lot about factory life and working with unions; in fact, I was in the ETU for most of my time at Cossor Electronics. I was mixing with lots of people and varied cultures. It was fascinating, and I was not only enjoying the experience – I was learning.

When working at Cossor Electronics I became involved in a problem-solving forum that was both unique and, in my opinion, good practice. It requires a particular mind-set and the ability to be a bit imaginative. I found it enlightening, intellectually challenging, and enjoyable. It was set up to look at production problems, technical engineering problems, sometimes procedural and occasionally practice-related, the latter often involving staff practice. My expertise was in methods of working, process and project planning. The forum was solution-focused and did not attribute blame. Discussion was open, with participants encouraged to contribute. Out-of-the-box thinking was welcomed. People were listened to respectfully, and no idea was ridiculed or put down. Negativity was not allowed. Each person was allowed five minutes maximum to present their ideas. Obviously they could answer questions and contribute later in the process. The forum was a safe place, designed to brainstorm and, in doing so, tease out a solution. The most important rule of all: you had to hang your ego on a peg outside the room. I found it totally liberating. I discovered in the years since, particularly in my police service – certainly in the higher ranks – such a process was seldom, if ever, used. There were rarely safe areas in which to openly and honestly offer an opinion without being interrupted, put down and – in some cases – ambushed and ridiculed. Rank, it seems, equips the bearer of that station with perfect, unassailable knowledge on everything. Such a pity, and such a barrier to progress. I found the police service to be, for many, a 'career-driven' organisation, where some were guarded and unwilling – perhaps unable – to openly contribute to a forum like the one I have described. There were obviously exceptions, but they were far outweighed by the hewers of wood. I find that politicians, in the main, possess the same traits.

# CHAPTER 4

THE year of 1969 was momentous in many ways. Northern Ireland saw riots as the troubles flared. Two of the aeroplanes I had worked on during my Ferranti days came on stream. Is that a mixed metaphor? Concorde's maiden flight was in March, followed in April by the Harrier 'Jump Jet' entering service with the RAF. The Beatles launched their last album, and the ten shilling note died. On the 29th March, the Grand National was won by Highland Wedding at a price of 100 to 8. I was not in the factory that weekend; I was in Scotland getting married. I think every person in the factory scooped the jackpot that day. Not many months later, the first man walked on the moon. I worked on for a while and, as I did, I studied at night classes and got qualifications in Mathematics, English and Geology. I also qualified to be a member of the Institute of Work Study Practitioners, initially as a Licentiate member. The lure of getting back to Scotland was too strong, however. Within two years I was on the move again. I got a job in Aberdeen County Council as an Organisation and Methods Officer. I left some good people in Essex.

A house in Peterculter awaited. Work was based in an office in the centre of Aberdeen city, with my 'beat' stretching the whole of the county. I enjoyed the job, and I really enjoyed working with the characters I encountered across the county. I happened across the occasional communications issue. The further into deepest Aberdeenshire one ventured, places like Strichen, Methlick, Chapel o' Garioch and Clatt for example, the broader the language. Doric, certainly to my untrained ear, was challenging enough when being addressed individually. However, when listening in to a conversation between a group of 'county' dwellers, one starts to wonder what country you are in. I used to love it. I could only look on in awe – or perhaps that should be listen in awe – then get someone to explain later. The Doric, to my mind, is as important as Gaelic to our culture, and I think we should make more of it. It is a wonderful sound, so earthy, organic, natural. We must not lose it. On the road I worked out of the council depots at Ellon, Aboyne, and Port Elphistone. I had an assistant, Duncan McNab, who had worked on the farms for years. He used to point out bothies in farms as we passed, then regale me with suitable bothy ballads. 'Aikey Brae' being his favourite. In between all that, we did work. A lot of my work involved negotiating with trade unions; that could be difficult.

Change management was central to my job. On occasion, one would come across a situation that required someone to change the way they worked. Sometimes it was obvious to all. Not always. One particular task proved tricky. Some rural roads narrow through time as the verge grows and encroaches onto the tarred surface. In these circumstances, the grass and turf has to be cut back. I encountered two massively different approaches to this. In one area a single worker on a tractor towed a trailer with a 'ploughing' device, called a shoe, attached to the back nearside of the tractor. The driver simply ran it along the verge, where it acted like a plough and folded the intruding turf into the shoe where a rotating part flicked it into the trailer. One operative could cut back about fifteen miles of verge a shift. Another area had a road roller, a lorry and two walking operatives; four staff in all. At the back nearside of the road roller was a vertical spike. It sliced along the verge, thus separating a section. There was no shoe or other ploughing type of machinery. The two walking workers shovelled the loose turf into the back of the accompanying lorry. Four workers and two vehicles. They managed about six miles a shift. So, one worker with tractor and trailer, fifteen miles; four workers with road roller and lorry, six miles. How does change management work? Not as obviously as one might expect. You might think: simple. Instruct the staff to use the more efficient process. I agree that is exactly what many organisations would have done. Discussion was held with staff and unions. They were reluctant to change from a method that had served them well for years. They argued that single crewed process required someone who had worked on farms for years and was used to ploughing. Perfectly correct. There was a training issue. I agreed that training had to be set up. However, in the interim, instead of issuing operating procedures instructing the tractor method, I designed an interim bonus that related miles completed to staff hours, all reduced to a lowest common denominator that paid out by the hour based on the efficiency of the hour. It was up to them how they worked, certainly in the short term and until training was set up, but their bonus would reflect their method. That lasted for a few months until they agreed to a retraining programme. We were able to agree on the more efficient operating procedure, and they all bought into it. They were hard workers. Change can bring anxiety and distrust. Explanation, honesty, discussion, listening and allowing time to adjust all helped them come to terms with and accept the change. There was no requirement for confrontation. Years later, when working as a police officer in communities and for a time in Central Regional Council as a seconded police Inspector, I found this a useful experience.

Back to Aberdeenshire. Not many years later, the accountants of the council removed most of these tasks as part of a cost cutting exercise. Jobs were lost, and redundancy notices were issued. They did not engage in change management. Most organisations do not engage in the niceties, or perhaps the inconvenience – the bother – of change management. The police service certainly did not. The logic employed seems to have been, perhaps still is, very top-down in my experience. 'I am in charge; just do what you are told.' To be balanced, however, in some circumstances that might be the only way. I was gaining experience in dealing with people and negotiating through potential conflict situations. Having a clear understanding of the aim was crucial. Lessons that would help when I got to the police; not that such a notion was in my head at that time. I worked for another couple of years with the council until another path had to be chosen.

> 'I say it is useless to waste your life on one path, especially if that path has no heart.'
> 'But how do you know if a path has no heart?'
> 'Before you embark on it, you ask the question: Does this path have a heart? If the answer is no, you will know it and then you must choose another path.'
> 'But how will I know for sure whether a path has a heart or not?'
> 'Anybody would know that. The trouble is, nobody asks the question: and when a man finally

realizes that he has taken a path without a heart, the path is ready to kill him. At that point very few men can stop to deliberate and leave the path.'

Carlos Castanada
*Teachings of Don Juan* (1968)

\* \* \*

It was the autumn of 1973. I was twenty seven years old. My young son, seven months old, was sitting on the living room floor in the middle of a large white blanket. His mum and I were searching him and his clothes for *Ceratophyllus hirundi-nis* and *Oeciacus hirundinis*. To be honest, I would not recognise either. There was a big empty glass jar on the blanket. Actually, it was not empty. On the bottom was a very small thingy. It may well have been one of the former; we did not know. What we did know was it was an intruder, a parasite. The former named is actually better known as a 'house martin flea', a nasty blood sucking critter. You guessed correctly. Our house had several house martin nests under the eaves. We resided in a top flat apartment in a council block in Peterculter on the western outskirts of Aberdeen, near the main Aberdeen to Braemar road. We had been visited by the council pest control officer, who had advised us of the perils of house martins nesting on your building. It appears their nest can be infested by twenty or more ectoparasites, and often some will migrate inside the building and find a human host. The two most popular would appear to be the two I named. They, the pest control officers, left the jar and advised we search our son, his bedclothes and his clothes. We had to check our own clothing. We only ever found a couple on the wee one. We took our captured species to be identified. The pest control returned and spread powder and removed the nests, which were empty of young house martins by then. If you are interested, we had captured a house martin flea. By the way – so you can get a timescale to this – Zolton Varga played for Aberdeen Football Club then. I used to wonder if Ceratophyllus Hirundinis was also a Don. I recount that incident, not only because we found an infestation on my young son, but because I found something else. I found a dream reawakened. A realisation, and it was as vivid as finding the house martin flea on my son. So, with captured flea in the jar, I chose that moment to tell my wife that I needed to move on from Aberdeen County Council. She asked me why. I told her I wanted to become a police officer. That is all I ever wanted to be, and at my age perhaps this will be my last chance. Her reply was short and supportive. 'If that is what you want, just do it.' A walking Nike advert, years before they even thought of it.

Decision made: just get it done. House martins had absolutely nothing to do with my decision. I have often thought of that moment, and my police dream that had lain dormant. An old aunt has since told me that she always knew I would be a police officer. Not only was I certain that I wanted to join the police service, but I was equally certain it would be north of Inverness. I did not immediately start the ball rolling, as I wanted to run it past my dad. A couple of weeks later he and I were in the bar of the Rothes Arms Hotel in Glenrothes. He had moved again, and the Co-op in Glenrothes was where he was at that point. His last Co-operative, as things turned out. It was a rare occasion to find us in a bar together; in fact, I do not recall another such liaison. My mum had died earlier that year, June 1973. I tried to visit dad as often as I could. He was an extremely self-sufficient individual, and never gave any indication he needed support.

Mum had suffered from cancer; various outbreaks, over many years. She was a survivor, but there comes a time – no matter how spirited and stoic – when death arrives. We had been told towards the end of 1972 that mum would not live that year out. She spent a lot of time in her bed. She was reading Isaac Asimov's *Foundation* trilogy, and was in a hurry to get it finished. Her doctor was hurrying her along, as he was also reading it. Her copy, that is. As mum finished the first book, he took it away. Then the second, and so on.

It was a poignant, muted Hogmanay as we headed into 1973. New Year was big in our household, much more important and emotional than Christmas. We never partied during Hogmanay; drinks were charged and we waited, glasses poised, for the bells and the New Year. Our toasts to family and friends, past and present, were meaningful and heartfelt. Be assured, we did party after the bells. But not that year. Mum had joined us and sat quietly in the corner of the living room. It was midnight, we were entering the new year, and I just stood looking at her, hesitant. I did not know what to do. What was there to celebrate? Looking at her and thinking about her. She smiled and raised her glass, as if telling me it was fine; life is what it is, death is as real as living. Celebrate what we have and had. Tears were running down my face as I took that sip then hugged her. She whispered something to me I will never forget. It was not a secret. It was a message of hope, because that was mum. She said, 'Dying is a consequence of living; don't be frightened of it. Please be what you can be. And remember, they told me I was going to die before New Year. They don't know everything. I will live to see my first grandson; I can go then'. Our first born was due in April

1973. Yes, the infested one. He was born on 20<sup>th</sup> April, and mum died on the tenth day of June.

That night in the bar in the Rothes Arms, Glenrothes, I told my dad about my police dream. He was less than enthusiastic, and tried to talk me out of it. He said I was not suited to be a police officer and, interestingly, he did not think I was 'hard' enough nor my character tough enough. That conversation was perhaps the only meaningful one dad and I had ever had in the twenty-seven years of my life. I never forget it. I was not angry; I was disheartened. I think I was also a bit lost, as the main influence on my life was trying to turn me from my dream. I wondered if I was being foolish for even having a dream. Do working class people have dreams?

Anyway, I said I was only thinking about it and changed the subject. I loved my parents, and really doted on my dad. Heroes do not occupy much time in my thinking. I do respect a few people. But heroes? Not really. That is different. However, in my longish life I can say there are three people who fit into the hero category for me. Physicist Richard Feynman and then, rating above Richard, my brother and my dad.

I think I probably disappointed dad. I frustrated him in some ways. I have no idea what he wanted of me or what he thought I should have achieved. We never spoke about anything like that. Sad to relate, really. I honestly have the belief that he did not rate me very highly. I don't think he appreciated – perhaps understood is a better word – how hard I tried to live up to him. He was one of the bravest men I ever knew; he feared nobody. He was not a bully; he was not a 'hard man'. He was honest, had integrity, and was definitely not born to follow. In fact I don't think he ever learned to walk backwards. Not based on Stalin or Soviet Order 227, 'Not one step back', but pretty similar. He never saw his reflection in me, and sadly never would get that opportunity. He was wrong that night in the Rothes Arms. I did join the police service a few months later and, within six months, dad was dead. I regret, selfishly, that he never got the chance to see something in me he had never known.

He was such an influence in my life. Some years after, when I had about six years' police service, I was stationed in Tullibody, Central Scotland Police. It had a fearsome reputation as a seriously hard community, and some out-of-town officers were reluctant to attend calls there. There was a regular route in the village, one patrolled on busy weekend nights. The 'mad mile', we called it. On it were the four main hostelries, and each carried its fair share of weekend merriment and drunkenness as well as the occasional to regular 'incident' requiring police attendance. The Inn, The Top Club, the Bottom Club, and the Abercromby Arms Hotel. All quite close to each other, and situated around the small Tron Court, the shopping precinct in the village, forming a natural circuit as far as patrolling was concerned. Some nights it honestly was hairy, and could be a bit scary. Normally two officers paired on weekend nights. They circled the 'mad mile' in the van. An older officer once gave me some sage advice. If you find you are on on your own (as happened occasionally) and Alloa cannot supply assistance, don't patrol the 'mad mile' on your own. Drive to the Ditch Farm road end and stop passing vehicles and carry out document checks. You will be working, but you will be out of harm's way.

I was on my own one busy Friday night. As the pubs and clubs were emptying, I got into the police van with the intention of driving down Stirling Road, Tullibody, to its main junction with the Alloa to Stirling road at the Ditch

Farm. Yes, I was about to hide at the Ditch Farm road end as advised and carry out alternative police duties. I was no distance down Stirling Road when my dad appeared in front of my windscreen, looking at me. As vivid as day. He asked me what I was doing and told me I was not raised to hide. I should get back to where people needed me and do my job. I pulled into the layby in Stirling Road and wept. I dried my eyes, turned the van around, went back to the police office, parked, got out, and locked it. I spent the next two hours on my own, walking the 'mad mile'. Calling in to each premises and keeping visible. I never forgave myself for nearly letting him down. He would never have hidden; he would not even have contemplated hiding.

# CHAPTER 5

**M**Y dream of joining the police, however, was tempered with a touch of reality. I had tried to get in twice before, and had been turned down both times. In 1962 or thereabouts, I applied to join Stirling and Clackmannan Constabulary as a cadet. I got an interview and sat some kind of test at their headquarters at Randolphfield, Stirling. I remember it was still the actual Randolphfield house, since demolished. My application was rejected because my English grammar was below standard. They also commented on my lack of general academic qualifications. I did not even reach a medical – probably just as well, as that would have ended my aspirations anyway. A few years later, sometime in the late 1960s when I was living in Whitecraig, Musselburgh, I applied for a second time. This time Lothian and Peebles Constabulary would put me to the test and again find me lacking. They had no quibble with my academic efforts. They discovered my lazy left eye and my quest to don the chequered hat again bit the dust. Willie Merrielees was the Chief Constable of Lothian and Peebles Constabulary at the time I was rejected, on medical grounds. I found that ironic, as he had fingers from his left hand missing and was four inches below the regulation height of five feet ten inches when he joined as a constable. He had other hidden talents I suppose. He was also a comic book hero and featured in *Valiant* comic between 1991 and 1994.

So as I headed to the selection process for Ross and Sutherland Constabulary in early 1974, I was not confident of success but soldiered on nevertheless. My entrance examination had been organised within the force area I resided in at the time. That was how I found myself at Bucksburn police office one early afternoon, nervously waiting. I was not alone. Several other equally nervous candidates also waited. The form-filling formalities soon over, the sergeant explained stage two: the written test. He described it as a mixture of arithmetic, English language, reasoning, and logic. He added that it would be carried out strictly against the clock, as part of the test is to gauge how the applicant operates under pressure. When we were all finished, I was asked to wait behind. He explained as my test was for another police force he would mark it right away and let me know how I had fared. On his return he said he was going to do something a bit unorthodox. He let me know I had passed, adding: 'I have never had a higher pass mark. Would you consider joining our force?' I thanked him and stuck with my first choice, Ross and Sutherland Constabulary. An old fashioned loyalty thing; I had started with them, and felt it the right thing to do to continue with them.

Two or three weeks later, I headed to Dingwall and went through the first interview. I must have done well, as I was asked back for a second interview. This time my wife accompanied me. The Chief Constable was present at the second interview. At the time I did not think anything of that. Years later, when I had more experience, I learned that was not the format in other forces. The Chief Constable of Ross and Sutherland was Kenneth Ross, and without doubt I rate him as the best officer of that rank I ever encountered. He was charming, open, and welcoming. He said he regarded Ross and Sutherland as a family and he took each appointment seriously, making a point of greeting all new officers and where appropriate their spouse. He had many kind words for both my wife and myself. However, he said something directly to me that I have never forgotten. He simply said, 'I welcome you to the the the Ross and Sutherland family. I want you to enjoy your service and remember, you hold an important role in the community; never forget that and never abuse it'. He concluded with a short statement: 'make haste slowly'.

A police officer had to seek the permission of the Chief Constable to marry in these days. I was unaware of that when being interviewed, and perhaps bringing my wife to meet the Chief Constable at my initial interview process was about that. Did he just want to be assured that she was acceptable? Perhaps I am being uncharitable. His support of me a few months later, as I will relate, evidences my initial positive view of him. When I worked in Central Scotland Police a few years later I saw a letter, dating from the 1930s. A Sergeant was reporting to the Chief Constable his opinion as to the suitability of a woman one of their constables wished to marry. The officer had written to the Chief Constable seeking permission to marry. The Sergeant carried out background enquiry about the woman. His enquiry was not at all positive regarding her character or the character of her relatives. The officer was refused permission to marry her. I did not see whether he resigned the service and married, or whether he stayed in the service and broke off the engagement. That practice continued in the police service until well into the 1970s. There were a few things in the police service in those days one was either not allowed to do, or that could only be done after permission was granted. Buying a house was not allowed. Going to certain 'at risk' foreign countries was either forbidden, or permission had to be granted. Permission to grow a beard had to be sought and was seldom granted.

The next and final part of my recruitment was my medical examination. I was sent to the Ross Memorial Hospital in the town to see the police surgeon and undertake my medical. I remember thinking, 'Oops, they've got this in the wrong order; they needn't have wasted their time'. I was a bit anxious. Doctor MacLachlan was a really pleasant and decent person, and made me feel a bit more relaxed. He quickly got the business done and announced: 'You are very fit; exactly what we need. You have passed'. I was puzzled. There had been no eye test. Taking my courage in both hands, I blurted out, 'You've missed the eye test; I will fail'. He was completely unfazed. 'Don't worry; it's a formality. I have never seen anybody fail.' I told him I wouldn't pass it. I have a lazy left eye. He said, 'It can't be that bad; let's get it over with'. I failed. He was taken aback and said, 'You have failed. Your left eye is a problem; you really cannot see well with that eye'. I obviously agreed. He then said, 'your right eye is twenty twenty'. He was silent for a few moments, an eternity, before he spoke again. 'You know, they are so keen to get you started. You are the type of person they, we, need in the police service. What does a lazy eye matter? You are in. I wish you well in your career.'

Since that date and that decision, I have witnessed people's natural courage and common sense in decision-making becoming increasingly suppressed by an unchecked rise in political correctness, health and safety, and blame culture. Decision-making has ceased to be an objective-led process that considers the problem to be solved, or the victim, or what are we aiming to achieve? No, it has become increasingly internalised, with the person making the decision placing themself at the centre. How will the decision affect me? Decision-making has also become an emotional process; objectivity has taken a back seat. I was once asked by a Superintendent to explain my decision-making process. I gave him my version, and he disagreed. 'Your decision has to be based on the following: where can it come back and catch me out?' Sad but true. However, I mislead. That is not decision-making, and someone who thinks like that is not a decision-maker and should not be allowed into the position they hold. 'When the world is destroyed it will not be destroyed by its madmen but the sanity of its experts and the superior ignorance of its bureaucrats', as John le Carré once put it.

The police surgeon in 1974 who carried out my police entry medical examination did not internalise the decision. He looked objectively at the issue, weighed up the evidence, added some common sense, and made an outcome-based decision. He was no coward. I will contend that if I were to attempt to enter the police service today, I would be unsuccessful. Over the next thirty years as I rose through the ranks to Chief Inspector and served a lot of people in a lot of communities, not once – not even a tiny bit – did my lazy eye ever make a whit of difference to my performance. It never at any time disadvantaged me and, more importantly, it did not disadvantage the communities and the people I served. Likewise, being four inches below the regulation height and missing fingers on his left hand seemed not to have disadvantaged the 'comic book hero' who rose to be Chief Constable of Lothian and Peebles Constabulary. My police career, my dream, was underway.

As it happened, my dream had financial implications. When working at Aberdeen County Council my annual salary was in excess of £10,000. On joining the police service it dropped by more than half that amount to under £5,000. I cannot remember the exact figure. In 1978, when I had transferred to Central Scotland Police, the Edmond Davies report into police pay and conditions awarded us an increase of 29.7%. That would take the lower paid to over £5,000 per annum. The then-Labour Home Secretary, Merlyn Rees, is quoted in Hansard saying the increase would be implemented by 1$^{st}$ September that year, 1978. It wasn't. In 1979, Labour lost the General Election and a Conservative government, with Margaret Thatcher at the helm, replaced it. It was she who implemented the recommendation about police pay. Many suggested it was to keep us 'on side', as there were plans to tackle some of the more powerful unions. I had no idea at that time about the motives of government, whatever colour it may be. I was married with two children and the wage increase was welcome, because financially it was a struggle to make ends meet. In the few years before the pay increase, a lot of experienced officers left the service, many never to return. It has been suggested that I chased my dream at the expense of my family. That was never the case, and they knew that. What they got, in return for less household income I confess, was a dad and husband who had found himself and was actually happy with his lot. There was a way, certainly in the area I worked, of helping out with the bills. I agreed to participate in a pooled arrangement of working on farms during rest days. One officer kept a record of our shift rotas and was the conduit for farmers in the area. If a farmer needed someone to do a shift – picking fruit, lifting potatoes, bailing hay, anything really – they simply called the 'gang master' and he would call round and get the required number of officers. We got £1 an hour and, occasionally, a bag of the produce would appear beside your car as you were leaving.

My career started at Ross and Sutherland Constabulary on a Saturday, 23$^{rd}$ March 1974. My first posting was to the Traffic Department based in police headquarters, Dingwall. On relating that to officers over the years, they are a bit skeptical. The Traffic Department? Are you having a laugh? You were not authorised to drive the beat car, never mind a traffic car. But I was not having a laugh. The first person I met that day was a police support worker, Doreen. We still keep in touch to this day. Her husband was also a police officer, and a bloody good curler. I spent that first day filling in forms, reading police reports, and looking at maps of the force area. I also made a lot of tea. In the afternoon, one of the officers took me out in a traffic car and showed my round some of the area. We drove out to Tarvie on the Ullapool road just short of Garve and had a bacon roll and a cup of tea at the filling station. In these days it was easily recognised – no, not just by the petrol signs. There was a larger-than-life-sized statue of a man wearing a white coat sitting on a bench beside the pumps. That statue, carved out of wood, was there for years, and was only moved back nearer the building – now a café – a few years ago. The officer who showed me the sights of Tarvie and Garve was the same officer who drove the Universal Carrier to the top of the Struie Hill, as mentioned earlier in this book. Then it was back to Dingwall, and off home to my lodgings in the town. The Sunday involved a bit more learning about the force, and then two actual tasks. I had started work. My first real duty as a police officer on Sunday 24 March 1974, still innocent of police uniform, was calibrating the speedometer in each of the two traffic cars stationed at Dingwall. They were Triumph 2.5 litre petrol injection machines. I held a stopwatch as the driver drove on a long straight part of the A834 road, heading west out of Dingwall. Between Dingwall and Fodderty, the straight is over half a mile in length; enough distance for the two posts that mark the measured half-mile. Holding steady at thirty miles an hour, I clicked the stopwatch on and off at the posts. Check the time against the distance. Speedometer calibrated. Job done. Essential evidence, as I was to discover.

A van was travelling south-west on the minor road between Easter and Wester Rarichie on the Fearn peninsula. It was a wet Sunday afternoon in early March 1974. The occupants had 'jumped the budget' many years before that date; the husband was driving. He was thirsty, so his wife clambered into the back of the moving van and – among the detritus of old blankets, clothes and more – she unearthed a Primus stove which she primed and lit. Where she got the water to boil I cannot tell you. Anyway, water is in a pan precariously balanced on the lit stove. Tea is the planned outcome of the activity. Fate intervened, as you probably guessed. Something on the road caused the driver to swerve. The travelling chef, perched in the back of the van, was caught off balance and could only look in horror as boiling water and energetically burning stove pitch over into the blankets and clothing. The driver, on hearing his passenger scream out an expletive, looked behind to see flaying arms and blazing blankets. His wife was doing her best to beat them out with her bare hands. He instinctively reached behind with his left hand, having freed it from steering duties, in order to engage it in frantic fire fighting duties. Attention diverted, his right hand, still engaged in steering duties, pulled a fraction to the right – as it will in such circumstances – causing the still-moving van to veer to the right across the road and through a fence. As fate would have it, the land dropped steeply down from the road on that side. The van careered down the steep slope into the field, bouncing and rolling, before coming to rest amongst a herd of bemused cattle. The back door burst open during the accident, and flames poured out. Luckily and thankfully, both occupants quickly emerged from the van – dazed, shaken and bruised, with minor burns to their arms and hands, but suffering no serious injury.

Writing up a summary of that road accident was my second task as a police officer. Having calibrated speedometers, I was now transferring information from road accident report forms into the official force road accident book. Every road accident the police attended had to be written up on a road accident form by the reporting officer. Forms then wend their way to police headquarters where, before being filed, a summary of the information was transferred into said book. It was quite boring work and, after an hour or so of such sleep-inducing labour, I came across the tale of the travelling tea party. Perhaps due to my boredom, coupled perhaps with my zany, pictorial sort of humour, I could not help visualise the whole incident. I struggled to stifle my laughter. The sergeant eventually emerged from his office to enquire into the source of my mirth. He was quick to rebuke me and remind me that laughing at the misfortune of others was not called for. He asked me if the kettle was on and, as he turned away to return to his office, I could swear I saw a smile on his lips.

As my service got into its stride, I would soon meet the occupants of the 'tea' van and their immediate and extended family. They were a family of Tinkers who resided and travelled across most of Ross-shire and had done for many years. I use the 'Tinker' term advisedly, unashamedly, and with not a trace of derision. In my time in the north and later in the Central Belt, I came across many travelling families. I have sat in their houses – Reid, Williamson, Bradshaw, McPhee, Stewart, and more. I have also drunk tea in their 'benders', and listened with bemusement as they spoke 'Cant' in my presence. It will be of little surprise to know that I had little or no idea what they were saying. I am not sure where the word originated; however, old Scottish Gaelic has a word 'cainnt' which translates to 'speech' or 'talk'. A similar Irish term is 'caint'; hence 'Cant', I suppose. Some suggest it was developed as a form of secret jargon. Well, it worked as such in my case. A couple of the words I do recall; 'manishi' was a woman, 'gadgie cove' meant a man. I also heard what sounded like 'lorrycar' and I took that to be lorry. 'Scaldie' referred to us 'normal' folk, bidin' in hooses. 'Bender' was the tent. They carried tarpaulin sheets and would locally source branches, ideally willow, which they would secure into the ground and bend over into a kind of tunnel over which they stretched the tarpaulin sheet. Lo and behold, a 'bender'. I urge you not to follow my instructions to construct a shelter of your own; I never mastered the technique myself. But you will get the idea. I prefer Tinker to other terms. During my many contacts with travellers, I would ask about how they would describe themselves. 'Tinker' was preferred over 'Gypsy Traveller'. The term 'Scottish Traveller' was also acceptable. I can say most of these conversations were with Tinkers in the north of Scotland. The word Tinker derives from the Irish, 'tinceard', meaning tinsmith, mender of pots and pans, sharpener of tools. The whole area is ancient and confusing. What might offend in one area might not in another. There is no doubt, however, that whether Tinker, Gypsy, Gypsy Traveller, Scottish Traveller or whatever, they – as a race or collection and mixture of races – have been persecuted over the centuries.

In my later policing life as a Chief Inspector, I represented my force and, on occasion, the Association of Chief
Police Officers in Scotland, on various working groups, committees and meetings involving the Scottish Government,
Health Services and Local Authorities on the subject of Diversity. The considered wisdom was to label our travellers as
'Gypsy Travellers'. I remembered my cups of tea, benders and
Cant, and my conversations with actual living travellers on
their origins, their race and their name. I thought, 'nonsense;
the term is not accurate, nor is it inclusive' – and to some of
my 'friends' in the north, it was puzzling. A centralised system
does that; it operates, for its own benefit, on the principle of
the 'lowest common denominator', and in doing so excludes so
many. A parallel: in the United States there has been an
equally strident brigade of the politically correct, who have
decreed that 'Native American' will be the designation for the
people the European illegal aliens cleared out. Meanwhile, the
indigenous peoples are happy and proud to be Indians, and
actually use that term to describe themselves. I am happy to
call my cousins, Indians.

The Tinkers I encountered in the north were like anybody else. Some were prone to push the boundaries of the
law, some were difficult, most were simply decent people –
just like us scaldies. A colleague of mine, with responsibility
for an adjoining police area, had many years of experience in
dealing with communities and with Tinkers who passed
through. He had been, for a few weeks, trying to persuade
one group to move on from an area. They had no permission
to set up camp, and the land owner was losing patience – both
with the police 'inaction', as he saw it, and with the immobile
travellers. Despite several promises to move on, they stayed
put. The officer was experienced and resourceful. He had a

certain sympathy with the Tinker fraternity, and persecution was not on his agenda. However, they were in breach of the Trespass Scotland Act and liable to arrest, without warrant. He had better get something done, short of criminalising them. Having ascertained there were several children involved, he called at the camp and spoke to the assembled adults. He mentioned the children and the fact that they were not at school, it being a school day. He said he assumed they would have exemption certificates, giving authority to keep the children off school during the term. He explained that he was really busy and did not have time to inspect documents that day. However, he definitely would be back the next day and would want to examine all the certificates. Agreement was reached and he headed off to his important meeting. He sent his Sergeant out to the camp next day. When he arrived, there was no camp. A solution had been reached, and nobody had to be arrested or criminalised. It was, and probably still is, a stop-gap solution to an age-old question. I think instead of debating and getting into a lather about what we call certain groups, we should spend more time in seeking sustainable answers to the harassment faced by certain members of our society. Yes, they have a different way of living; it does not mean they are wrong, just different. There is so much talk about the vibrancy and colour brought by different cultures associated with immigration. We have a colourful and vibrant society in our midst. Embrace it.

# CHAPTER 6

I GOT my uniform on the Monday, and was sworn in by a local Justice of the Peace. My warrant card followed later that day. Another step; my goodness, this really is happening. My first full week in the service was spent moving dead bodies from Dingwall to Inverness. There was no post mortem facility in the Ross and Sutherland Police area. All sudden deaths had to be taken from wherever the occurred in the force to a temporary mortuary in Dingwall. A sudden death is when a person dies and the doctor who pronounces life extinct – a quaint wee phrase, I have often thought – does not know the cause of death, and therefore cannot issue a death certificate. Any violent death, accident, suicide or murder, for example, falls under that category. A 'normal' death, like a heart attack, that happens in a public place, even if the certifying doctor is aware of the cause, may also be designated as a sudden death. In the case of a sudden death, the Procurator Fiscal will normally instruct that a post mortem be carried out to establish the cause.

So first thing every morning that week, I accompanied the civilian driver to the temporary mortuary building in Ferry Road, just opposite the Ross Memorial Hospital. One had no idea, day on day, what would face you. So every morning that week it was with trepidation that I opened the door of the building. It was not the prettiest week of my service. There were bodies every day, most old but not all. There was a nine year old boy, and there was a male who had died as a result of a 'hit and run' road accident in the west. One morning we really struggled because of the smell. An unfortunate young man had drowned in the Beauly Firth. His body was not found at the time. Weeks later – the very week I was on 'death transport' – a local farmer spotted his body washed up on mud flats. It was not a pleasant journey that day. I had no idea that so many people could die in one week and would require to be subject to a post mortem to establish cause of death. I had never seen so many bodies.

A few years later, not long in Central Scotland Police, I was involved with a sudden death. I needn't have been; however, I was doing a favour for a colleague. I started duty at six o'clock one evening to be met with my day shift colleagues hard at work typing what was a sudden death report. The officer dealing with a sudden death had to have a report with the Procurator Fiscal by the next morning. He asked me to do him a favour. He said he did not want to see another dead body in his career, and would I accompany his other day shift colleague to take the next of kin to view and identify the body prior to the post mortem examination. The unfortunate lady had lain dead in her apartment for about two months. She had sons, but they had not seen her for more than two years. We made contact and got them to the mortuary. I had never dealt with a sudden death since joining Central Scotland Police, and did not know the procedure. At the mortuary my colleague established that the two sons were happy to view the body in the actual room where bodies are stored. They did not require that we take their mother into the 'viewing room' and cover her with a sheet, then pull it back to let them see her face. I was unsure about this. However, as it was my first sudden death in Central Scotland Police I went with the flow. First mistake. The four of us trooped into the storage area. There were a row of metal doors along one side. These were the refrigerated storage shelves; three shelves arranged vertically behind each door. My colleague explained that if the two sons stood to one side he would open the door and pull out the tray containing their mum's remains. They agreed. I was standing directly in front of the refrigerated door, a few feet out. My colleague opened the door to reveal three trays, and three pairs of feet. Our body was on the top tray. One day, no doubt, it will be my turn to be in such a tray. Well, till that day arrives I will never forget what happened on that fateful night. Confidently and with purpose, he grabbed the handle and quickly pulled the selected tray out. As the feet were to the front the tray needed to be brought out to the fullest extent so the sons could see their mum's face and identify her. My colleague had the tray nearly fully out and the weight was distributed between his pulling hand and the tray runners. He explained later that, for an instant, he somehow assumed the tray was like a filing cabinet drawer and had a stop. The fatal flaw in his understanding of the mechanics of the mortuary tray. He soon realised his mistake when he pulled the whole tray off its runners. The inner end of the tray then dropped a few inches and stuck on a part of the freezer below. At that point – and it all happened in an instant – he was taking the whole weight of a dead woman and a seven foot of metal tray on the fingers of one hand. He then lost his reason all together, and he let go. With the inner end balanced on a part of the freezer's metal frame, the other end dropped like a stone, creating a chute. The lady had been washed and was quite soapy. She slid down the slide like a scene from some macabre film, continued across the full width of the room to stop with a shudder against the far wall. I had to take urgent avoiding action or she would have swept me off my feet. As quick as a flash, my colleague apologised and said there was a fault in the drawer. He then calmly asked if they recognised her. They did. We hustled them out and I drove them home. We never heard another word about the incident. If it had been up to me, my colleague would have finished in one of the vacant trays. There were none.

Back in Dingwall, after the Friday morning body run, the officer in charge of the Traffic Department took me to the canteen and bought me a bacon roll. He asked how I felt. Was I alright? I said I was. My bacon roll was consumed with no problem. Seems I had passed that test, if that is what it was. And if it was, it was not the last.

My next test took place the following week. My police driving competence test. I have called it that because I am not sure what else to call it. It was like no other test given to police drivers I ever came across again. I was fully uniformed, and had been for a week. I was getting better at using the police radio. But I was still a passenger. On the Tuesday afternoon I was in traffic car, Tango 2. The Traffic Department Inspector intercepted our journey and told me to get into Tango 1 and drive. He did not say why. I drove, as instructed, to the traffic lights in the centre of Dingwall and stopped. No more than one hundred yards. He made me turn left onto Tulloch Street. I then followed his directions as we twisted and turned through Dingwall to eventually come to a halt in a woodyard, where he got out and made me wait. After a short delay the Inspector got in the car and told me to drive to police headquarters, down past the academy. It is not there now, as PFI gave it a new home. At the rear of HQ he told me to stop and wait. He got out and looked about the small back yard. He instructed that I reverse into the tight parking space he was indicating with pointed finger. I did. He then pointed to a really awkward parking place right in beside the building and told me to reverse into that space, which I did. He instructed me to get out and wait. He headed inside the building and, a few minutes later, came out with a document that he made me sign. I did not get a copy; something that proved a tad of an issue ten years or so later in my career. He told me I had passed, and I was qualified to drive police cars and police traffic cars. He then told me I was driving the Lord Lieutenant the following Saturday. In the event I did not drive him, and in fact spent the whole day – more than twelve hours – parked at the Skye ferry jetty at Kyle of Lochalsh watching for a blue car with front nearside damage. We were looking for the car that had knocked down and killed a pedestrian in a hit and run road accident some days before, near Dornie. Incidently, the victim was one of the bodies I had transferred to the Mortuary at Inverness during my first week in the job. We did not see anything of note.

Back to my driving test. I had driven no more than two or three miles, never exceeded 25 miles an hour, all in-town driving. Having satisfied the Traffic Inspector I was a competent driver, I would never have another driving test or driving course ever again in my thirty years of service. No three weeks at the police college. Nothing. Similar to telling fellow officers that I'd started in the Traffic Department, my short 'one-off' driving test again met with comments like 'you have got to be joking'. I was not joking. I was a Sergeant in Central Scotland Police, a dozen years or so after my 'driving test', when an Inspector in the Traffic Department was getting his house in order. He could find no trace of my driving record or having qualified to drive police cars. He contacted me. I simply told him I passed all that in Ross and Sutherland Constabulary. Did they not send my certificate when I transferred? He resolved to sort it out. I never heard of it again, and quietly completed my thirty years police service without one recorded driving blemish. I had two that were not recorded, but they can wait until later.

I got into the police by the vision of a clear thinking doctor. I got authorised to drive police vehicles again by another unshackled man of self-determination. You will now begin to understand why I do not get exercised by systems. They have their place, but remember they are a guide; they do not make decisions. Today, in the single Scottish Police Service, some senior officers do not make decisions. The Sergeant is told to wait while they refer to the Standard Operating Procedure (SOP) on computer. It is my understanding there are about seven hundred SOPs and guidance documents in this modern police service. I call it dumbing down, removing initiative, creating robots. Follow that logic and a day will come when nobody will have the ability to think for themselves or make a decision. It is Orwellian; it is Communist centralisation at its worst. It is actually scary. Is there a benefit? Not that I can think of. Or perhaps there might be one. The Sergeant could have looked at the SOP her or himself and read what to do. Thinking of my previous life before the police service – organisation and methods and work place efficiency – one could make a good argument to remove the more senior officers. The higher ranks could then become redundant. Now that is a money saver.

My Traffic Department experience in Ross and Sutherland was about to come to an end. After about two months I headed to the Scottish Police Training College at Tulliallan.

The Basic Training Course lasted one month, and was quite intense. It was a mixture of physical training, the criminal and road traffic laws, general police duties, and powers in relation to dealing with each. It came complete with marching; bulling boots till one could recognise oneself in the reflection; ironing shirts and uniform; squaring away your bed space and more, all carried out with the added psychological pressure of everything being carried out to a ridiculous timescale. A five minute limit between classes being the cornerstone of the psychology strategy. If adjoining lessons were classroom-based, that worked out well. However, many of the activities were not classroom-based, such as lifesaving lessons in the pool, marching until you got it perfect, and other pursuits like seven-mile runs or negotiating your way round an obstacle course set by a psychopath. Five minutes to get showered, dried and back in uniform, and into your classroom and seated. After one such session we were sprinting along a corridor, buttoning up shirts, fastening trouser belts, forcing feet into boots, socks wet from poorly dried feet, when a Fife officer grabbed my tie and put it around his neck. Seems he had lost or forgotten his. Such was the high level of institutionalised induced stress that we really were on edge. Our home forces were supplied with reports about our performance. Forces took them seriously. The first two years of a police constable's service is a probationary period. Your service could be terminated at any time during that two years with no reason given, other than the quaintly worded 'not likely to be a suitable police officer' or some suchlike career-ending phrase. Not properly in uniform was a black mark. I wanted my tie back, I had not lost it. I grabbed him and asked for my tie. He laughed at me. It was obvious he was trading my tie for his black mark. He was instantly on his back with one very 'charged and motivated'

Ross and Sutherland officer kneeling on his chest with one hand on his throat. With the other hand I retrieved my tie.

Muir of Ord was my first actual proper police posting in a community, starting on day two after my Basic Training Course. It would be my first step into a community as a police officer, and the first step towards understanding the social mores within a community – certainly from a police perspective. I had been exposed in the 'tighter' communities of factories; this would be different. Or would it?

I, with a mixture of excitement and apprehension, turned up for my first shift. I was in plenty of time, and was met by the office clerk who was busy typing. After introductions she pointed out my tray and some things about the office. I read some documents and my joining instructions. I was getting my bearings when the lady told me there had been a road accident. I asked her if the rest of the shift was attending and should I join them. I am sure she was smiling, certainly inside, when she informed me the rest of the shift were not in fact at the accident, quickly adding 'you are the shift'. I was, and probably looked, a bit in shock. I said, 'am I on my own?' She quickly affirmed and told me that the Sergeant would likely be in to introduce himself about midday. I sheepishly asked for directions to the accident. I really had little idea of the geography. She showed me on a map. I then asked where the police car was. I got it out the garage and was about to set off when she waved me to stop. I opened the window to be asked, 'do you know your call sign?' Furnished with that useful information I set off, hopefully in the direction of the accident. I soon came across the carnage. There was a car on the verge and a second car on its roof, broadside across the road. The road was blocked. There were other vehicles and a few people milling about. I walked forward slowly – well, not too slow, but certainly not running. I wanted to look in control, and I thought running would not give that impression. I remember thinking: stay calm, and look as if you know what you are doing. Two were not 'milling' anywhere; they were obviously injured, though not seriously. They were sitting on the verge being attended to by others. I spoke to the two casualties and confirmed they were shaken and probably in shock. I radioed headquarters with a status report, asked for an ambulance, a breakdown truck to clear the road, and some assistance to direct traffic. I remember thinking, 'what have I forgotten?' I got details of witnesses and ascertained the circumstances surrounding the accident, as well as marking the relative positions of the cars with chalk and establishing the point of impact. The rest was a bit of a blur, because within minutes there was an ambulance, a traffic car, and a beat car from Dingwall. And before I knew it, probably down to adrenalin, everything was under control; the road was cleared, the cars moved, and the injured away to hospital. I informed the control room. All that was left for me was to get statements, ascertain if there had been a traffic offence, and get the various reports completed. I have no idea how I achieved all I have just related, or how I remembered what to do. I must have switched to autopilot. I was concentrating so much, I felt in a daze. Or should that be a zone? It all seemed so quick and, whilst being apprehensive as I travelled to the incident, my training took over and nerves disappeared. I had attended a few road accidents in my two months in the Traffic Department, and that obviously helped. I also have to give credit to the Police College and the course I had just completed. I already said it was quite intense, and now I know why. Some time later I related the event to a colleague. He laughed and told me it was not rocket science. Get there, get an ambulance, get evidence, clear the road, and write a report. What's hard about that? My first actual, hands-on, fatal road accident was at Muir of Ord. A pedestrian had stumbled from the footpath into the front of a passing cattle truck. There was a full horse-shoe adorning the front grille of the lorry. His head struck the decoration, and he was killed instantly. It was at night and, as we worked by torchlight, my senior colleague informed me I was walking about on the brains of the poor victim.

Muir of Ord was the section station; the lead police of-fice covering the Black Isle, or Ardmeanach as some tell us was its original name. Meaning Holy heights, from *ard* for height and *manach* for monk. We just called it the Black Isle, but I wish we had used its ancient variation. I will relate two completely different tales; one fishy, the other not at all fishy. Their importance, in my opinion, is not just about what phys-ically took place. No, it is something else. Working in commu-nities is a privilege, requiring constant balance and diplomacy. Just as important is the ability to apply discretion, balanced by community needs, public order, and the law of the land. The notion of public interest is also an issue and, I would suggest, is the factor most associated with discretion. To achieve that balance, I contend, one has to be based in the community, be close to it, to demonstrate firmness and fairness. Only in that way will you have the slightest chance of gaining trust and delivering an effective service.

A report of an assault and robbery late one evening saw me team up with a local officer. We hurried to the re-ported locus: a derelict farm with some outhouses. A pension-er lived in one of the outhouses – you might call him a va-grant, that might be wrong. I understood he had once worked on the farm and chose to remain there after it went out of business. He was the victim. As we turned off the road and headed up the gravel track to the farm, I saw a figure staggering about on the track heading in our direction. In the car headlight the whole of his head was a mask of red; it was surreal. It was blood, his blood. He was well known about the village, and spent time in the bar of the local hotel. He had been there that night. It was difficult to get a clear picture of what had happened to him, as he was obviously in shock. He was able to tell us that when he got home two men appeared from behind a building and attacked him. They knocked him down and kicked him about the head and body. He gave what description he could. It had been two younger males in dark clothing. He really did not remember much else. They had taken his money, his breakfast eggs, and his pension book. After we got the poor man into the ambulance, we went to the hotel and asked around. He had been in that night, and left quite late. Nobody remembered any strangers. We scouted about the village and the area for a wee while, then I learned another trick of the trade. We drove away from the area for a couple of miles, turned off the road, put the lights out, and simply waited. It was sometime after midnight and the place had closed down for the night when we drove back into the village. As we travelled the main street, we saw two males walking in our direction. Young men in dark clothing. They did not run; probably had nowhere to go. I actually don't think they knew it was the police; I guess our headlights hid that. We spoke to them, explained what we were investigating, and got them to sit in the car. We informed them we suspected they were responsible for the robbery, and told them to turn out their pockets. One had the old man's pension book. There was no sign of eggs and, while they had some cash, they claimed it belonged to them. They had no weapons. They were detained, and we set out to take them to Dingwall

Headquarters to be further interviewed and processed. We had hardly set out when they both became very aggressive; verbally aggressive, rather than physically. They seemed to be directing their ire at me. They said they knew where I lived and that my wife was going to be raped when I was out working. I have no idea how much of that was based on actually knowing, or just nasty threats. Whatever, it was getting louder and the threats were getting more personal. I suddenly realised we had turned off the road as the car bumped across rough ground and came to a halt. My colleague, as he was alighting from the car, asked if I could fight. I did not understand what he meant. Once out, he pushed the seat forward to allow the person sitting behind him to get out. I was not sure what was happening. I soon found out. The guy behind him refused to get out of the car. My colleague simply got back into his seat and said: 'Well, it's up to you. Don't let me down'. I should explain, yes, I was quite fit. I played rugby, mountaineered, and for a brief spell did a bit of boxing. But I had little experience of no-holds-barred 'street fighting'; my life had not been like that. Yes, I had stepped in to aid my younger brother when he was bullied at school and had dealt with my own bullies – of whom there were few – but nothing since. I got out, not really sure what I was expected to do. I let the one who had been threatening me out the car. He immediately went for me, like a greyhound out the traps, and head butted me on the chest, knocking me backwards. He was then right on to me in a thrash of fists. I regained my balance and my composure, and thought *fuck, this is real*. Once I had regained my poise it was not an even match. I waited on his next rush at me and kind of smothered him in my grasp and refused to let go. He kept trying to headbutt me, but I kept him close. We both tumbled to the ground and, for a few minutes, we writhed about accompanied by much cursing and expletives, heaving this way and that. He unsuccessfully tried to bite me. I got him in a headlock and applied pressure. I held on for 'grim death'. He eventually gave up, and I dragged him to the car and put him in the back. I was covered in mud, had a graze on my face – no idea how that happened – and one hand had bad gravel rash. Apart from gasping for breath, he seemed fine. We headed for Dingwall and completed the procedure. Later I asked what it was all about. My colleague told me policing is not all about paperwork, neat and tidy evidence and clever interview techniques, outmanoeuvring suspects. Sometimes to achieve making the community safer, the thin blue line, out on point, might have to assertively hold the line. Twenty-twenty vision after the event is always easy for the drivers of desks. They will always be uncomfortable with that view, but they are not out here. It is not about bullying, but sometimes you have to step up, because if they think they can do it to you, then who is left in their way as they head for the old man in his outhouse? 'In terms of tonight, there were two issues. I know the families of the two we arrested. The one you tackled is a particularly nasty individual; he was trying you out, testing you. He had never seen you before; it's kind of instinctive. You will have noticed I was not challenged. I knew I wouldn't be; it was all about you'. He added, 'you will do well'. I heard no more about the incident, and was never threatened again. Well, not when working in that area. They both admitted their involvement in the assault and robbery and, some time later, they received short prison sentences. The old vagrant never really got over the incident and soon after went into a home.

A few weeks later I was again with that officer. It was about midnight, and we were on the low road beside the

Beauly Firth. It was a calm night and there was a fairly full moon. Visibility was good. He told me to slow down and drive down to the water. I turned the engine off and coasted the last few yards. No slamming doors. The water was like a mill pond. Being the probationer, I took the 'off-shore' part of the task. I could see two rows of floats stretching out away from the shore into the firth. The one furthest left did not go too far out. It was set up nearest the small white cottage that nestled on the shore. The floats on my right stretched much further out into the water. I removed my tunic and waded out into the Firth. When the water was at the top of my thighs, I grabbed the net and pulled at it till it started to move. An inquisitive seal snorted over to my right as it bobbed about watching my every move. I simply pulled the net hand over hand toward the shore. My colleague on the shore pulled it onto the grass and coiled it into a pile. Before long we had 110 metres of modern monofilament drift net on the shore. No fish. We stowed it at the police office and I headed home, still soaking wet.

I had only been in the service four or five months and I had dealt with a serious road accident on my own, had a full on fight with a robbery suspect, and waded into the Beauly Firth to remove an illegal drift net. Quite full on, and yet I had been told by some of my south-based colleagues that policing in the north was boring, quiet, and I should wear slippers. Whether they were right or wrong, who knows? One thing I did know. It sure beat the pants off negotiating bonus schemes with unions. A couple of weeks after the wading incident I asked what was happening to the net, expecting we would be interviewing a suspect. This was my first lesson in decision-making in the public interest; something I will make further reference to later. My colleague was smiling and said: 'You are still learning about communities and their needs'. He told me he gave it to two old pensioners in the village; they lived in cottages along the shore. Their nets were old and torn. They simply shared it by cutting it into two nets. 'We will not be taking any further action'. Along that part of the Beauly Firth there are several old cottages. In years gone by, they were occupied by estate workers, crofters, and some old fishermen. Most of them put out an old drift net in front of their homes and caught the occasional salmon, and still do. It is an ancient practise and predates the Salmon and Freshwater Fisheries Act, which, in spirit, was probably not intended to catch these old guys. Anyway, further along the Firth there is a fishing village, and one of the commercial fisherman had taken to slinging his longer, more modern net out in front of the local nets. In effect, plundering their catch; their ancient right. The locals asked if something could be done. Something was done. They saw that as a fair solution, carried out by a fair police service. What we did was in the public interest.

Policing communities need not be complicated; a simple solution often provides an acceptable answer. A centralised system with Standard Operating Procedures and career aspirations would have struggled to find such a just solution. Not long after that, we were again patrolling Ardmeanach when the very commercial fisherman – whose net had been recently redistributed – passed us in his car heading in the opposite direction. We suspected salmon! By the time we got turned, he had taken flight and had gained a bit on us. We could see him a fair distance in front, heading into the village of Munlochy. We sped through the village and, as we emerged onto the junction with the Fortrose to Dingwall road, we had lost him. We raked about for a while, to no avail. The following week he told my colleague that he had turned into a field and stopped behind a hedge, hidden from the road. He waited for a couple of hours and headed home. He had about forty salmon in his car. No harm, no foul. Last laugh to him. Not many years ago, well after having retired from the police service, I was in a popular pub restaurant in Inverness. The proprietor, who had owned and run several eateries in the area over the years, was reminiscing with me about old times, like old farts do. He had known the commercial fisherman I just referred to, who passed away some years ago. He was aware of the salmon chase and the net mystery. Small communities are like that. 'Touch ane, touch a',' he laughed. How does Visit Scotland expect us to keep locally sourced fresh salmon on the menu if we do not source it locally? It is the cornerstone of our tourist economy.

# CHAPTER 7

B Y August 1974 I was out of lodgings in Dingwall and living with my wife and young son in a rented farm worker's cottage at Garguston, a couple of miles into the Black Isle from Muir of Ord. The weekly rest day's drive from Dingwall to Falkirk to see my family could stop. It was a torturous drive in those days. No Kessock Bridge, and no dual carriageway on the A9. I had only been living in the new farm cottage about a month when the Muir of Ord Sergeant came there to to tell me my dad had been found dead at home in Glenrothes. I was not long back in the force from my Basic Training Course at Tulliallan. I drove south. He was in his bedroom, and his fishing gear was in the corner as if ready for a day on the loch. A glass with whisky still in it was on the bedside table. My dad subscribed to the Reader's Digest, like a lot of people in these days. The latest edition was lying on the bed; it was bent back at the article he had been reading. Ironically, it was entitled 'How to cope in a crisis'. I smiled. My dad would say that after the day in France when German soldiers had used him as target practice, thankfully not very accurately, every day was a bonus. His bonuses had come to an end. I had lost my mum and dad in just over a year. I was twenty-eight years of age, and I felt like a ship without a rud-der. He would never get the chance to reassess his opinion as to my suitability to be a police officer. As I grew up through the 1950s I had no real idea how hard life was for my parents, and other parents. As I get older and allow my memories to drift back over these early years, it becomes clearer the day-to-day struggle they had, each and every day. In allowing yourself that perspective, the love you had – have – for them grows. I was not consumed with grief at either of my parents' deaths. Should I have been? I was sad, and I did shed a tear. I was angry, however – certainly in terms of my dad. He had gone to war as a teenage youth, and spent five – hard – years in a prison camp, along with thousands of other young men. He got home to have his efforts largely ignored, air-brushed out, as if he, they, had failed in some way. He never got over feeling betrayed. Then, never really coming to terms with the experience, he died at fifty-four years of age. My parents taught my brother and me to be pragmatic, realistic. Life is a series of hurdles; the sooner one understands that, the easier it will be to cope. My dad was the most reasonable, practical man I ever knew. I never saw him panic. I missed both parents, and the older I get the more I miss them. As fate would have it, the officer who was dealing with my dad's sudden death was also not long back from his Basic Training Course at the Police Training Course at Tulliallan. I noticed he had found his tie.

My days on Ardmeanach were destined to be short. There was a village called Hill of Fearn further north in Easter Ross. The Chief Constable had decided to reopen the single officer station at Fearn. It had been closed a few years before. I never did find out why it was now being reinstated as a police office, although jaloused it had to do with the development of oil rig manufacture at Nigg and perhaps political pressure had been applied. I did know, however, that I was heading there. It is never that straightforward. I had actually been informed I was heading for Brora. Another officer was destined for Fearn. That officer questioned the posting. He was reassigned, and I got Fearn. So, seven months' service – still in my probationary period – I was bound for a single officer station. My probation seemed to be on the right tracks. Colleagues who expressed disbelief at my lazy eye episode, followed by my 'arduous' police driving test, were aghast at me being posted to a single officer station whilst still in my probation – in fact, not even a third of the way through it. Whatever anybody thought, it was all true.

Before I got to Hill of Fearn, however, I had a shock. I received a witness citation to appear at a trial in Dingwall Sheriff Court. My first trial; not my last. My calibrated speedometer had been active. The week after I was involved checking the accuracy of the speedometer, it had been used to catch a speeding driver. He had pleaded not guilty. I was a bit nervous. I should not have worried. I only had a very minor role – a walk-on part, as my more experienced colleagues would say. I was in the witness box probably no more than two or three minutes. The defence lawyer did have one or two simple questions for me, probably just to assure the court I was who I said I was. He did ask if I would tell the court what calibration meant. I stayed in the court to observe and learn. I was interested in the thoroughness of the Procurator Fiscal. He had six witnesses for what seemed quite a low-key offence. I should say, alleged offence. The two police officers who stopped the accused and reported him were the main witnesses. I spoke about how I calibrated the speedometer, and the officer who drove that day agreed with my version. A sergeant spoke about checking the accuracy of the stop-watch using the Greenwich 'mean time' pips on the radio. Finally, a man from the local council spoke to the accuracy of the measured half-mile posts. The defence was simple. He admitted speeding, but not at the speed cited. I don't think the Sheriff was too pleased. He asked the defence lawyer if he had heard him correctly. 'Your client admits to travelling at more than thirty miles an hour'. The defence lawyer explained: 'He disputes the speed cited by the Procurator Fiscal'. The Sheriff asked, 'so what speed will he accept?' The defence would accept forty-seven miles an hour, and not the fifty-two miles an hour cited. There was a discussion involving the Procurator Fiscal, the Defence Lawyer and the Sheriff, during which the latter – sounding a bit annoyed – said: 'Your client admits to travelling well above the speed limit, and you think it acceptable to waste the courts time on trivia?' He then announced that the Crown would accept the amended speed, and found him guilty subject to that amendment. I don't think the amendment made any difference to the sentence. I found it entertaining. And so I had survived my first trial and got a verdict.

My second trial was also road traffic related. This time it was driving whilst having consumed alcohol and being over the legal limit. I again was the corroborating officer. We had observed a male driving erratically, became suspicious, and stopped him. His breath smelled of alcohol, so he was asked to provide a breath specimen. He did, and it was over the limit. His second breath specimen was also positive, over the limit. He was reported, and pleaded not guilty. We were about to be given a lesson in clever defence work. I was first to give evidence. The Procurator Fiscal set the scene and got me to talk through the circumstances. The defence lawyer had little to ask, although what he did ask was crucial.

'Officer, can you tell the court where you breathalysed my client?'

'At the locus', I replied, a bit puzzled as to what he was getting at.

He said, 'I am sure you did breathalyse him at the locus, but where exactly was my client when asked to provide a specimen of his breath?'

Still not sure where this was heading, I replied 'in the police car'.

The next question was immediate: 'Yes, but where in the police car?'

'In the back seat', I responded.

'What made my client get into your police vehicle?'

I replied that my colleague had told him to.

'Thank you, officer. No further questions.'

The Sheriff thanked me and said I could leave. I took a seat in the public benches. My colleague went through the same questions from the Procurator Fiscal and the defence lawyer. The instant he confirmed the position of the accused when breathalysed, the defence lawyer asked 'why did my client go into the back seat of your vehicle?' The response, similar to mine, was because he had asked him to sit there. There were no further questions, not even re-examination from the Procurator Fiscal. My colleague sat beside me, keen to find out the defence's next move.

The Procurator Fiscal moved that the case had been proved and sat down. That marked the conclusion of the prosecution case. The defence lawyer immediately made a 'no case to answer' submission. There followed a short debate, during which the defence argued that a member of the public – particularly one like his client, with no previous dealings with the police – would have no clue as to police terminology or procedures. When told, or even asked, to get into the back of the police car, his client – quite reasonably – thought he had no choice. In effect, he thought he was being arrested, and to all intents and purposes he had been. As a person can only be arrested after providing a positive breath specimen and not before, the police procedure was flawed. We had arrested a suspect – his client – before we had evidence. After listening to the debate going back and forward for a time, the Sheriff made his judgement in favour of the accused. No case to answer. The accused went free. I learned from that, and never again did I breathalyse any person inside a police car. More importantly, from that day forward I studied and made sure I knew all my powers in relation to every offence and crime.

It was always my understanding that the police was a community service and when I joined it was, without doubt, a service. I understood there had to be an element of enforcement, but, principally, it was a service. So was I correct or I just being being unrealistic, fanciful even? It is not only an interesting question; it is crucial to understanding the police function. I believe that question is not understood, certainly by many in our communities, and I will suggest by many within the police itself. I further suggest that confusion, that uncertainty, allows the unscrupulous within its ranks – supported by the 'blind eye' of politicians – to constantly push the boundaries until it becomes more and more unrecognisable. As power creep advances, so the spectre of a police state becomes more of a reality. I will return to that thought, that worry. To get a handle on where we are now, and perhaps how we got here, it will be useful to go over some of the history, but not a lot of it.

In Scotland between 1667 and 1930 an organisation called the Commissioners of Supply was the forerunner of County Councils. They were based in Sheriffdoms and their original and principal function was to collect tax. However, they expanded their remit and carried out many of the roles now performed by County Councils. The Local Government (Scotland) Act 1889 saw most of their duties move to Local Government, and in 1930 Commissioners of Supply ceased to exist. However, when they did exist, the Commissioners of Supply for the Stirlingshire area had some interesting discussions and deliberations about the police. In 1840 they increased a constable's retaining fee from £3 per annum to £5 per annum. They also specified a constable's duties as follows: 'intercept and put away vagrants or suspicious characters – to interpose on occasions of petty irregularities tending to a breach of the peace and give prompt attention to any case of actual crime occurring in their neighbourhood of which it would enjoined them to send immediate information to the general Superintendent'.

In 1974, the year I joined, The Police Duties and Procedures Book was supplied to all new recruits. It is a thick tome; however, a useful starting place. I will mention only the duties prescribed under the Police (Scotland) Act 1967: General duties and jurisdiction of Constables:

(1) Subject to the provision of this Act, it shall be the duty of the constables of a police force,
    (a) To guard, patrol and watch so as -
        (i) to prevent the commission of offences,
        (ii) to preserve order and
        (iii) to protect life and property.

A bit different from the 1840 variety. Early references to crime and how it should be dealt with do not always mention police. For example, the Parliamentary Register in 1594 has an entry condemning certain crimes and even naming the clans responsible. The crimes cited are theft, robbery, oppression, and sorning. (The latter meaning extortion – in particular, free quarters and provisions.) The entry goes on to actually outline the clans guilty of such behaviour, and including many that will be familiar to this very day – perhaps even your own: Clangregor, Clanfarlane, Clangun, and broken men of the surnames Farquharson in Braes of Mar, Grahams in Menteith, McNabbs, and many more. While that is far removed from how things will be presented today, it still states that prosecution will require two witnesses. Something that, as I write, some argue is not necessary. A political decision, and not related to fairness or evidence – and in my opinion, fraught with danger.

Policing, in the modern sense, was developing in Scotland from about the turn of the nineteenth century. A portion of the early police responsibility included, in addition to a specific responsibility for crime and disorder, looking after roads, footpaths, water supplies, and the disposal of rubbish. There are earlier historic references to actual policing. Let me start in the mid eighteenth century, with Sir John and Henry Fielding, half-brothers who lived in London. They were concerned with the effects of crime in their society and, in the mid-1700s, with the help of Government in the form of a budget to pay expenses, they jointly set up a group of citizens who would investigate crimes and be responsible for prosecuting offenders. They did not have uniforms and probably, because of that, some referred to them as detectives. Part of the philosophy was that it would be better to prevent crime happening in the first place. That group of non-uniformed citizens was called the Bow Street Runners. They were confined to the City of London. I think their main focus was on enforcement, and probably one would say they were a force. Interestingly, their presence was not universally welcome. Some felt it had a negative impact on their individual liberties, and also there was seen to be conflict between a police force and the tradition of local authorities. Policing and ideas of policing were to abound in that era. Among others, Patrick Colquhoun, a Scottish judge, opined that the function of policing should be an arm of Government, controlled by the judiciary. He also said their main purpose should be by their presence in communities, to prevent crime and disorder, and to apprehend offenders as required.

Then it was the turn of the 'Bobby'. The most famous development probably was in 1829, when Sir Robert Peel established the Metropolitan Police Act. It allowed for a uniformed force of one thousand officers to patrol the City of London. They were famously, or perhaps infamously, labelled 'Bobbies', after Robert Peel himself. The name stuck, and to this day is still synonymous with uniformed policing throughout the UK. In fact, in the Highlands it is still in common use. When I policed in Fearn a century and a half later I was called the Fearn Bobby. I regarded that as a term of endearment. Perhaps I was kidding myself? In 1839, the County Police Act allowed for policing modelled on the Sir Robert Peel idea to spread outwith London. Even then, I think it was principally about enforcement. Even with the spread of policing there was still debate about how it would – or should – interact with the notions of individual rights and the collective needs of society. I think a debate about this area of the social contract is relevant to this very day. Despite 'Bow Street Runners' and 'Peelers', the police service in Scotland had still not cemented itself as a mainstream, perhaps essential – dare I say, irreplaceable – service. In October 1844 the fate of policing in Stirlingshire came under threat as the Commissioners of Supply evaluated the need for policing. The note of their minute on this subject read: 'Communicate with conveners of the counties of Dumbarton, Lanark, Perth and Clackmannan in order to ascertain how far these counties are disposed to abandon their present police establishments providing neighbouring counties concur with them in doing so'. I found no other reference, and assume policing remained as a county service.

Moving into the 20th century. During World War One. October 1917, at Passchendale with the battle raging in the mud and rain, the troops needed to get an urgent message back to headquarters. A courier was sent out into the battle to try and deliver the crucial message. It would normally have taken less than half an hour to complete the journey. The messenger had not travelled far before coming under German fire, somewhere near Menin Road. One round struck home and passed directly through the body of the messenger, breaking one leg and passing out through the back, missing the spine. The courier did not lose the message and, despite terrible injuries, kept on to finally deliver it some twenty one hours later, before dying the next day. For that feat, above and beyond the call of duty, the Dickin Medal was posthumously awarded. That feat was carried out by messenger pigeon number 2709, one of thousands to serve and die during that war. Homing pigeons were an important form of transport. When other communication links were compromised, non-existent in some cases, the pigeons could be relied on. They carried messages directly from the front line back to base. I assume that such was their importance to the war effort, the Government saw the need to control them at home. The Police Service had an important role in that regard. A role that was directed by the provisions laid out in the Defence of the Realm Regulations 1914. Pigeons were something the police had to take account of. To be more accurate, homing or carrier pigeons. This Special Order, sent out to officers of the Stirlingshire Constabulary on the first day of October 1914, illustrates that responsibility and was penned thus:

The regulations provide as follows:
No person shall in any area which may be prescribed by order of the Secretary of State keep or have in his possession any carrier or homing pigeon, unless he has obtained from the Chief Officer of Police of the District a permit for the purpose (which permit may at any time be revoked) and the Chief Officer of Police may, if he considers it necessary, or expedient to do so, cause any pigeon kept in contravention of this regulation to be liberated.
The area to which the above applies now embraces the whole of the United Kingdom.
For the purposes of getting together information as to the keepers of these pigeons in the County, Constables in charge of detachments are to get in touch with the secretaries of any Homing Club in their District which are affiliated with the National Homing Union, or any similar association. Inquiries are to be confined to such people in the meantime. All members of the National Union have been asked by their Union to co-operate and assist the police in every way they can. Lists giving

names and addresses of all persons who are known to possess pigeons of the classes named are to be prepared and sent to this office, through Divisional Superintendents, as soon as possible. When these lists have been received arrangements will be made to have all known pigeon lofts visited along with trustworthy members of Homing Clubs or others who have special knowledge of these birds.

It goes on a bit longer, and ends by articulating how a contravention of the regulation shall be dealt with. I found that part extremely funny. It comes at the end of the actual regulation part of the order and states: 'A police officer may, if finding the situation necessary and if expedient to do so, cause any pigeon kept in contravention of this regulation to be liberated'.

I had a vision: Constable liberates pigeon from 'doocot'. Pigeon shakes its feathers, flies around the houses for a few minutes, like they do. Constable leaves locus of the crime looking for the nearest kettle. Job done. Realm well and truly defended. Having been liberated, the treasonable pigeon comes home to its doocot and coories in beside its unliberated chums.

About that time, the secretary of the Carron Bowling Club kept racing pigeons. When playing bowling matches away from home, he always took one of his homing pigeons. After the match he affixed the score to its leg and released it. The score was always home before he was.

Pigeons caused a smile some years later. Not that I am suggesting they are normally that funny. I was Sergeant of a unit at Camelon. Our telephones had been down for nearly a week. One of the officers was interested in, and kept, homing pigeons for the purpose of racing. On the Thursday of that

week he brought in a small wicker carrier basket containing
six homing pigeons from his loft in Stirling. During our lunch
break we were given a mini lecture on pigeons, shown wings
spread out and what various feathers were called. Lecture
over, pigeons back in their carrying basket, we headed outside
to release our celebrity feathered custodies from a grassy area
next to the office. As we trooped out the office to witness the
release we were met, on the stairs, by a telephone engineer,
complete with toolbox. I asked who he was, as if it was not
obvious. He said he was here to fix the telephones. I told him
he was too late. We would not be requiring the telephone
anymore; we have invested in alternative technology. He
looked a bit puzzled. He followed us to the grass area and
watched in disbelief, turning to laughter, as six pigeons carefully flapped their way out of their basket, ascended into the
sky, circled over our position and headed off in the general
direction of Stirling. I honestly believe that engineer will have
dined out on that story for years.

I came across these interesting, perhaps amusing, Chief
Constable's directives and orders from the police archive.
Note the language and style:

### 17 October 1914
If Airship distinctly seen, or engines heard, tele-
graph or telephone (whichever quicker) to HQ
Scottish Command. Telephone No. 36 Post Office,
Edinburgh.

### Special Order Nov 10 1914
Central Belgian Refugee Committee for Scotland,
HQ in Glasgow, have asked for and been granted
permission by the Chief Constable to send refugees into any part of the Stirlingshire Constabu-

lary Area, excepting the parishes of Airth, Grangemouth and Muiravonside.

It is interesting that the Chief Constable gave the permission. I am not sure if that would be the case today.

### Special Order Nov 9 1915
Owing to depleted strength of the Constabulary the annual census of the population will not be taken this year.

### Special Order May 4 1915
Members of Constabulary to assemble for uniform fitting. The men are to wear the same underclothing as in winter.

On the subject of uniforms, I came across an order in a logbook, still with the police. I think it was the Bonnybridge or Denny logbook, dated about the same era. It simply ordered officers not to wear their uniform trousers in bed.

### Chief Constable's Order Nov 30 1931
Stopping Vehicles; officers rely too much on lamp at night and hand signal in daylight. In future they are to use their whistle at the same time as lamp or hand signal. This will attract the attention of any other occupants on the spot and discredit statements made afterwards by occupants of the vehicle concerned that they were unaware of the attempt to stop them. It is, in certain conditions, possible with lights reflected on a wet surface for a driver to overlook the flash of a police lamp.

## Chief Constable's Order Sept 1934
Arrest of a Blind Person.

I include this latter order because it is the first evidence I have seen of gender equality being displayed in a police order, or a legal document for that matter. It concerns how an officer will carry out the arrest of a blind person. All reference to the person uses the female pronoun, all the way through. She or her, never he or him. This is 1934, long before gender equality was highlighted and probably before the anomaly was even recognised. This is at a time when he or him referred to both sexes, in just about every law and legal document. So why was the order written like this? The writer does not explain. So I will offer my own explanation. I set myself up to be knocked down. I think because the subject is sensitive – dare I say, touchy feely – the author turned convention on its head and used the female pronoun. Simply that. One might argue that in itself displays sexism.

And lastly in this interesting interlude, I refer to another arrangement during World War Two. In order to support the war effort, Constables were often diverted from normal police duties to work on farms. In this case the Chief Constable decreed that six Constables be directed to carry out ploughing duties in local farms.

To conclude my deliberation on the police as a service or a force, I make reference to a 1976 study by Robert D. Storch in the *Journal of Social History*, entitled 'The Policeman as a Domestic Missionary: Urban Discipline and Popular Culture in Northern England 1850-1880'. He highlights the fact that hitherto most studies into policing concentrated on their activities in preventing crime and public disorder. He argues that they were about more than that, and provides evidence about how unpopular they were. It seems the public did not consider them as a service, and saw them as oppressors. While the study is about their role in rural areas in the north of England, it may well translate to other areas and certainly to similar rural areas in Scotland. The police were seen as an arm of municipal and state authority, and their activities directed to control or manage the behaviour and institutions of the working class. Storch refers to it as 'acting as a lever of public discipline'. It is perhaps significant that at this time there were other movements afoot with designs on changing public behaviour. Storch refers to these movements as urban middle class elites, hell bent on educational, temperance and recreational reform. Supporting this middle class voluntaristic reform, approaching from a different direction, was the police officer and his truncheon. The police therefore complimented, and were as important in this urban 'Change Strategy', as the Unitarian 'domestic missionaries' who roamed the cities of the north at that time. Hence the Domestic Missionary reference in the title of Storch's study. In this role, the police were hated and seen as an unwelcome intrusion into working class life and their recreational customs and activities, at the behest of the higher classes. Police activities included cracking down on foot racing, and on ale houses and pubs – including making sure these establishments did not operate at times of divine service. They also started moving on groups gathering in the street, particularly in the vicinity of public houses and much more. This tactic was referred to as the 'move on system'. The police were seen as lazy parasites who did not really work for a living. Other derogatory terms used at the time were blue plagues, blue drones, and blue locusts.

In short, the police were not a service, they were a force: enforcers. What I find interesting was, where did they direct their enforcing activities? It seems not to have been at the middle and upper classes. It would appear that their behaviour was acceptable and not requiring police intervention. I argue that whilst things did change over the years, that basic premise about where we should mostly direct our activities has not changed that much. We police in an age of double standards and hypocrisy. A close look at Storch's full study evidences that while things have moved on in terms of the way we express ourselves and the subtlety of our more modern approach, deep down – at core level – there is so much that remains the same. We are cloaked in a thin veneer of civilisation. To repeat something from earlier, I do regard policing as a service, and when I joined Ross and Sutherland I did join a service. I had not thought about who the service was for. History shows it was designed to keep lower classes – the working classes, the dangerous classes – in order. To amend or restrict their behaviour. It continues today. The government, supported by health experts, put measures in place to restrict smoking. They are attempting, through propaganda and pressure on producers and retailers, to reduce our use of sugar. I also contend that the 'named person' legislation, which is being debated as I write – but has been adopted by some local authorities anyway – will have more effect on the vulnerable families than the those who can afford a lawyer, to misquote from Andy Wightman. Alcohol is also in that same drive, with minimum pricing being pursued. Something that is more likely to impact on the poorest, and not make one whit of difference to others. In terms of the latter, even the temperance societies would have struggled to explain away this ancient evidence from the Bible, where it contradicts the drive to reduce alcohol in society: 'Give strong drink to him who is perishing and wine to those in distress; let them drink and forget their poverty and remember their misery no more' (Proverbs, 31: 6-7).

These days we see an increase in the use of private security or guarding companies. For example, many of the more exclusive city apartment blocks hire private security to look after their safety. On the other hand, council-run apartment blocks – unable to afford private security – will rely on the police for that purpose. One might argue the police will see their role as controlling the occupants, as opposed to ensuring their security. While there is a truth in that, I feel the police – while 'acting as a lever of public discipline', to borrow an earlier phrase – should strive to achieve more of a 360 degree focus. I genuinely believe the police have developed from the 'missionary' days and moved on to deliver a more all-round service than originally intended. I think there are still gaps, and on occasion decisions not to pursue or prosecute certain people expose these gaps. I am not sure the gaps are all about class anymore. Celebrity and establishment paedophilia, as well as culturally-driven sexual abuse of young girls – such as in Rotherham – evidence some of the gaps. In such cases, the police and the prosecution system step gingerly, and on some occasions step aside for fear of offending minority cultures, certain religions and/or influential people, who might be able to impact a career. An interesting thought. Whilst serving in the Policy Unit of Central Regional Council some years later, I was party to this comment: 'The better-off areas – Dollar, for example – do not need police patrols. They are well off enough to have insurance'.

There was a time when police were deliberately recruited from the lower working classes and from farm stock. The logic being that they were used to physical hardship, were strong, and would work long hours in any weather. It was also believed they were used to being obedient. What psychology was used to pit them against their own kind? The studies of Frederick Winslow Taylor about work place psychology might give some insight. A uniform, a guaranteed wage, being part of a structured team and security, might just do the trick. The service today recruits from a much more eclectic base, most well educated, some with a career path in mind, but not all. While that does not guarantee perfection, and in fact can – and does – bring its own problems, my point is that on average there is a better chance of creating a more sustainable, creative and committed, dare I say, a more educated workforce. To support that view, I have worked with and amongst them. Of course we were not all perfect, but the majority I encountered were committed, honest officers who would – and did – put in that extra pound of effort to keep the people in their community safe. Importantly, they saw the police as a service, no matter the machinations of senior management or, dare I say, politicians. I once suggested at a senior officer's meeting in Stirling that if headquarters was dumped in the River Forth with us still at our desks, the Sergeants and Constables would just carry on delivering the service. Trust them.

# CHAPTER 8

IT is October 1974. Having completed seven months police service and still in my probationary period, I am about to be transferred to Fearn. My family will move from the farm cottage on the Black Isle to a detached cottage in the village, Hill of Fearn – the main village on the Fearn peninsula. The police office being a single room within the Police House, with a separate, self-contained office door at a gable end of the building. The peninsula lies at the northern end of the Great Glen Fault. On a map of Scotland you can trace a straight line from it through Loch Ness and Fort William to Oban. It is about fifteen miles long by about five miles across at its widest part. In addition to Hill of Fearn, there are six other villages on the peninsula. Portmahomack at the northern tip, Inver in the east, the seaboard villages of Hilton, Balintore and Shandwick, on the west flank; they run into each other like a single settlement. To the south is Nigg. The latter more of a hamlet than a village. The village of Hill of Fearn was established in 1240 with a monastery that, in later years, became Fearn Abbey. Still there to this day. There is evidence in the peninsula of Pictish habitation long before that and, based on the 'skull' I make reference to later, evidence of Neolithic habitation.

The oil boom was well underway before I found myself emulating Hamish Macbeth at Fearn. Within the Fearn beat was the Nigg complex of Highland Fabricators, where the biggest dry dock in Europe – certainly at that time – was situated. Because of the number of workers employed at the yard, however – as many as three or four thousand on occasion – the site owners, Brown and Root, Wimpey paid the police board for a number of Ross and Sutherland police officers to actually work inside the complex. Shift arrangements meant that only one officer was likely to be on duty at a time. There was a police office on site and, just off site, Highland Fabricators had bought a small 'but and ben'-style cottage, completely renovating it for the officers' use. Meals were obtained on site; in short, a good posting. In terms of practical policing, the on-shift site officer and I would, when required, team up. On occasion I would support them on site, and vice versa. A good arrangement, not just because I was fed on site once in a while. In addition to that, Highland Fabricators provided accommodation for a few hundred of their workers at the site. When I first arrived at Fearn, that accommodation was provided on one retired passenger ship, the *Highland Queen*. It had first been named *Princess Elizabeth* when launched at Fairfields yard in Govan on 16 January 1930. It had a name change to *Pegasus* in 1960 before receiving its third name, *Highland Queen*, when bought by Highland Shipping Company to be used at Nigg as accommodation. In April 1976 it was towed to Zeebrugge and scrapped. Initially there were two accommodation ships. The sister ship to *Highland Queen* was *Hermes*. It was launched in the same yard, and in the same year as its partner. It was called *Princess Joan* prior to *Hermes*. It had a slightly shorter life, and was scrapped at Inverkeithing on the Forth late in 1974. The floating lodgings were replaced by a purpose-built accommodation block. Inhabitants were riggers, welders, painters, and whoever was required to build the rigs. These guys were from all over the UK, and could be quite lively. There was the occasional alcohol-fuelled incident requiring police intervention. There was also a lot of contact from other police areas enquiring about this person or that person. They were interesting times, sometimes involving positive police action. One famous incident, previous to my arrival, involved two officers on the water side of the outer ship, keeping clear of a few of its wilder inhabitants who were intent on checking out if the officers could swim. The situation was brought under control, and the officers stayed dry. As someone said, it was 'the wild west'.

Policing communities is not rocket science. It is about being in the community, it is about gaining trust, and it is about honesty, fairness and integrity. It is about providing support and making decisions that are just, fair and firm when required, and are relevant in that particular community. It cannot and never will be achieved by centralising policing to a location remote from the area one is policing, and it is not aided by faceless control centres and call centres and a 'one size fits all' mentality. How could such a model ever hope to make sense of the intricacies of the Nigg and Kildary Rabbit Board, for example? Being a single station officer requires one to be organised and dedicated. I think it requires a deal of confidence, mingled with a splash of courage. I do not suggest one is faced with danger every day, if ever. No, it is just that you are alone and there are communities looking to you to deliver a sustainable service, and it your duty to do that. Taking account of the situation on the ground and making decisions that are relevant to the local circumstances goes with the territory. One does not, and cannot, police in a vacuum.

So what happens in an Easter Ross rural single station beat? The same as every other beat in the country. Just different actors on different stages using different props. It is all about people and their behaviour. Much of a police officer's work – in any area – is routine, involving road accidents, assaults, antisocial behaviour, various enquiries, crimes and offences to sort out and investigate, courts to attend, sheep dipping to inspect, reports to write, and so on. Fearn was no different. The intensity and the pace have to be balanced with the number of officers available to patrol and deal with situations. In the next few pages I will relate some of the everyday, normal – perhaps mundane – things I got involved in when working in Fearn, as well as some actual incidents. I will try to keep the 'mundane' to a minimum. Perhaps routine is a better description. Each will take the form of a short story; a wee tale. All absolutely true. If I have missed any detail, put that down to memory. They are designed to give you a flavour, a snap shot in time, of a Highland police beat.

A typical day for me would start with sorting my mail, doing the filing. I then headed out into my beat, carrying enquiries and attending at whatever incident might arise. Enquiries ranged from those such as getting a statement from a witness to a road accident, enquiring into a theft, doing a firearm certificate renewal, attending at sheep dipping, getting statements for police in other areas, and so on. Firearm certificates were the responsibility of beat officers. The rural beat of Fearn had a lot of farms and, consequently, firearms. Therefore there were a lot of certificates to check. It was an invaluable way of getting to know the beat and the people. Years later when I was in Central Scotland Police, the system changed and a dedicated civilian team was created for that role. I think that was a mistake. Police officers lost contact with a group of people in their community and, with it, the knowledge that entailed. In Fearn it did not take long before I was carrying a load of my own enquiries and situations to deal with. There were Police politics looming, however, which I will refer to shortly.

My posting to Fearn marked a change to policing in the area. The station had been closed for a few years. It was now to be reopened. I was not first choice to take up the post. Maybe I was not even second – who knows? The station was now functioning again. Tain, about seven miles or so north on the A9 road, was my nearest support and that is where my closest supervision Sergeants were stationed. I will take this moment to mention three officers; I probably should not single these three out, as many other officers were top quality in the force. However, the three I mention were hugely instrumental in my early development, and I learned so much from them. Constable Angus McKay, my mentor during my first seven months, remains a friend to this day. He was a special officer. Very intelligent and resourceful. He understood people and was respected by all in the communities he worked. Sergeants Henry McMillan and Donnie Beaton in Tain were the perfect example of community police Sergeants. All three of these officers were gentle giants – not necessarily in build, although they were imposing, but in character. They were caring men who put their officers and their community first, and did not suffer fools gladly. Their knowledge of the community, of the law and of their powers were second to none. I learned so much from them. They were also very supportive, particularly knowing my position in Fearn.

I was out with Sergeant McMillan one evening. He was mentoring me and explaining some of the intricacies of remote rural policing. There had been some reports of the odd sheep going missing in the Tain area. We obviously were aware of that, and kept a watch during our patrols. I asked Henry how a sheep could get stolen. 'Did they shoot them?' He laughed, and told me he would demonstrate one method that might be employed. He made me drive the old Bedford police van onto the Struie Hill road. The van had doors that slid back. It was a summer evening. There were sheep lying on the grass verge beside the road. He spotted one lying on the nearside verge. It was facing away from us, resting. He got me to steer in close to the verge, driving very slowly. He slid open the passenger door, held on with his right hand, then leaned right out the van. As I slowly passed the beast, he grabbed the far away horn of the sheep and swung it inside the van in an easy flowing motion. I was not really prepared for that, and nearly drove off the road as I was assaulted by a flurry of flailing hooves and legs. Less then five seconds, and one sheep in the back of the van. It was that easy. A lesson in rustling. We deposited the bewildered sheep back on the verge and drove off. I was on a sheep learning curve.

At the end of my probation – two years' service – I had been at Fearn for nearly a year and a half. The last step in completing probation in the police service was the final confirmation exam. I sat it at Tain, in the Sergeant's office. Sergeant McMillan was the invigilator. I was the only person taking the exam. It was time-limited. He opened the sealed envelope and laid the paper face down on the desk. He then apologised and said he had to make an urgent telephone call and left me in the room, with the exam paper. He returned ten minutes later, and I sat the exam. I was appointed soon after that, and I became a real police officer. I was nearly thirty years of age. Not long after my confirmation, I happened to be typing a report in the muster room at the Tain office.

When it was finished I signed my name under my title, Police Constable. I had tears in my eyes. I was a real police officer. My dad never got a chance to understand what it meant to me.

Now, to the police politics I referred to before. My posting to Fearn had not met with universal approval. There was some disquiet among some of the officers, as well as the local branch Police Federation representative. They argued that because I lacked experience, I was a danger to myself, the community, and to my fellow officers. None of that was ever mentioned in my company, but it was bubbling. Knowing what I know now, I realise it had nothing to do with my lack of experience. It was much more fundamental. Prior to my arrival, Fearn was part of the Tain beat. It emerged that a couple of officers had taken the area under their wing and had a lot of contacts and things going on. Suddenly this imposter had been parachuted into their fiefdom. Their protests must have reached the higher echelons of the force, not that I knew at that time. I suspected that all in the garden was not rosy. I worked shifts – yes, even although I was a lone officer. Incidents in the Fearn beat were either left for me to deal with or, if that was not appropriate, they would be dealt with immediately and a note would be left for my information. Certain officers did not bother to let me know. To put this in perspective, these officers were very much in the minority. However, as they correctly pointed out, their duty to respond to calls from the public outweighed my feelings. They accused me of being precious. I reasoned that while the first part of their argument was correct, it was not about me. It was about continuity of service and simple, good, sustainable policing. Service to the community came before before their pigheadedness or my preciousness. If a follow-up was required, or if a similar incident occurred, it made sense that the officer responsible for the area had a handle on what was going on. Annoyingly, or perhaps pathetically, they knew that.

It all came out one day when I was out on duty. A message over the car radio instructed that I return immediately to my station. I had two important visitors. We did not have personal radios in those days. I was puzzled, and actually thought I had relations visiting. How naïve. There was a car in the driveway. I was met in the office by my wife, who ushered me through to our living room. The Chief Constable and his Divisional Commander were eating my biscuits. Both of them stood up and told me to sit, reminding me they were guests in my house. I was impressed by that courtesy. He did not need to say that, but he was – as I had always believed – a decent man. Rank need not be an excuse to hide your decency. However, over the years I met some who did not display even a modicum of decency. It probably had nothing to do with their rank; they simply were not decent people in the first place. The Chief then told me he was aware of some disquiet amongst some officers about my posting to Fearn. He told me to ignore such talk, adding that he had chosen me for the post. He said I had already displayed maturity beyond my service, and that he believed I was the right person for the task, adding that if people continue to question his decision, I had to refer them to him. He went on to talk in general terms about policing. He said that a police officer, especially one in uniform working in a community, has a special role. People will be delighted if you acknowledge them. You do not need a reason; speak to them, make them feel you are there for them, which you are. If you are out and have not met somebody or have not seen somebody for a while, then just turn your car and drive to wherever they are and make yourself known.

You have a responsibility to all people in your beat, so get to know them and become visible.

On the subject of visibility in communities, a farmer in the Fearn area – a widow – stayed up late most nights doing the farm books and other office work. The farm was isolated. She was nervous, and asked for my vehicle call sign. She liked to listen to the police radio. She asked me, when working late, to check something out using my radio. Anything. She listened, and knew my call sign. Hearing me out and about in the area made her feel safe.

Police officers never outnumber the communities they serve. Nor should they. In the main, communities find their own level of what they will accept and what makes them feel comfortable and secure. Working as a lone officer is a privilege on two counts: the police service trusts you to represent them without daily supervision and, secondly, being able to express yourself in a community as 'their' police officer is the highest honour a serving police officer can achieve. I do not care what rank you might achieve.

Yes, you have to understand your community. It is not difficult, but you have to work hard to find that understanding and gain their respect. You must not confuse them as to your role. One minute you might be helping the local doctor lift a patient from the floor back into bed. You might assist a farmer with his firearm certificate. Or you could be the one to impart tragic news to a family. You certainly will have to report some for committing some offence or other, and you will have to arrest someone on occasion. It is all part of your job. I explained it this way once: if you want your lights fixed, get an electrician; if you want a steak, go to the butcher. A police officer is also an important part of the community. Not supplying butcher meat or fixing lights, but providing a policing service and, if it means someone gets arrested, that is what will happen. Nobody should fall out about it. That would be nonsense. Would you fall out with your butcher? At all times, one tries to be non-judgemental, fair, balanced, and treat people with dignity. Remember that popularity is what politicians and entertainers crave. Discretion is one of the main pillars of police work, and is not only a strength but the first step in any public interest decision in the criminal justice system.

* * *

I was heading into Tain from Fearn one evening, not too late. As I approached where the minor road from Fearn meets the A9 trunk road, a few miles south of Tain, I saw the local mobile shop as it turned north – the wrong way along the one way slip road that takes vehicles from the north into the Fearn road. It then, without stopping or slowing down, emerged onto the main road and continued north. The driver was obviously under the influence of something. Perhaps he was ill, or maybe there was a mechanical issue, maybe with the steering. The mobile shop was swerving all over the main road. I was unaccompanied and called for assistance. The nearest help was a bit away, and would take about fifteen minutes to reach my location. I stopped the swerving vehicle. When I approached the driver – someone I knew well – I could smell alcohol. When assistance arrived, some time later, I breathalysed the driver. His test was positive. I duly processed him and filed a report to the Procurator Fiscal. He took no action because I had stopped him driving without corroboration. I was completely aware of that when I stopped the van. My decision was made to protect the public. It was a straight public interest decision. Winning a court case was not top priority that night. I did get lectured about my actions, and was advised that I should have used my blue light to warn other road users until assistance arrived. That was definitely an option. However, I rejected it and decided to remove any threat. Was I correct? Should I have waited for assistance in order to have more chance of winning a court case, having the culprit banned from driving and – in doing so – making the roads safer for longer? Or is taking immediate action to protect the public at the time, even if it risks losing a court case, more of a priority?

A local tradesman, with his own company, had problems with alcohol. He had already lost his driving licence because of his problem. I was aware that he continued to drive whilst disqualified. I called at his office one day and warned him that I would not turn a blind eye and, if I saw him, I would arrest him. He apologised and assured me it would stop. It didn't, and I did arrest him. He lost his licence for even longer. Despite that, our relationship continued to be amicable.

A few years later, when living and working in Tullibody, there was a local politician who resided in the village. Incidentally, he came from the same village in the Fearn peninsula as the tradesman. The politician asked me to call in at his house one night and, after a cup of tea and a discussion about a local issue, he told me he had a present for me from a mutual friend in Fearn. He handed me a bottle of good single malt whisky, still in its cardboard box. There was a message written on the box: 'Tae the Fearn Bobbie, I hope it fuckin' chokes ye'. It was signed 'Bo Bo'. Yes, the tradesman I had intercepted driving whilst disqualified. I was honestly moved by that gesture, and the humour involved. He was a good man and he understood.

A butcher who lived in the village, on occasion, would drink and drive. I was aware, but did not actually see him doing that. He lived near the police house. Early one morning, while I was in bed, I heard a vehicle revving and then the engine stopped. I looked out and saw the butcher being helped out of his car by his wife. I was on the late shift that day, starting at five o'clock. I called at his house just after six o'clock. He was at home. I asked to speak to him alone, but he insisted that his wife be there. I explained my suspicions and what I had witnessed earlier that morning. I told him that his behaviour was not only illegal, but that it was dangerous and unacceptable. 'I will catch you and report you. It is what I do.' There is nothing personal in that. He was so apologetic, as was his wife. He assured me he would never do it again. I went to leave, and he said that his wife and he were just about to have steak for dinner. Did I want to join them? I really struggled with my sandwiches later. I never heard of – or witnessed – him driving in that state again, and in fact I saw him using a taxi for a while after that.

It was not all about alcohol and driving. Poaching salmon and illegal shooting of geese were big pastimes on the peninsula. The area is surrounded by good salmon waters and, apart from poaching salmon, there were – certainly in my day, and for a couple of centuries before that – several salmon fishing stations around the coast. The main fish farmers were the Paterson family. The accepted legal method of fishing is by fixing a large 'bag' net to the seabed about one hundred yards or so out from the shore. It is simply a big elongated net box with entrance on the shore end. The box is not active, not fishing, until a leader net is affixed to it. It is a floating hang net, attached to the shore, that is called a fixed engine. The other end is affixed at one side of the bag net entrance; an arrow-shaped narrowing enclosure. When the leader is deployed, the fishing process is active. Fish naturally follow the shore line and the 'leader' net funnels them into the bag net past the narrowing entrance, trapping them. A local farmer on the peninsula, Douglas Gordon, has written a comprehensive article on salmon fishing in this area, entitled 'Salmon Stations Around Easter Ross Peninsula' (2015). Needless to say, some did not heed the niceties of licenses or legal fishing methods, and used a drift net from a small boat to catch the fish. Drift netting like that was – and still is – illegal. I was aware it went on. However, I have to say that it was not top priority. But it was breaking the law, and as part of my duties in trying to understand my community I was required to find out as much about this activity as I could. In particular, who were the poachers? It was obviously a clandestine undertaking, and typically took place in the early hours of the day. I found out where the popular spots were, and basically did a nightshift. (I still had to do my rostered dayshift, however; no rest for the wicked.) So on the nights I had been told salmon poaching was likely, off I set – alone, armed only with a pair of binoculars. One night, the poaching was happening on the Moray Firth side of the peninsula; below the cliffs at Nigg, near King's Cave. I drove onto the Hill of Nigg and parked near Bayfield Loch. I then hiked over two kilometres down to the cliffs. I sat for over an hour and watched them poaching. Visibility was reasonable. There were four men, and I knew three of them. I was not sure where they were going to land and, as I watched, they headed north along the Firth. I eventually lost sight of them. However, I had more information about peninsula activities and that would be useful.

Loch Eye was a different kind of poaching. Well, it was not actually poaching. During the season, Grey Lag geese can be shot. Loch Eye was a favourite roosting spot for them and other species of geese. It was created a bird sanctuary on 19<sup>th</sup> September 1974, just about the time I landed. The Order prohibited entry at any time into the prescribed area, which I marked on my map. Offenders would be liable for special penalties under section 12 (2) of the Protection of Birds Act 1954. Interestingly, it did not protect birds from being shot – even on the loch – assuming one shot from distance and did not actually trespass. The law can be a bit lacking on occasion. It was my duty to dig deeper.

And so, back to sneaking about in the early hours. Hidden in bushes beside the loch, I observed as some locals wandered over from the nearest road armed with shotguns. One was a long-barrelled goose gun. The poor craters were roosting with their heads turned in when the shooting started. Several were hit. I was on my own, and had a plan to disrupt the activity through the courts. I should have known better, and I should have stood that night and stopped the carnage. Mind you, that would not have been a sustainable position. This had been going on for many years with no illegality involved. However, I thought the protection order might give me an angle. I visited the Procurator Fiscal in Dingwall and explained my dilemma. I proposed resorting to the Firearms Act 1968: 'Trespassing with a Firearm'. It states that a person commits an offence if, while he has a firearm with him, he enters or is on any land as a trespasser and without reasonable excuse. The term 'land' in this section includes land covered with water. Anyway, my plan was scuppered, as the Procurator Fiscal did not agree the law was relevant to this situation and what I proposed was not in the spirit of the law.

My next plan involved getting the support of other officers and the dog branch, and catching the offenders in the protected area. So on a cold moonlit frosty night I was driving back to the Fearn office when black ice intervened. After a few breathtaking swings left and right on the ice – skilfully countered by spinning the steering wheel this way and that – I was just as suddenly off the black ice, and my opposite lock manoeuvre was mistimed. I drove straight over the deep ditch on the nearside of the road. Beyond the ditch the banking was higher than the road, with a fence running along it. The next thing I knew I was on the higher banking, travelling parallel to the road, snapping fence posts on the way. All I remember hearing was snapping wood and strands of fence wire squeaking as they scraped over the car. All very surreal, and with a slow motion effect in the car headlights. Then the ignominy of it all. The car slowed to a halt, then gently slid down on its side into the ditch, with me still inside. It was completely on its side. The driver's door was below me, and water was coming in. The only escape was through the passenger door. Because the car was on its side, the door I needed to use was above my head. A car door is heavy. It was also just that awkward distance above my head, so I struggled to get purchase. Eventually I got it shoved far enough up to get my shoulders through. I have no idea what I was standing on to get the last bit of leverage, but with some brute strength and adrenalin I was out. I was able to step directly on to the road. A car stopped and gave me a run back to my office. I had damaged my head and my right knee; just 'walking wounded'. I telephoned the Sergeant in Tain; it was Donnie Beaton. He assured me all was well and that he would deal with the accident. He would get the local garage to remove the car and sort it overnight. I told him it was worse than that. He laughed. About an hour later he called me back and agreed: it *was* worse than that. He would have to report it. About an hour later, the on-call Chief Inspector arrived at the office. My wife let him in. I heard him ask if I was alright, adding that replacing cars is easy; replacing good officers is harder. He came in and all he talked about was my condition, telling me not to worry. As he left, he told me to get into Dingwall in the morning and get a replacement car. I did exactly that. It was a bashed-up mini, but it drove well. I never heard anything more about the accident.

Years later, in Tullibody, I attended a disturbance in a house late one night. As my colleague and I left in the police car, I was driving and had to reverse out between parked cars, at the same time looking up at the window of the house we had just been in, watching to ensure that the situation did not flare up. I reversed into the back of a parked car. The back corner of the van collided with rear of the car, low down and right in the middle. It crumpled. There was no mark on the police van. We knew the car owner, and woke him and his wife from their slumbers. At first they thought it was bad news; the kind police officers bring. On learning that I had damaged their car, they laughed and put the kettle on. He came out and saw the damage. His first thought was about me, and the trouble I might get into. He asked what happens now. I explained the process and that I had to report the accident. He spoke to his wife. They did not want me to report it, and asked if I could just get it repaired. After being assured they definitely did not want the incident reported I agreed to the repair option. The car was duly repaired at a local garage. I went to pay the bill and asked if I could pay it in two instalments. The owner said he would check with the accountant, his wife. She took the bill from me, ripped it up and threw it in the rubbish bucket. She said, 'Ian, you – and the rest of you in Tullibody – work so hard for us, long hours and sometimes dangerous hours. There is nothing you will not do for the community. If we can't show our appreciation for that service, it would be a bad day'. Nothing more was said; not then, not ever. Working with and for decent people is like that.

On the subject of bumps in police vehicles, one officer – during my time in the north – was convicted at court for careless driving. A total miscarriage of justice, according to the officer. However, the Sheriff was the least of his worries. He had the Chief Superintendent to face. He drove through to the hearing in a police vehicle. He received one hell of a telling off and was told he would never drive a police car again: he was 'banned for life'. He informed the senior officer he had driven through from Easter Ross in a police vehicle. The Chief Super stared at him for a moment, then said 'Okay, you are banned for life – when you get back to your station. Now get out of my sight'.

One accident in treacherous icy winter roads saw a police car plunge into a Highland river. It was pitch black, and the only illumination came from the car's headlights. Both officers managed to get out of the car into the freezing river. One got ashore, but in the dark lost sight of his colleague. Desperately, he searched about and shouted 'where are you?' Then the answering, factual – but comically understated – response came: 'Sure; I am over here!'

'What are you doing over there?'

'The breast stroke.'

That was what it was like. No big issues, no career destroying reports – kind-hearted bosses who blustered and shouted and got things done and got respect, because they would walk though fire to save you the next day. None of the last two, true stories involved me, but they are indicative of a level of camaraderie and team spirit that permeated every rank and gave the service a heart.

During my service, certainly for the first twenty years or so, checking firearm certificates – including examining the actual firearms, counting the ammunition and ensuring safe, lockfast storage – was the responsibility of the front line Constable in his or her community. It was carried out on a monthly basis. One therefore had to visit the certificate holder at home and physically carry out the check. On one occasion, whilst in the north, I called at a large house occupied by a Law Lord. Discretion prevents me from divulging his identity. On arrival, I was shown into a large drawing room, or perhaps library. How was I to tell, a young man from a prefab in Bonnybridge that was smaller than that room? However, one identified it. In any event, the Lord was deep in conversation with his guest when I entered the room. By the way the other person spoke, I assumed they had both attended the same school, or perhaps they had a similar calling. The Judge was well organised, and I soon completed my examination. I was about to leave the warmth of a roaring fire and the wood-panelled, book-lined room and head into the cold night when he asked me: 'Are you having a busy night?'

'No', I replied, 'just getting on with some paperwork'.

He then quoted small section of the Police (Scotland) Act to me – the bit that allows a Constable on duty to consume alcohol, if given permission by an officer in charge of the relevant police office, or by a senior officer. There were certain considerations to take into account that legitimised that permission. The Lord did not trouble himself with the latter and, sticking with the former, said 'in my position, one may conclude that I hold the rank of a senior officer, wouldn't you say?' I could find no fault with his logic. He nodded, and motioned me to take a seat. As I sunk into a serious Chesterfield, he handed me a crystal glass containing just the correct amount of the finest single malt. Not your vulgar, working class measure. There followed a very convivial evening. You will be reassured in the knowledge that his firearm certificate was in order.

That quaint introduction to firearms and the police masks the other side of that coin. Checking licences was not the only time that police officers came into contact with firearms, sometimes with a tragic outcome. Since the 1800s, there have been twelve officers killed on duty in Scotland as a result of firearms being discharged. Eleven of these were straight-out criminal, and one was as a result of a tragic incident involving the drunken actions of a third party. Amongst the former was the only recorded death of an officer from the various police forces that eventually were clustered together in 1975 to create the Northern Constabulary. Constable Thomas King was based at Nethybridge, Inverness-shire. He worked alone. On 20th December 1898 he said cheerio to his wife and children and headed out to team up with Constable John MacNiven, from the nearby Boat of Garten police office. Their intention was to arrest Allan MacCallum, for whom they had a Sheriff's arrest warrant. MacCallum had notoriety as a poacher. He was known to Constable King. He was known to reside in a 'but and ben'-type cottage near the hamlet of Tulloch in nearby Abernethy Forest. He was eventually traced, though not before threatening the officers with a firearm. The officers split up and King confronted MacCallum, who immediately – and apparently without warning – shot the officer, fatally wounding him. He made good his escape into the forest. After a huge search, he was cornered and arrested a few days later, hiding in a barn at Tomachrochar. MacCallum was later found guilty of Culpable Homicide, and avoided the death penalty. Constable King was laid to rest in the graveyard at nearby Abernethy Kirk, Nethybridge.

I was not immune to the occasional firearms incident. Most officers are not. My first close encounter happened to be the closest; there were others, but not like this one. About 9.30pm one evening I was relaxing whilst watching a 'police training' film on television. It was *Kojak*: 'Who loves ya, baby?' It was as near as I would get to a training video in these days. The office telephone rang, and kept ringing. I answered, to be informed from HQ in Dingwall that they could not raise any Tain officer; could I attend a robbery in progress? I was given the address in Balintore and instructed to radio them when I got to the incident. Uniform on, blue light on, first stop Balintore. I was there in minutes. I rushed into the house to find the two victims – a husband and wife – in a distressed state. The robber had fled with a loaded shotgun and a box of shotgun cartridges. I was joined a short time later by the Sergeant from Tain. The accused was known to the victims. He was the brother of the husband. He had held a knife to his sister-in-law's throat, and made his brother get a shotgun and ammunition. When he got it, he ran off into the dunes behind their house. He still had the knife. He intended shooting his wife. She resided in Alness with the children. We immediately arranged for a watch at that location, got some reinforcements – that would be about six officers – and spent a fruitless two hours or more searching about in the pitch black through endless sand dunes and along the shore. Our only illumination being our hand-held torches. We had no idea which direction he had gone in, and it was a big area with miles of unlit coast and scrubland. The CID had taken over the enquiry, and they obtained the necessary statements and other productions. About two o'clock in the morning we gave up for the night. The watch on the house in Alness continued. I got a few hours' sleep and was awakened by my jangling telephone just before seven o'clock that morning. It was the robbery victim from Balintore. He knew where his brother was hiding. I called Tain for assistance. A single detective officer arrived. The two of us headed for Balintore, to be informed the robbery suspect was about a mile along the shore amongst the sand dunes in his old caravan. The detective and I drove there and found the caravan. It was like a scene from *Broadchurch*. The door was locked from the inside. I banged on the side of the caravan and told him to come out. A male voice, from inside the caravan, told me to fuck off. I got the jemmy – the crowbar – from the back of my police car. Standard issue in Ross and Sutherland vehicles. I wedged the jemmy into the outer door flange, a caravan door opens outward, and I started to force the door open. The following conversation and actions cannot be found in any firearms instruction manual or guidelines.

Accused: 'You'll wreck my fuckin' caravan!'

Me: 'If you don't open the fuckin' door, I'll wreck you and your fuckin' caravan! Now open the fuckin' door and be standing with your hands up and nothing in them.'

Accused: 'Okay, okay! I'm opening the door.'

I stepped back, and the door started to open. I put my right elbow inside the door and forced it open. I was still holding the crowbar. The accused had jumped back. He was holding his hands high. There was a knife in a ledge beside him, and a shotgun on the floor at his feet. I grabbed him and pulled him outside. We fell down the steps. He did not struggle. My colleague pulled him to his feet. He was arrested, and removed to be interviewed by the CID in Tain. The shotgun was empty; however, there were live shotgun cartridges lying about in the caravan. He eventually pleaded guilty to several offences, and received a term of imprisonment. He was not really a bad man. Alcohol abuse and a wrecked marriage; his life was in tatters. He was a poor soul with no hope. A prison sentence probably did him no good. I knew him, and I was confident he would do me no harm. Despite what I believed, there is always a scintilla of uncertainty; a sense that tells you to be very careful. Maybe he was drunk, maybe he was not thinking straight. Hence the need to take control: the shouting, the use of firm language, telling him exactly what to do. I actually used his name whilst urging him to leave his caravan. Every situation is different. One has to rely on judgement, experience, and the particular circumstances faced. You have to be confident and decisive – and crucially, assertiveness has to underpin your every action. His brother and sister-in-law recovered well after their ordeal.

A senior officer friend of mine, whilst in charge of a senior crime group in the 1970s, told about planning to deploy armed officers in response to an armed gang. Only trained and certificated officers could be issued with a firearm. He instructed they load their weapons. One officer was struggling, and kept fumbling and dropping his bullets. My friend asked if he was alright. The detective Constable replied: 'No, I am quite nervous. I have never handled a gun before.'

His boss was taken aback. 'How did you get the gun?'

'I just queued up with the rest of the guys.'

He was sent back to the firearm store to return the weapon and did not take part in the operation. Oops.

# CHAPTER 9

THINGS have moved on since these halcyon days. In terms of my own career – in addition to the incident of the caravan on the dunes – I was involved in four other firearms incidents during the next twenty five years or so. They are never 'simply routine'. Two were dealt with, and resolved with, no drama other than the Tactical Advisor being at odds with my handling of one incident. An advisor is the expert; however, decisions are made by the officer in charge. I considered his advice, and took a slightly different course of action. He was a bit put out, but – on reflection – agreed I had a point. Firearm recovered; no drama. The two I will recount were interesting in different ways.

When working in Tullibody, information was received that a well-known drug dealer – and thoroughly objectionable member of the community – had a firearm in his house. The CID took charge and obtained a firearms search warrant. Two armed detectives, carrying handguns of some type, called at the Tullibody office with a warrant to search the suspect's house. They hatched a plan to execute the warrant. I kept thinking, 'there is likely to an execution all right: mine'. Similar to my comment about one of my previous firearms incidents, the tactics employed in this one are also not likely to be top of the pops in any firearms training or tactics manual. The suspect lived in a terraced house. There was a small front garden area with a short path to the public footpath. On either side of the gate was a neat privet hedge, about three or four feet in height. The plan went as follows. My uniformed colleague and I march up to the door, knock, and stand waiting on suspect to open it. We have the warrant and, if he opens the door, we present it to him and enter the house, keeping the door open. Clint Eastwood and John Wayne will quickly follow. All I could think whilst waiting on the door to be answered was that we were right in the crossfire. If this idiot has a gun and pokes it out a window, or the door or anywhere, what will the two behind us do? We were not wearing Kevlar or any other protective clothing. In fact, this was about 1980; I am not even sure Kevlar was invented. Shot from the front and back: now that would be an epitaph. Even his own guys shot him! In any event, he did open the door and we never did find a firearm in his house. I learned many months later that he did have a shotgun, and he kept it strapped above a roof truss in his loft. Whether he had it that night, who knows? If he had one, it was never found. He died while still a young man, and we never found out if there ever really was a gun.

The other incident involved being actually shot at with a high-powered rifle. Luckily it was not aimed to actually hit David or myself, and was only warning us. I cheat a bit with this story, because I was off-duty at the time and climbing in the Scottish mountains in Glen Lyon one winter. The bullet 'ripped' over our heads, quite close. A high-powered rifle being discharged sounds very different if you are at the business end of the discharge than if does if you are on the safe end. It's a bit like ripping cloth, although I thought it sounded like a quick-flying baritone bee. Some hours later, David and I caught up with the 'shooters' and remonstrated with them. They admitted it was them who had fired at us, and said it was because we were on their hill when they were heading out to stalk deer. They were only trying to frighten us off. There are many other incidents I am aware of when police officers have put themselves in the line of fire to do their job and protect the public.

The subject of police and firearms can raise some people's temperature. Routine patrolling whilst armed is one of these contentious, touchy subjects. Certainly it is a subject which generates a lot of differing opinions. For what it's worth, I reluctantly went with the development of certain Traffic cars patrolling with armed officers. Their ability to quickly attend a firearms incident was reasonably compelling. My only caveat about this whole argument is that the general public is not in possession of the same information available to the professionals, and therefore not in a position to make a considered decision. I believe that many of today's decisions about policing are greatly 'influenced' by politics, with dogma taking precedence over evidence. When serving, I did not agree with every high level decision. If I was given a platform to have a legitimate say, I did. I then got on with my job. I was not in favour of beat officers routinely carrying firearms on patrol. My default position today remains the same. I will qualify that with a reference to context. There may well be intelligence – information – that requires officers to carry firearms. In such cases, the Chief Constable has every right to deploy armed officers. The decision is made as a result of a legitimate and real concern. While it may be reasonable to inform politicians about the decision and – perhaps, dependent on circumstances – also reasonable to inform them why the decision was taken, that is the only role they should play.

Deployment of any police resource, including arming officers, should be professional police decision. Politicians have a role, and that is producing legislation. They may well have a role if a Chief Constable acts outwith her or his legal remit. However, they – politicians – have no role in operational policing decisions, nor should they, and to allow them such a role is to take a dangerous path. Take heed to the words of Lord Denning, in the English Court of Appeal, while accepting that the police are answerable to the law, reiterated the cardinal principle of police independence: 'No minister of the Crown can tell (the Commissioner) that he must, or must not, keep observation on this place or that; or that he must, or must not, prosecute this man or that one. Nor can any police authority tell him so. The responsibility for law enforcement lies on him. He is answerable to the law and to the law alone'. In short, while referring to the Commissioner, he was talking about every police officer being individually responsible to the law for his actions.

A post-script on armed police patrolling in our communities today. There are records of the police having access to arms going back nearly two centuries. Many had armaments under lock and key, and issued as and when thought necessary. However, there are also instances where officers carried firearms on routine patrols. After the murder of two Metropolitan Police officers in 1844, night patrols were routinely armed with revolvers. During the Crofters War, or Protest, of 1884 (whatever view one takes) over high rents, the lack of security of tenure and access to land, the Chief Constable of Inverness-shire was loaned fifty revolvers by the War Office. I do not know if he issued them to officers. In 1823, the Local Council (Stirling) – meeting in the Justiciary Court Hall in Stirling – agreed to appoint ten or eleven steady men as watchmen (Constables) with a Superintendent to regulate their movements. A committee to oversee them consisted of the Provost, First Bailie, Dean of Guild, and convener of the seven incorporated trades ex officious, with five respectable inhabitants. It was similar to the plan of the poor scheme. Each watchman was provided with a lantern, a rattle, and a formidable weapon – the same as the police in Glasgow and Edinburgh. They were given routes to patrol the town of Stirling, right down to the river. The patrol in the churchyard was to be every half-hour, and the watchman on that patrol was to have a gun. This was at the time when body snatching – or 'resurrections' – were rife in Scotland, and it was felt the Town Guard needed to be supported. Some body snatchers had a reputation for being violent. This decision was brought to the townspeople's attention by the Town Drummer. It is not clear what a 'formidable' weapon was, although one historian suggested that a truncheon could be such a weapon. There is a view it may well have been a cutlass, as it was not unusual in some areas for cutlasses to be carried by police. By the way, the 'rattle' was a large wooden rattle, sometimes called a fire rattle. It was rotated to attract attention. So the question of arming the police is not quite so recent. There were no immediate news outlets, television, radio, mobile telephones, Facebook, Twitter, or whatever else that is about today, so perhaps that is why there is no record of any dissenters to that situation. The Stirling watchmen were disbanded in 1857.

* * *

It all started at the weekend dance in the village hall at Inver. To be exact, just outside the hall. A young male partygoer was obviously not handling his mind-altering substance too well, or perhaps he was suffering from rejection. Whatever the reason, he was in a foul mood and was struggling and fighting with another male who looked like he was not that interested. My intervention to calm things was met with a torrent of abuse and profanities. I arrested and handcuffed him, then deposited him in the back seat of the police car. I was slowly driving off through the gathering crowd when a friend of our guest opened the back door of the vehicle and dragged the prisoner out, pushing him in the back to assist his escape. My prisoner instantly disappeared into the throng of excited young people, who closed ranks to block my way and encouraged him to run. He was soon lost in the unlit recesses of Easter Ross, coming to rest in a deep, water-filled field drainage ditch. Not that I knew that. I had no idea where he went. He may have drowned, had two passers-by not heard his cries for help. By then I had given his seat in the police car to his 'helper'. My original prisoner subsequently pleaded guilty. However, his 'helper' did not. That was how I found myself giving evidence at one of the strangest trials it has ever been my pleasure to attend.

My evidence was relatively straightforward, with only some debate about what was a pull and what was a shove. I was quite clear what I saw, and how I interpreted the accused's actions. Then it was the turn of the defence. The accused took the witness box and told the court his version of events. The defence concentrated on intent: a crucial element in criminal prosecution cases. He had not intended to help the prisoner escape. He was merely going to give him a cigarette, and was just as surprised at his actions as anybody else. At that point the Sheriff stopped him, and asked the defence lawyer if his client had just admitted opening the police car door. The lawyer agreed. Before either the accused or his lawyer could say anything else, the Sheriff announced him to be guilty and asked if the lawyer intended continuing with this line of defence. The lawyer was taken aback but soldiered on against unsustainable odds, continuing to argue that the case was all about intent and there was an absence of intent in terms of his client's actions and the prisoner escaping. By this time the Sheriff had the bull by the horns and ploughed on with his questions. In effect, he was doing the Procurator Fiscal's job for him. The Fiscal just sat quietly. 'Would my learned friend agree with me that if one is arrested, handcuffed and placed in a police car, that car is a lawful place of custody?' The defence agreed. The Sheriff went on, 'so now one is out of the police car and locked in a cell, is that a lawful place of custody?' The defence knew where this was going and was powerless to stop it. He agreed. The Sheriff continued, 'your client walks into the cell area and opens the cell door to give his friend a cigarette. The friend runs away. Would your client still be pleading not guilty?' The lawyer continued to plead intent – or, in fact, lack of intent – to no avail. The defence solicitor, unhappy with this whole interlude, asked if his client could be allowed to continue with the defence. The Sheriff looked at him and said, 'if you insist; however, he is guilty'. The accused rambled on for a few more minutes. The Procurator Fiscal had no questions, and the defence had nothing more to add. The Procurator Fiscal stood to move that the accused was guilty, but never got the chance. The Sheriff butted in and said 'it's alright, Mr Fiscal; he is guilty'. Then, with no hesitation and before anybody could utter another word, added: 'Can I see his previous convictions? He obviously has them'. The Sheriff Clerk dutifully handed the sheet of previous convictions to the Sheriff, whereupon he looked through them, looked at the accused over the document, and said: 'Ah! I see you are a thief, and I see you have also interfered with the police before. I am going to send you to prison'. The Clerk then went over and whispered something to him. My Lord took a moments' pause while he reflected, then announced, 'I am informed I have to stop sending so many people to prison; they appear to be filling up. Well, I will not send you there. In that case, I will impose a monetary sentence. Fined £200. Now get out of my court'.

Another trial day, another case. It is the lunch recess. The Sergeant and three officers are in the lounge of the Royal Hotel, Tain, just opposite the Sheriff Court. We have dined and are having a refreshment. In the far corner of the same lounge sits the Sheriff, the Procurator Fiscal, and two defence lawyers. They also have eaten and are, like the police officers, having a refreshment. It is ten minutes past two, and the court was due to resume at two. I was feeling a tad uncomfortable and suggested that we head back over, in case we are called. The Sergeant wisely retorts: 'Who is going to call you? They are all here'. We leave a short time later, and court resumes. A few days later I bumped into one of the lawyers and mention being a bit uncomfortable at lunch that day, mentioning the Sergeant's remark about not rushing back as the main players are still at lunch. The lawyer laughed and said 'that is exactly what the Sheriff said, referring to the police'. My main point is, the Sheriff was dining with the prosecutor and the defence. They are not at war; they are honourable professionals. They would do nothing to compromise their clients or, in the case of the Procurator Fiscal, the victims. Nor would the Sheriff compromise either. Anybody seeing conspiracy or 'collusion' is the one to be wary of. Sheriff Ewan

Stewart, the subject of these two tales, was only notorious to the elite establishment, power figures in the south, who seemed to regard him – unjustifiably in my opinion – as an embarrassment. To many of those he directly influenced, he was a clear-thinking, if a touch eccentric, supportive and loyal person. I would go further and say he was an honourable, free thinker. Put simply, he was a decent person and brave man; a man of principle. I greatly admired him. He died at his home in Wick on 9 October 2000, aged 74 years. Tributes mentioned his generosity, kindness, humour, and lack of pomposity. I like the latter comment.

I will return to death and road accidents briefly. Over the years I have witnessed and dealt with many instances of death on the roads of our country. Every single one of them was a huge tragedy for families and friends. I have previously mentioned one. The following two are somewhat different, if only because of the number of fatalities. I mention them for a reason, and will explain as the stories unfold.

Not long before being sent to Fearn, there was a road accident on the A9 trunk road not far from where I stopped the mobile shop a few years later. It was on October 20th 1973, not long before I joined the police service in Dingwall and almost one year before I took over that beat. I had no role in the accident, but the tragedy resonated for years in the area with the police and I never forgot about it. Five teenage schoolchildren, seventeen years to fourteen years of age, were walking south on the A9 road when they were mowed down by a car being driven by a male person. The five young people were killed. On that same road nearly two years later, just north of the village of Evanton, there was another terrible crash; a tragedy. I was off duty and driving my wife to the hospital in Dingwall. It was in late September 1975; I think it was Wednesday the 24th. I was stopped by a build-up of traffic; in fact, it had come to a halt. There was a blind bend up front and I could not see what the hold-up was, so I walked forward. After seven or eight cars I could see round the bend into a dip. On the opposite side of the road, facing north, was a stationary heavy lorry. Crumpled up low, in front of the lorry, was a pale blue car. It was in a mess. It had not long happened. There were some people standing about, but nobody at the car. I hurried forward. I could see three people lying in various positions within the wreckage. I checked them, feeling for pulses and any sign of life. I detected none. I asked someone to get a telephone in the nearby industrial estate and summon the police and an ambulance. I then asked the other people milling about if they would make sure no other vehicles got to the scene, and to keep people back. I returned to the family in the car, cleaning out their airways as best I could. When doing that a lady knelt beside me and asked if I thought any of them were alive. She called me Doctor. She was a nurse. I told her I was a police officer and no, I did not think anyone was alive. She agreed, and asked what we should do. I said, 'nothing really; just keep doing what we were doing and at the very least give the onlookers hope'. I did not want them thinking the car occupants were all dead. In reality, I did not know what to do. Police and ambulance were soon on the scene, and I was able to melt into the background. My wife was late for her appointment at Ross Memorial Hospital in Dingwall. The dead were a family of three. The mum and dad were in their forties, and their son was nineteen. They were killed instantly.

I mentioned these tragedies for a reason. The first is to show what police training does to a person. It changes – perhaps conditions – one, and equips the officer to walk towards danger. Or – if not danger – tragedy, mayhem, or chaos. And it teaches one to stay calm, stay focused, and take control. With reference to that triple fatal road accident, I could have stayed in my car. Any off-duty police officer can stay in their car, but they don't. It is not what they do. They are police officers and there is a code, a duty. Secondly, in terms of these two tragedies, neither sparked a national emotional response. There were no services in some Cathedral or other; there was no national mourning or fundraising for the victims' families. The 'left behind' simply dealt with their grief and got on with their lives. Today a similar event, certainly in the Central Belt, almost stops the nation, led by a twenty-four hour, self-serving, hysteria-inducing media. It does not make me feel comfortable; I get no sense that any of the outpourings of grief are genuine.

Senior police officers go through a lot of media training, during which they are taught to express their condolences for the bereaved in a public display. They do that at the top of their input. I was taught the self-same thing. To me it looks wooden, scripted, and certainly not genuine – as if they fear the consequences of missing out that bit of the script. Mostly the person making the utterance does not know and has never met the bereaved. Save your tears for when, or if, you actually meet the bereaved, and direct your feelings to them with dignity. Above all, keep it private. Tragedy is no platform for a PR script. Who grieves for the individual killed two days later at a different location? Only their nearest and dearest. It is no less a tragedy.

While there was the occasional serious crime and serious assault to deal with during my time in the north, I never had a murder. Unfortunately, they did happen. The one that sticks with me was one of the most publicised incidents in

Scotland at that time. To be accurate, the incident involved the disappearance of two people. The incident is not classified as murder. It remains a missing person enquiry. If found dead, the cause will have to established. Only then can it be classified. I am pretty sure about what I think.

It began on 12<sup>th</sup> November 1976. There was a mother, Renee McRae, and her four year old son. Her car was found burned out in a layby beside the A9 trunk road that night, a Friday. The layby is at Dalmagarry, about fifteen miles south of Inverness and just a mile or so north of the Tomatin junction. At the time there was a Little Chef restaurant at that junction. The Sustrans cycle network now passes through the layby. I am sure few cyclists will have the slightest notion of events at that spot over forty years ago. Various enquiries took place over that weekend to trace the car owner. There was no 'sinister' element at that time. As the enquiries panned out over the weekend, it became clear something was very wrong. These enquiries were delayed initially, as some of the main players could not be traced. By the start of the week it was apparent that two people could not be accounted for. Mrs McRae and her young son. A major missing person hunt began.

I was working in Fearn at the time and was directed, as were other officers from the Easter Ross division, to report to police headquarters in Inverness for briefing at eight o'clock on the Tuesday morning. I was now working in Northern Constabulary. After the amalgamation in 1975, Ross and Sutherland Constabulary was no more. The Easter Ross contingent had an early start and travelled together. It was long hours and hard work during the week or more that I was involved. Typically we were split into teams and sent to locations along the A9 to search. We covered both sides of the road. Each team – perhaps ten officers – had a leader, sometimes with a megaphone. We formed a straight line from the edge of, and at right angles to, the road, across the verge as far as we could stretch. The distance between searchers depended on the terrain. We had to work as a team and keep in a straight line, whilst maintaining the same spacing between us. Our team leader kept us concentrating, either at the top of his voice or the megaphone's limit. Open ground allowed us to stretch further away from the road, whereas thick undergrowth, bushes and trees meant we were closer together. Sometimes we were able to walk upright and other times we crawled, particularly in dense undergrowth and trees. It was cold, however mostly dry. Not always. Mid-morning break was provided by the wonderful Scottish Women's Rural Institute – the SWRI – who appeared in a vehicle and fed us tea and snacks, without fail. Lunch was brought in police vehicles. A special treat late in the afternoon was when a police van came along. We clustered around and the officer opened the back and dispensed life-saving elixir. Well, as near as he could get: in our case it was single malt whisky.

We searched both sides of the A9 from the top of the Slochd, all the way north to the top of the hill at Daviot, just outside Inverness. That is a few miles. Some of the search areas were perhaps more strategic than others. I was on two of the latter. One day we were driven six or seven kilometres down a minor road, east from the A9 at Dalmagarry along the Findhorn River. The tarred road stops at a farm called Ruthven. An estate track continues for the last couple of kilometres to Shenachie. The map indicates a rope bridge at that point. There is no bridge. There is a rope pulley system with a box. Some might call that a bridge. To cross the river, one clambers into the wooden box and then pulls on the rope, hand over hand. The box, swinging dizzily back and forward, slowly progresses to the other bank. The box comfortably carried two nervous passengers that day. After getting a dozen or so to the south bank, we lined up and – directed by megaphone man – the search began. The line of searchers on my side – because I did not go over – stretched well up the south flank of the Tom na Slaite hillside. We walked slowly, and scanned every tussock and clump of heather. When I looked to my right and left, the sight was impressive. A line of searchers from hilltop on the north, right down to the Findhorn and the same – if a bit shorter – on the other side. I thought it looked like a military manoeuvre; a Roman Legion marching forward. We stayed in formation and searched all the way back to the A9 road. It was a disciplined display of teamwork that day and, if I am allowed comment, quite impressive. It was a long, slow day. Just short of the main road the river swings left, to the south, with no crossing point. Decision made, the south bank brigade simply plunged into the river and waded across. They certainly deserved their limb-thawing elixir that day. We had been joined by a number of soldiers a couple of days before, and they stayed with us all the time I was involved. The search lines were alternately a police officer and a soldier. The other search I was involved in, perhaps more strategic than the Findhorn, was from Daviot along a side road to the east of the A9. During the late afternoon a senior officer appeared and stopped the search going any further. We were instructed to return to HQ and await further instructions. There was a brief delay in departing, occasioned by the arrival of our afternoon refreshment. We waited at HQ until a decision was made about continuing the search. I learned later that, as we were approaching some houses, one of the owners objected to our presence. After a while we were stood down and returned home. I understood later that a compromise was reached, and other officers continued that search. That was my last day on the Renee McRae search.

One incident, however, I have to relate. We had been searching for a week or more and, while it was tiring and hard work – and long hours – I never heard any dissent. We worked so hard to get it right, and we were confident we would be successful. Our enthusiasm never wavered. As it transpired, our confidence was misplaced. Whilst searching near the Little Chef at Tomatin, we had to cross a field containing some cattle and a large bull. Halfway across the field the row of searchers, including me, were becoming a trifle uncertain. We were corralling the cows into a corner, making them uneasy and trapped. However, it was the bull in the other corner we had eyes on. Our uncertainty was justified. Suddenly the bull took over. He had been standing by the gate, watching us steadily moving forward. I assume he also felt trapped. Perhaps he was just protecting his harem; who knows? I do not speak bull. (Others may have a different opinion.) He snorted, then – with no other warning – charged right into our ranks. Fully-fledged Tulliallan-trained police officers and equally well-trained soldiers, scattered like nine pins, each intent on saving themselves. We cleared that fence like Olympic hurdlers. Then we lay about in hysterics of laughter. Diners at the Little Chef no doubt chuckled.

Another day, down near the Slochd summit on the east side of the A9, we had to get over a deer fence – not for the first time. This time, however, we were in the company of a dog handler, Kenny, with his large and beautiful German Shepherd dog called Simba. It could not climb a deer fence. Kenny climbed to the top and, between him and I, we shoved and pulled Simba to the top. I climbed up and held onto Simba while the handler got down on the other side. I gingerly lowered his dog to him. I was less frightened of the bull.

I travel that road often. I never pass without thinking of the poor woman and her young son. I do, however, raise a smile at the bull location, the Little Chef (now long gone), the situation of the dog over the fence, and the Findhorn waders. Such memories. It is still a live enquiry, and that restricts me from referring to some of the evidence of which I am aware. However, I do have an opinion. Somebody knows exactly where Renee and her son are. I have no doubt who that somebody is. Years later, when a smart-mouth or two in Central Scotland Police made unwarranted remarks about our ability in the north to solve the mystery, I was a bit upset. Why do people with little or no knowledge of events, circumstances or situations feel it is reasonable to make sarcastic, demeaning comments? Why do I ask? The world is full of such arrogant people and, by making such remarks, they expose themselves for the shallow persons they are.

# CHAPTER 10

THERE was a Royal Visit at Highland Fabricators in 1974. The visit was to include the police accommodation, the 'But and Ben' cottage. The visit was going well, on time, with no hitches. The Queen was walking along the line of dignitaries, saying hello, or whatever the Monarch says on such occasions. End of the line was the top man of Brown and Root, Wimpey; a big Texan. Normally as cool as a cucumber. Next to him was his head of Personnel and Public Relations. I got this story from him. As the Queen got closer, the top man seemed to get more and more agitated, as if he wanted to say something. But he did not. He was twisting his wedding ring and looking more and more uneasy. The Queen was getting really close. The top man, after meeting her, would then escort her on the rest of the tour, including calling in at the police accommodation. The Queen was only two or three people away when the top man, unable to contain himself another moment, leaned to his PR man next to him and, in a strangled whisper, said 'get the cops to take their fuckin' drawers off the washing line!' The head of PR, just about to be introduced to the Queen, glanced over to the cottage and – to his horror – saw what his boss had been seeing for the last few minutes: police shirts and underwear flapping in the breeze. It was sorted in time, embarrassment averted.

Sometimes the spouse of the single station officer had to fill in if the officer is out on duty. A citizen producing driving documents to be checked was a regular. Two distressed birds of prey were dealt with by my wife during the course of our stay in Fearn. Not at the same time. A young peregrine falcon was found on a road verge. The motorist who found it had the presence of mind to throw his jersey over the falcon, thus calming it. He then deposited it with my wife. I dealt with that on my return. The same with a long-eared owl. It too was found, apparently disorientated, by the roadside. This time a handy cardboard box was used to enclose and calm it. It seems both birds were blown off course by heavy storm winds and got lost and exhausted; not the same storm. Hence the reason they were so easy to catch.

On the subject of flying, Morrich More by Tain was used extensively by various 'friendly' air forces – mostly ours – to carry out practice bombing. Sometimes spectacularly at night, when parachute flares were dropped to illuminate the night sky. Mostly, however, it happened during the day, especially on good visibility days. Fearn was directly on and under the path of the bombing run. The planes were low when they turned over our house into the last leg of their bombing or strafing run. As they levelled off, you could see puffs of smoke along the wings as the planes loosed their armaments. There were different runs, depending on the bomb or other armament being tested. It made no difference what they were testing; they all were seriously noisy. The first few times they flew past, the children came into the house crying as the planes screamed overhead. Some days there would be four planes following each other on several runs. It was ear-splitting. The wee ones soon became used to it and did not flinch. In fact, they took not one blind bit of notice. Nor did the residents. Apart, that is, from Brigadier Pricket who lived in Loch Eye House on the far side of the loch from the village. He had designed and made a 'jig' of sorts. It was of wood and one held it as a plane passed, lined it up in the sights, which consisted of a two small pieces of dowel at each end. If the sighted plane was inside the dowel markers, all was fine. However, if it did not fit then it was flying too low and the Brigadier was on the warpath. He always called me and the person in charge of the flight, whether at the nearby range or at Lossiemouth. It seemed there was a minimum height for these planes; 250 feet, if I remember correctly. The RAF officer always apologised and promised it would not happen again, which it undoubtedly did. I probably failed in my duty, for I never did work out how to properly deal with the Brigadier's complaints. Was I supposed to track the pilot down and report him to someone? Often they were NATO exercises and the planes were not even British.

On the subject of RAF planes, an account which did not involve me but rather an officer I knew, stationed in Fife. An aircrew member from RAF Leuchers in Fife had been involved in a road traffic accident. My colleague needed to speak to him, and so he popped along to Leuchers to be told the person he needed to see was over Germany on manoeuvres. He asked when it would suitable to call back. The person he spoke to asked if he could wait a minute. When he returned, he asked the officer if he wanted to take a seat and have a coffee; the person he needed to see would be back within the hour. He was.

Being the only officer and actually residing in the village, I felt it important to participate in some of the village community events. Whist drives, beetle drives, and more. I was approached to start a youth club. I agreed on the proviso that at least two other adults participated with me. The local garage owner and a painter in the village agreed. Prior to getting it up and running we visited two other youth clubs. They were council-run, one in Alness and one in Dingwall. We also spoke to some local parents and, more importantly, some local young people. Our first decision was to run the youth club one night a week. Our second decision was to reject most of the advice we had been given by the Community Education teams we had met. We did not write a constitution. We believed it to be too controlling, bureaucratic, and – frankly – we thought it smacked of control. We simply started the club, gathered all those who attended on the first night round in a circle, and asked them how they wanted it run. They came up with seven or eight rules. So we went with them. They also voted on a committee, all young people. They acted like the board and we three adults, in effect, worked for them. It worked like a dream.

We had one incident that tested the whole ethos of the club. One of the older boys lost his temper during a table tennis match and deliberately stamped on the ball. One flat table tennis ball. In keeping with their own rules, 'deliberate breakages will be paid for, or you do not get back into the club', the offender was asked to pay. He refused. He was barred immediately, and they did not let him back. Two weeks later he came back and paid. He was immediately made welcome. No recriminations, no issues; simply welcomed back into the fold. The committee were all younger than him, boys and girls.

Finding a skull was an interesting interlude. On Monday 19th January 1976, a sudden death with a difference came my way. It came with a history – a long history, as things turned out. There was house-building going on in Balintore. Children were playing on the developing Abbotshaven site one day when they dislodged sand from an embankment. A skull rolled out and skeletal remains could be seen. Shock horror! The children took the skull to school, and their head teacher put it in a shoebox and contacted the police. I headed to Balintore and viewed the site. I then removed the skull, still in the shoebox, to the Fearn Police Office.

Oh, a small diversion. Is it a police office or police station? When I first arrived in Central Scotland Police to work at Tullibody, police reports were typed up by the officer and handed to a Sergeant for checking. One Sergeant had an issue with my style of reporting and sent my first three reports back to me, red ink prominent. Most of it was semantics and trifling things about phraseology. However, one thing seemed to really annoy him. My use of the term 'police office'. The word 'office' was, deeply and with feeling, scored out each time and replaced with station. I had to enquire. His response? 'You might have called them offices in the north, but down here we call them stations'.

Where am I? Ah, the skull. It seemed obvious to me that this was nothing recent. I contacted Tain and, before long, I was making tea for an assortment of detectives and a few Bath Stars. For the uninitiated, the pip worn by senior officers is correctly called a Bath Star; something to do with Heraldry. So the next time you witness a group of senior police officers, you will be perfectly within your rights to refer to them by the collective noun, in these terms – 'Bath Stars'. Drinking tea and eating biscuits helped the thought process. Should we start a major investigation? 'Have you', addressing me, 'taped off the area?' I explained that I had been at the location and where the sand had broken away from the embankment, there seemed to be a stone barrier. Maybe a wall? Without digging it out, I cannot tell. I then opine, 'Sir, it looks like something really old'. Eventual agreement. The CID will have a look, and we will wait for their opinion. Look they did. Their opinion; this is ancient, we probably should get an archaeologist. And we did. The next day, one arrived from Inverness and agreed that the skull was indeed ancient and that the stone barrier – the wall I described – was not a wall, but a coffin of some sort. The archaeologist came back the following week with assistance and specialist tools, and proceeded to unearth – carefully – a 'double short cist burial', an ancient grave. Inside was a second skull and bones. A cist being a small stone coffin. Hence my reference to a wall. It was the grave of an adult and child. The initial estimate of age was probably circa two thousand years. It was really interesting. A detailed report of the findings and the dig, along with photographs, was sent to the Procurator Fiscal. Later, the bones were sent away for dating and expert analysis. They were found to be Neolithic: 5,000 to 5,500 years old. The child was estimated to be two years of age, and the adult was thought to be a male. No estimate of age given. The remains are kept at Inverness Museum, and can be seen by appointment. I still have a copy of the initial archaeology report. There was no evidence of foul play, so the detectives heaved a sigh of relief and went back to practicing their fingerprinting skills – on each other.

There was a full-blown industrial dispute, ending in a strike, at Highland Fabricators when I was there. I will cover that incident in a section about the three bigger strikes I was involved in as a police officer. Fearn had many surprises. A lobster on my doorstep. A red deer carcass, ready to be cut into roasting size pieces, delivered to my wife and dumped in the middle of the kitchen floor. I arrived home for supper that night to be met by my wife at the door, with the words 'what am I supposed to do with this?' The local General Practitioner asking me to visit so he could share some of the fish he had caught that day and have a chat. He was of the opinion that communities were best served when the professionals serving them could meet up once in a while and relax over a drink. It was like that. Seriously decent people, and I had the fortune and the privilege to be their police officer for three years. It was not only the people of the peninsula that made it special. It was the amount of good police officers, the camaraderie, the support at every level I encountered during my time in the north. The best three years, by far, of my whole career. I missed it when I left and I miss it now.

Fearn was the defining term of my police career. It was where I was taught and learned the benchmark for policing in communities, and also what was meant by the moral compass of policing. No matter where I policed after that, in my heart I was The Fearn Bobby, and I was proud of that. And no matter the bullying I would face many years later, by officers who had no moral compass, I knew who I was. They could never understand. My experience in Fearn taught me to hold my head high. That is why I am unabashed in naming my book *The Fearn Bobby*.

Before moving on from Fearn, I will relate a story that – certainly to my mind – typifies what I consider real community involvement and developing trust. The officer is happy that I use his name. One of my near colleagues, stationed in Tain – Harry 'The Horse' Munro – was on duty one snowy evening. A complaint was received that a group of youngsters were disturbing the neighbourhood with their antics, shouting and yelling whilst sledging. The Inspector ordered Harry to get out and stop them sledging. Harry was taking a long time about this, so the Inspector headed out to check. When he reached the locus he saw Harry sledging, in full uniform, along with the children. There was much merriment, but no annoying shouting and yelling. Harry had got them to be a bit quieter. The Inspector was furious, but soon calmed when seeing the funny side.

Then it was time to move on. Word on the street was that I was bound for Lochboisdale. Part of the development of officers in Northern sometimes included a spell, three years or so, on the islands, the Outer Hebrides. Nothing official, but certainly in the wind. At the same time, my wife wished to be nearer her mother in the Central Belt. Dilemma. I had no desire to serve further south. However, life it is not always about what you want. We had two young boys at that time, and my wife did not drive. I was out and about on duty for hours; she felt trapped. It was not that she did not have some good friends; however, the mother and daughter bond is strong. So south it was. I reluctantly started the transfer process. I honestly felt like a traitor. The Chief Constable had put his faith in me, against opposition, and now I was jumping ship. I felt I was betraying his trust. The process did not take very long; a few weeks. I still remember the day we filled the moving vans and drove away from Fearn. I had deep feelings of sadness about leaving, and trepidation about where I was heading. I was destined to move directly to Tullibody in Clackmannanshire. Not only was life going to change. I was about to experience a shock.

# CHAPTER 11

MY service took a new path in late 1977, when I moved from the Northern Constabulary and landed in Dodge. Apart from a break of just over a year, when I went into the CID then a spell in Tillicoultry, I was there until promoted in 1983. CB radio use was popular in these days, and Dodge was the code name for Tullibody. The village has a history going back to four thousand years BC and perhaps older. When it was a settlement, the Neolithic remains found in my previous police beat, Fearn, would have been alive and no doubt operating in a similar settlement. On occasion, my thoughts would drift to Neolithic times when dealing with one or two of the local characters. Tullibody's CB nickname fitted it well. There was no OK Corral; however, there was a place or two I could have recommended for that title. Tullibody, Clackmannanshire, had a population of seven or eight thousand when I was there. I referred earlier to Bonnybridge being 'gritty'; Tullibody was just as 'gritty'. Before anyone gets offended, it was a seriously good place to work and the residents – who were, for the most part, loyal and supportive – were decent, hard-working, honest folk who were a pleasure to serve. Like all communities, no matter how big or small, there were a few characters who challenged my theory; there always are. I spent the vast majority of my police service in Central Scotland Police; twenty-four years. Over the next few chapters I will, as far as time, space and my memory allow, give an account of front line police work in such a community, certainly as I delivered it, followed by my experiences and perspective from various management positions. I cannot – and I am sure the reader would not encourage me to – cover every incident, even if I could. So I will try to recount some of the more interesting situations, as a front line Constable and then through the ranks into management as well as how certain departments support front line community work. I will intersperse my narrative with comments on my view of some of the issues I encountered. Toward the conclusion I will give some of my thoughts on the whole concept of a single police force and perhaps why, in my opinion, some of their headline-grabbing policies are, to my mind, flawed.

Alluding to some of my earlier comments and thoughts on communities, Tullibody was no different in many respects. However, I found it generally busier, a bit more intense, and in some ways harsher than my earlier experiences. I gave an account of a test I was subjected to when not long in the police service in Ross and Sutherland. It would prove to be no different in my new arena. Testing out the new police officer was the early winter sport of 1978. The setters and invigilators of these early tests were the Gizz. They were the local dominant gang. They could be violent. Members of the Gizz were mostly teenagers, typically 17 and 18. There were no schoolchildren. I was the new boy in town and, in no time, I was christened 'rookie cop'. Tullibody had four officers at that time, covering all shifts from nine o'clock in the morning till two o'clock the following morning, seven days a week. It was not possible to be paired up every shift. The rota ensured pairings at the busiest and potentially riskier times. However, policing on one's own was a big part of the job. I was used to that. On such nights I often heard the cry 'rookie cop' ring out. My first real 'test' was a bit scary. One night I encountered a group of them in Tron Court, the shopping area of Tullibody. There had been an incident. They were a bit hyper and loud, and seemed angry about something. I spoke to them about their language and the noise they were creating. There were domestic dwellings above the shops. As I spoke to their 'leader', he started poking me quite violently in the chest with his finger. He was threatening me, and he was doing so in a loud voice. His pack were emboldened and crowded in closer. Telling him to back off seemed to antagonise him further. I assume alcohol or some other substance had been consumed. He prodded his finger into my chest once too often. He had obviously not read any Jack Reacher books. (He wouldn't have; they had not been written at that point.) I grabbed his finger and violently forced it back. I mean, right back. He screamed and went onto his knees pleading with me to let him go. I told him to tell his gang to back off or I would tear his finger off. I kept up the pressure. He stayed on his knees, squealing. The gang was uncertain how to react, so I just kept the pressure on his finger. We had reached an *impasse*. I was not sure how any of them would react if I let go, and I sure as hell could not stand like this all night. The threats to me started to grow again. I took out my personnel radio and called for assistance. Within five minutes, a crew from Alloa attended. We cleared the area, and I arrested old finger poker. He was charged with assault and was subsequently fined.

They had not finished with me, and soon a second 'test' was set. I was patrolling alone one evening and saw about a dozen of them sitting on a wall. As I passed, they gesticulated and shouted my nickname. Endearing creatures. I pulled over and got out. I was immediately surrounded, and their leader that night – the brother of a well-known, difficult family – instructed one of his crew to 'hook the black bastard'. It was no racial slur; it related to my police uniform. Up stepped a particularly 'difficult' young man. In the years that followed, he was convicted of some serious assaults. He was taller than I was. He said 'you are getting it, you black bastard'. A free and original thinker he was not. I asked if he was the chosen one, and told him I was having a busy night and really did not have a lot of time. He just stared at me and stepped closer. I then told him there had to be rules, because a police officer in uniform is not allowed to hit anyone unless they are hit first. 'So you need to hit me first and, when you do, make sure you kill me,' I said, continuing, 'because if you don't, I will fuckin'' kill you'. He was getting louder verbal encouragement by now, and one told him to hurry. As I prevaricated and worked out my tactics, I slowly changed position until I had my back to the gang and he had his back to the police van, facing me and his pals. I added the next set of rules, and said 'I will count to three, and you hit me'. I did what I had planned all along; I cheated. I failed to count and simply punched him hard. He went down on his knees, gasping for breath. The supporters in the stalls had seen enough. Cries like 'oh, whit ur ye dein?' were loudest. I turned, and they were all walking back to the village centre. Their champion, meanwhile, was on his hands and knees, gasping for breath. I got him to his feet and made sure he was fine, if a little embarrassed. He stumbled after his gang and I got on with the rest of my shift.

The sequel to that little discussion came the very next night. Again on patrol on my own, I encountered the gang sitting at Tron Court on a wall near the chip shop. I got out and sat on the wall beside them. My previous night's challenger was not about. One asked me if I was looking for him. 'Not particularly', I replied. 'Well, he is in the chip shop', somebody said. Sure enough, a few minutes later out he came, carrying a bag of chips and something to go with them. He pushed a gang member over and sat beside me, saying: 'How are you? Do you want a chip?' I took a chip, and we all spoke for a few minutes. I had passed my Dodge initiation, and never had one more bit of bother from The Gizz.

It was Tullibody, however, and there were plenty other people and situations to give me bother. My nickname got shelved as well. Years later – a lot of years later – I met two of that group at another place and time. They were a lot older, men with families. As we spoke about old times, one told me that they knew I was not frightened of them. I asked how they came to that conclusion, not letting on that my stomach churned, just like everybody else's would in such circumstances. 'You got out the police car. The other police stayed in the car and spoke to us out the window.' My goodness; you learn something new every day. I had never thought of that. What I did was simply instinct and how I policed. Something they did not know, however. When approached the night I was to get 'hooked' – the night I spent talking and 'wasting' time – I was only stalling to work out what to do next, talking them down and looking for a moment to take control. In the toolbox of policing tactics, the most important is taking control. The same goes for meetings and in other forums away from the front line.

So I was six months into my new path and getting to grips with it; well, in the community anyway. It was not all plain sailing back at base. I had not realised how irritating some senior officers found transferees. That was what I was. I had transferred from another force and that made me different, not so much amongst my front line colleagues, but certainly with some of the senior officers. By no means all of them, but enough to be noticeable. I was called a transferee, in company, more than once. The really hurtful barb came from a Detective Chief Inspector one day in the Tullibody office. Funny, really; it must have made a deep, lasting impression, because it was uttered nearly forty years ago. I can still see him, sitting on the bench desk in the office, swinging his feet back and forward, whilst unloading his sarcastic comment: 'Oh, you transferred from the Northern; the force that cannot catch anyone'. I was furious and if he, like the head teacher all these years before, thought he had humiliated me, he was so wrong. Funnily enough, some years later – when I was a Sergeant and had delivered a speech to a group he was part of – he was asked by a local councillor 'why is Ian not getting promoted?' The reply came: 'Because he does not mould himself on his superiors'. Until the day I retired, I did not feel part of the Central Scotland Police family.

I had hardly got started in Tullibody, when the national firemen's strike came along. I cover that in a separate section. It was soon over, and I could get on in my new life again. I had not long got back into my rhythm and was dealing with vandalism to a pillar box. Someone had spray painted UVF (Ulster Volunteer Force) and other pro-Unionist logos. I was interviewing a suspect. He obviously denied it. I suggested that if he told the truth I would deal with it as a low-grade vandalism. If he insisted on lying, I would have no choice but to involve the Anti-Terrorist Branch. There was no such local unit in these days, reminding him that post boxes have the monarch's insignia thereon and therefore, as the property of the Monarch, his actions in daubing the emblem of a terrorist organisation on one could be seen as treason. I left it to him. He asked if I would not 'screw him up'. I assured him I was levelling with him. He admitted he had done it as a prank and said he was sorry. He was reported to the Procurator Fiscal, who admonished him. Working in communities brings all sorts of challenges.

In the early hours of one weekend morning I dealt with the report of a sexual assault on a young woman. It had happened in a public place, and she had no idea who her attacker was. Within twenty minutes, he went on that same night to expose himself at another location. My only real identification clue was his distinctive checked, lumberjack-style jacket. No, not what you were thinking. My enquiries were getting nowhere. The following weekend, I visited the locus of the crime about eight o'clock in the evening. I was accompanied by a colleague from Tullibody. I parked the vehicle, opened the windows on a cold, damp December night, and switched the engine and the police radio off. My colleague asked what on earth was I up to. I told him that I was convinced the male we were looking for was local and had not jetted in from Glasgow or Edinburgh. I added that we probably knew him and, if we sat quietly and thought, it would come to us. So we sat in the cold, car windows open, in the quiet, soaking up the atmosphere and letting our brains do the work. It was not long before I remembered something that happened a year or more before, in this very same area. A male person, who lived nearby, had undressed and displayed himself at the bedroom window of his apartment. Two local women witnessed it and reported him to the police. That jogged my colleague's memory. He remembered seeing that same male twice over the last few weeks. On each occasion, he had seen him walking in the direction of Tullibody on the low road from Alloa in the early hours of the morning. He did not think much about it, and assumed the male was just out for a late walk. He was always alone. The hair stood up on the back of my neck. We headed back to the office and found his name and address in our records. My colleague asked what I was thinking of doing. I told him we were going to give him a call. 'What are you going to say to him?' he asked, adding: 'Because if that's all you've got, he will walk'. I told him he needed to have faith. I did not know what I was going to say, but was confident I would work it out.

We went to his door, and his wife asked us in. Her husband, the person we were interested in, was present. I explained about the incident the previous weekend and that we were completing house-to-house enquiries. I asked if either had heard screaming about one o'clock in the morning the previous Saturday. The wife said she had, but assumed it was young people larking about. He responded by saying he had not heard anything. His wife, who was knitting, casually remarked – without looking up – that he would not have heard anything, as he was not in the house at the time. I was now getting warm. I asked where he had been, as perhaps he might have seen something significant. He said he had seen nothing, and had not heard anything. I asked where he had been. He gave a long, very detailed route, encouraged by my promptings and questions. I noted every detail, every twist and turn. I then asked if I could see the jacket he was wearing. I did tell him the suspect was wearing a distinctive jacket, and this would help eliminate him from any suspicion. His wardrobe held no such jacket. As he was closing the wardrobe door I leaned over and saw the sleeve of a jacket under the bed. I did not need to move anything to see it. He said it was his work jacket, and he kept it there because it was a bit dirty. He took it out. It was identical to the jacket described by witnesses the week before. I explained that to him, and then cautioned him and detained him. He was subsequently pointed out by two witnesses at an identification parade, and eventually pleaded guilty at court. I never heard the final outcome. But we got our man. The point of that story is about community knowledge and awareness, coupled with giving yourself time to work it out.

There was no Sergeant in Tullibody; we were a self-supervising unit and we were good at it. We worked closely, and constantly supported each other. For example, when on the late shift sequence of the rota, one could be nearly three weeks away from the day-dwellers in the village. So if one required an enquiry to be carried out during the day shift period, you simply left a note on the early shift to-do list. First job every morning, assuming there was no emergency, was to sort out the notes and then get out and do the early enquiries, whatever they happened to be. You would be afforded the same service. On occasion, one might wait on at the conclusion of your shift to accompany the officer starting his later shift, to carry out an enquiry that required corroboration. No overtime was claimed. It was teamwork, and we all did it for each other.

I have to say, sometimes one could get caught in something a tad complicated when volunteering to assist a colleague. I was due to start at six o'clock one evening. During the late morning I was rolling about on the floor playing with my youngest child. An on-duty colleague called at the house to ask a favour. Could I come out early and cover for him from two o'clock that afternoon, as he was going to the police golf and he was due to tee off at that time. I agreed. He rushed back about twenty minutes later to say that a sudden death had just been reported and could I start even earlier. I did, and walked into one of the most difficult sudden death enquiries I faced in my career. Perhaps awkward – or even unusual – might describe it better. The latter term is not to be disrespectful, but I am not sure how else to describe it. It was really a sad situation. I arrived at the house, and the parents directed me to an upstairs bedroom. Their son, in his mid-thirties, was in bed and obviously dead. The family GP was in attendance and, after I got his details and a short statement, he left the scene. The dead male was over thirty stone in weight. It seems he had not left his bed for a few months. He had been unable to even get to the bathroom, and not just to wash. So the scene was as one might imagine, although I did not have to imagine anything. I summoned the police surgeon and got some assistance to move the body. We did have normal-size fibreglass coffins. However, we had nothing that fitted our deceased. We resorted to a large roll of plastic which we laid out on the floor of the bedroom. We then, six of us, manhandled the unfortunate person out of bed onto the plastic sheet. We wrapped him in it and tied it up. The only stretcher we could muster was an old canvas job with wooden carrying handles. The problem was that we could not lift him. Another two officers arrived. Getting him downstairs was the next logistic to be solved. One officer at each corner of the stretcher was not enough. There was no room for anybody else, as the stairs were narrow. Luckily they went straight down with no corners. Our only option was to tie a rope to the stretcher and have officers above it taking some of the weight. The first floor landing ran from the top step of the stairs along their length, which meant we could see over, and two could take the strain with the rope and move along as the stretcher moved down to the hall. So far, so good. 'Best laid plans' comes to mind. With an officer straining and heaving on each corner of the stretcher, and with another two leaning over from the landing taking the strain on the rope, we started. We got a few steps down when disaster struck. One of the wooden stretcher poles broke, twisting the whole thing to one side, collapsing the stretcher. The top two stretcher-bearing officers let go, the full weight was now on the lower stretcher bearers and the rope crew. The lower bearers could not hold on, particularly given the added complication of our body lurching to a sitting position and disgorging his stomach contents over them. They let go, only managing to leap out of the way as the unfortunate man tobogganed down the remaining stair with his head bouncing off every step. It was a disaster, and expletives filled the hall. We gathered our wits and got the poor man out and into the vehicle that was to take him to the mortuary for post mortem.

I went into the living room to speak to his parents, who were sitting quietly and could not have failed to hear the carnage in the hall. I could not apologise enough. Their reaction was humbling. They had just lost their son, and they had heard our disastrous efforts to get him from the house. They could not have been more calm, more pleasant and more understanding. In fact, they apologised to me for all the trouble they had caused. They said it was a wonder we got him down the stairs at all, and expressed their gratitude. They honestly could not thank us enough. I do not tell that tale to humiliate him or his memory. I knew him and his parents, and even if I had not, it would not have been my motive. My only point in telling you this true story is to evidence the human face of police officers and how, in often trying circumstances, they remain dedicated and treat people in these situations with respect. As in this case, when it did not go smoothly and later

– much later – when they laughed and resorted to macabre humour, it was about their own failings and in no way about the unfortunate people they have been helping. It sometimes is the only way to retain our sanity. Lastly, a warning to any reader: think twice before agreeing to let a colleague away early to play bloody golf.

A police officer will face and deal with a lot of death in her or his service. I was once asked, when the local unit Commander visited me in Bo'ness many years later, to justify my officers' existence and explain what they actually did, as the community did not see them about on patrol as much as they would like. Among my presentation, in which I reeled off a whole stack of officer activity statistics, was one that made the audience gasp. In a typical year in Bo'ness, officers dealt with in excess of fifty sudden deaths. Marginally more than one each week. In terms of my management style and support of my various teams over the years, I did not smother my officers in supervision. I trusted them and allowed each to develop and grow without my presence, breathing down their neck. However, there will always be exceptions to that approach. One is when the death is suspicious; there is no choice then. The vast majority were not suspicious, and may well not need my input. However, if it was a 'difficult' sudden death, I would attend. My definition of that is one that perhaps has lain a few weeks, or may have some other 'unpleasant' circumstance. I always made an appearance at such incidents. Not to over-supervise; just to let them know they were supported.

To move on from this section, I will finish with one that left me a bit spooked. I was a Sergeant, and my officers were at a sudden death. The undertaker had been summoned before I reached the scene. When I got there, the doctor was giving a statement. The officer taking it was facing into the bathroom. The person had died in the bath. Whilst taking the statement, the officer stopped writing and said that the dead person's chin moved. The doctor was relaxed about this, as these things can happen. The second movement was more pronounced. Panic. Second examination followed. The under-taker was cancelled, and an ambulance was called. The old lady was removed from the bath, wrapped in a foil blanket, and whisked off to hospital. She recovered.

# CHAPTER 12

TULLIBODY was a busy and challenging posting. Not without its humour. I attended at the working man's club, the Top Club, one night, as a steward needed to report something. One of the members had been difficult earlier in the night. Too much to drink. He was being asked to leave, and took exception to that. The more the steward tried to reason with him, the angrier the chap got. Eventually the culprit shrugged his jacket off and threw it on the ground in front of the steward, who reacted immediately and punched him, knocking him down. The vanquished party gathered up his jacket and headed off home. The steward was reporting his version to me, just in case the other party complained about being assaulted. Which he did, later that day. I was working an extended backshift on the Sunday when a call was received that a male wished to report an assault. On attendance, I was met by his wife who made a coffee and told me her husband was going to make a fool of himself. The victim was in the living room, sitting in the corner. His nose did look like it had been in contact with a fist. It was red and swollen, and looked a tad skewed. I listened to his story, delivered with a certain nasal inflection, and laughed out loud – as did his wife. His version tallied exactly with the club steward's story. The crucial difference concerned the casting of the jacket at the feet of the steward. According to the steward, that was a sign of aggression – wanting to fight. According to the person I was listening to, it was a sign of peace: a sign of not wanting to fight. He was indignant; however, his temporary speech impediment kind of took the edge off his indignation. Once his wife and I stopped laughing at the ridiculousness of the situation, he calmed down and laughed himself. I did not investigate the incident further, and advised him to verbalise his thoughts next time and reduce his reliance on sign language.

There is a serious point however. In the case of any crime, once it has been established there has been one, the police are bound to investigate. Do not be misled by television dramas that always ask the victim if they wish to press charges. It is not their choice. I will illustrate that with one incident. A male was beaten unconscious in a bar. Police arrived in time to see him being put in an ambulance. He had regained consciousness. Police asked him what happened, and then, 'do you want to make a complaint?' He did not, and the police left the scene. I heard this over the radio whilst at another serious incident a few miles away. I met the officers who been at the 'no complaint' incident. They briefed me. I advised them to return to the locus, get evidence, and deal with the crime. In fact, I instructed them to get somebody locked up. They were adamant the victim made no complaint. I answered thus: 'The victim is a witness; he or she does not make complaints, nor is it his or her decision. The police are witnesses. They do not make complaints; that is the job of the Procurator Fiscal.' If he had been killed, who would have made the complaint? If a young child is assaulted, who makes the complaint? If the victim – a witness – refuses to make a statement, the case may well be much harder to prove. However, it still is an assault and requires to be investigated. We work in a community, and have a responsibility to make it safe. Allowing serious assaults to take place is not the way to make anywhere safe. If we step back, what message does that send? It is in the public interest that we act, whether the victim wishes to co-operate or not. Certainly in minor incidents one may well use discretion. That is a decision requiring judgement, and it may well be accepted. However, it is not up to the victim, and it must never be based on laziness. The officers did not get a statement from the victim. However, they did get plenty of other statements. A person did get arrested that night, and pleaded guilty at a later date. The police report included all the evidence with a caveat; the victim refuses to give a statement.

Back in the Top Club at Tullibody, one member had his membership suspended for a year by the committee. After a few weeks, his best friend asked for an audience with the management committee to appeal for his suspended friend. He argued that they were lifelong friends and spent every day in the club together; without his friend, he was lost. Would they consider reducing the ban? His appeal fell on deaf ears. He was about to leave and stopped.

'Can I make a second appeal?' he asked.

'This is a bit irregular, but in the circumstances we will hear you', said the President.

'Can I no' share his ban?' said the friend in desperation.

The President was perplexed. 'What do you mean?'

'Well, reduce his ban to six months, and ban me for the other six months.'

The committee agreed to this unusual request. A public interest decision.

I was working on my own one Sunday night. Strangely, the shift rota always had just a single officer on a Sunday night. It was one of the busier nights. I got a call to attend at the Top Club; there was a riot ongoing. I hurried round to be met in the car park by two officers from Alloa. That was to be the extent of the assistance. A quick decision, based on knowing my community. I was confident I would be safe enough. However, to introduce two strange officers? I was less confident about what might happen if they came in with me. Decision made. I asked them to stay in the car park and watch the cars; I would deal with the riot. I went into the foyer and looked through the small window in the swing doors. It really was a riot. I thought it had to be bad, because the committee would not normally call the police and liked to sort things out quietly. This was Agincourt with bottles and ash trays instead of spears. It was serious and the bottles were flying, as were the fists and feet. I asked that the hall lights be put on. I went through the swing doors. They opened onto the top step. The dance floor was a few steps down. The tables were on tiered levels going down to the dance floor. It was full, with over two hundred people. It was noisy. I walked down towards the main floor. I was grabbed by a male, shirt torn and blood on his face. He was well known to the police. He said he had been assaulted. He was probably not lying. I told him to get his wife and friends and get out before I got reinforcements and he got lifted. I could see assaults taking place. An ash tray passed near my head. I strode onto the floor and simply grabbed struggling males – yes, and females – and told them to fuckin' stop and get out before they were arrested. Within a few minutes it calmed down and they all trooped out. The club was empty in ten minutes. I followed the remnants into the car park and watched them drift off home. I thanked the Alloa guys, and they headed off.

On returning to the club I was met by incredulous committee men who said they could not believe I was on my own. I make a confession now. I was high on adrenalin by that point. Looking calm and in control can take a lot out of you. My logic was the same as the caravan in the dunes firearms incident. I knew these people; I was pretty confident they would not harm me, certainly not in that situation. I was their police officer. Working properly in a community, getting to know people, dealing firmly and fairly, does bring respect. Of that I have no doubt. You are their police officer, and that brings a level of insurance that an unknown officer may not have. Acting alone was also not threatening, not confrontational. The committee accompanied me onto the empty dance floor. I do not exaggerate: there was not a square foot that did not have broken glass on it. We crunched as we walked. I had a stiff drink and headed off. Just another Sabbath in Tullibody. I mused later that if I could have swapped my great coat for a poncho and a short cheroot, I might have made more of an impression.

* * *

The Abercromby Arms Hotel, certainly in these far-off days, had a reputation. It was rough. Another Sunday night, another stramash. As requested in an urgent, hoarse, whispered telephone call from the manager, I drove round the back of the premises and entered via the kitchen door. The manager was in a state; there had been trouble at the Sunday dance night in the extension. As we had discussed, I accompanied him into the hall and approached the main troublemaker. The plan was that the manager would tell him to leave. I knew he would refuse, that would complete the offence, and I would arrest him. Simple, really. We never got the chance. As we entered the hall, as if orchestrated – which it undoubtedly was – the culprit grabbed his wife, stood up and signalled to the band, who started playing. Instantly, the dance floor was full of dancing couples. I took over and instructed him to leave the premises. He refused by resorting to that age old phrase – popular throughout the western world, I assume: 'Fuck off!' I grabbed his arm and replied 'I will do that, then I will come back. And if you are still here, I will arrest you'. I went out and called for assistance. A short time later I was joined by a single officer, a young probationer. I have previously referred to how important it is to know your community. Well, I certainly knew the majority of my community in that dance hall and what I also knew was, this is going to be interesting. It was a completely different feeling from the night of the riot in the Top Club. This situation was so different, and I certainly did not feel untouchable. It is of no consolation to add, I was spot on: I read my community perfectly that night. I instructed the young officer what was going to happen, and to stick with me. I told him I was going to instruct a person to leave, he will tell me to fuck off, and I will arrest him. I will take hold of him and you will do the same. He is a big guy, and he will resist. On no account will you let go of him and on no account will you fall over. I added, remember, we are going to arrest him and we are taking him to the gaol, whatever else happens.

As we entered the hall, the same orchestrated pantomime took over. Music started up and the dancing commenced. This time they obstructed our passage. We got to our man and, as scripted, we went through the mating ritual complete with the verbals. There was a slight difference; as I grabbed his arm and told him he was under arrest, I added a phrase I had not learned at Tulliallan: 'We are fucking off, and so are you'. It was a 'light the blue touch paper moment', and all hell broke loose. We struggled, wrestled and sashayed him over the dance floor, obstructed all the way, verbal and physical intimidation being the order of the day. As we emerged out to the front, I realised my tactical error. Where is the police van? Bugger, I'd parked it round the back as suggested by the manager. Oops. It made no difference; the young probationer was soaring in my estimation – he was like a limpet, he was not letting his man go. We were surrounded by a baying mob, including a lot of our prisoner's family who had seen the inside of cells themselves on occasion. They were well-built, and no shrinking violets. Then it got a bit close for comfort as one of his brothers launched himself at me from behind, then jumped on my back with his arm around my throat. He pulled me back and I lost my grip on the prisoner, who struggled free of the young officer. As our prisoner ran into the night, I shouted to my colleague to catch and bring him back. Off he sped. I was preoccupied by then and, having struggled free, I was now facing my opponent who I had decided was going to join his brother in gaol. No matter how many angry people surrounded me, screaming for their champion to 'give it to the bastard', I had to only concentrate on him. He came for me quickly and swung a punch at my head. Haymakers are so predictable. I fended it off with my left arm then did something I did not learn in my boxing lessons. I did not retaliate with a punch. I figured that a punching match – with all his supporters waiting on their chance to join in – is a bad idea. I need to control the situation. So I stepped forward and grabbed him by his windpipe. I really grabbed it, and I pressed my fingers in so hard I could almost touch fingertips. As I did that, I forced him back against the wall of the hotel. He was gasping and trying to grab my arm to loosen the grip. People were shouting, 'You are going to kill him!' I shouted back, 'If anyone lays a glove on me I will rip it out!' Expletives followed me throughout my service, and tonight was no different.

We continued with this stalemate for a short time. Then the dynamics changed. The young probationer arrived back, dragging his recaptured prisoner, and at the same time I spied two police officers standing a distance away – yes, standing and not approaching. I shouted to them, and they reluctantly came to our assistance. They did not even register on my 'estimation' scale. Things got a bit nearer order then and, although there was still some resistance, we got the two accused handcuffed and into the newly-arrived transport. I then recovered my own van and, by the time I got it round the front, it had kicked off again and we arrested two of the supporting cast – both female. The manager closed down for the night, and we headed to the cells at Alloa with our catch. I lost my hat and my police tie that night, and never saw them again. I assume they adorned a trophy cabinet somewhere. The whole escapade eventually made it to Alloa Sheriff Court some months later. All four were found to be guilty, and all received fines. During the trial the bloke whose throat I became acquainted with told the court I had been jumping about like a hysterical spider. Lastly, my police house was no more than fifty yards from the Abercromby Arms, so while I engaged in this nonsense, my children and wife were sleeping peacefully.

Different night, same venue. It was about eight o'clock on the night of an Old Firm football match and there was trouble. No surprise there. Glasses had been thrown at the gantry behind the bar, breaking a couple of the liquor bottles. My colleague and I arrived to find all the staff cowering in the kitchen. There was a bit of trouble in the bar, right enough.

In the absence of bar staff, the helpful customers served themselves. It is not clear who was keeping the tab. We went in and soon became the butt of the joke – whatever it was. Witnesses were like hen's teeth. The bar staff also had amnesia. They had tried to clear the bar, without success. Only one solution. I jumped onto the bar and opened the glass cover off the large wall clock. It was eight thirty when I opened it, after a few seconds and a few revolutions of the hands, it was fifteen minutes after midnight and beyond their permitted License time. Still standing on the bar, I announced the bar was closed and they had exceeded their drinking up time. Two or three finished their drinks and we charged them with drinking after hours. We could not do that; they did not know. Problem solved. They all shuffled along to the Inn.

Another drinking venue in Tullibody was the Bottom Club. It was another working man's establishment. I have forgotten the difference, although I think it had a connection with the local authority and the Coalfields Regeneration Trust. It probably was more of a community centre, as it had badminton courts marked out in the big hall and football pitches out the back. They were not fooling anybody. I will not regale you with more tales of this club, although I could. On a Sunday – yes, the quiet day – buses would come there from other clubs throughout the west, mostly Glasgow or other mining villages. The usual pattern was to have an early lunch and a drink or two before the men would get out onto the football park and play football. Yes, in their suits. They did remove their jackets. They returned for more refreshments, then their tea, or – to use toff-speak – their dinner. That was followed by more refreshments and the dance. There was always a dance. That is where the trouble started. Always. Local woman meets visiting male, mud marks on suit trousers apparently not a turn off. Dancing commences with the usual lively rock or country and western number, then perhaps a slow dance followed – much later – by a smooch dance. Are you keeping up with the plot? Local males are now feeling a bit rejected; even the ones married to the smooch dancers. With noses firmly out of joint, the murmuring starts. It is now getting late. Fisticuffs are in the offing, to use a totally out-of-place nautical term. They are not in the offing for long before the Lone Ranger of Tullibody has to make an appearance. There are usually several complaints made. The Lone Ranger speaks to the bus driver and the organiser of the visiting party. Everyone is hustled onto the bus, and it leaves Dodge to jeers and the strains of 'will ye no come back again?' The more observant will see the glint of a tear in one or two of the ladies' eyes. It is not unknown for a Stonehouse local to be seen on Monday morning at a bus stop waiting on the Stirling bus.

It was not all fighting and frolicking, but hard-working men sometimes have to let off steam. The job of the police is not to prevent a perfectly natural activity, but to ensure that it does not result in injury to others. There were so many other duties. Routine stuff. We carried out checks on Liquor License extensions in premises with such a license; we also did reports on premises seeking such extensions. We may even do a report on road safety issues to avoid such situations occurring in our area. All warrants for people in our beat arrived at our office. Some were straight arrest, some were Means Enquiry and others were Extract Conviction. The office in these days was at the Cross, Tullibody, next to the Post Office and near the Abercromby Arms Hotel. It could not have been more strategically positioned. Most passed it at least once a week. Warrant hunting often relied on a sharp knock on the window. The passer-by, for whom an outstanding warrant existed, would simply come into the office. It was at that point local negotiations ensued. Usually along the lines of:

'How much is it for? I've no' got £130. I've got the wee one tae feed. I started work last week. Can you no' give me a couple o' weeks?'

'How about something now, something next week, and the rest by the end of the month? You okay with that?'

We managed our warrants and the community, and it worked – we had very few outstanding for long. Obviously there would be the odd time when we had to visit the 'non-payer' in his or her residence and actually arrest them. It was how communities worked. The Top Club was the main lender in the village. They had books with hundreds of pounds' worth of debt. There was no interest involved. It was just a straight-up loan. They always got paid back. It was a crucial resource in the village. I think the Bottom Club had a similar set-up. There were always hardships, and the clubs were a source of support. Legislators and other policy makers had little or no idea how these communities worked. The clubs kept a lot of decent people from the real money lenders and, if today, from the 'instant loan' merchants. The local police knew it went on; it did more good than harm, far more.

Crime was another big part of our work load. Theft, theft by housebreaking, assault, and more. A simple example of local policing might follow this model. I spot a car parked in the street. It has no Road Tax disc displayed, or one that is out of date. I call at the house where it is parked, establish the owner, and suggest if you have no Road Tax then you are likely to have no insurance. More often than not, that would be the case. Solution offered on the spot, with a twenty four hour limit: get your car off the public road and you will hear no more from me. That usually worked, in two ways. Illegal car off the street and a bit of respect, dare I say trust, for the police for handling the situation that way. In terms of crime in our community, we took a pride in keeping our detection rate high. It was funny, really; we were less concerned with the crime rate than we were in our clear-up rate. There were road accidents and more. It honestly was a busy place, and we worked hard. The community knew that.

There were the usual smattering of domestic violence incidents. Comments made in recent years by the Chief Constable of the Scottish Police Service suggested the police did not do their job properly in this respect. I, for one, took exception to his comments. He was in charge of a force where perhaps he was correct; I have no way of knowing. However, my experience was that we always treated victims of domestic violence with respect and listened to them. Often there was no actual assault, and evidence was sparse. When there was evidence, my experience was that we always arrested the suspect. As I say, some cases involved heated argument, with no physical element. In these cases, it was not always clear who was the worst offender. I attended at one such incident, which involved screaming and shouting – about not a lot, as it turned out. The woman wanted her partner removed, no more. The Matrimonial Homes (Scotland) Act was in force then, so removing either spouse or partner could be an offence in itself. As it turned out, he agreed to leave if I dropped him off at his parents' house. We got outside, just before the door was slammed shut and locked. Mr Charming then turned his attentions to me. I was on my own. Obviously still a tad annoyed, he flew at me. His attack was quickly dealt with, and – once he calmed down – I took him to his parents' home.

On another occasion, I was called to a house I knew well – though not from a domestic violence view. The occupants were a colourful couple, and police did have reason to know them. This call was about a domestic. Again, no personal violence, but certainly loud shouting and swearing. Both were giving it laldy when I arrived, again on my own. It was about seven o'clock one Friday evening. He had been working all day. He was a rigger, and it was heavy work. His wife had been in a hostelry most of the afternoon, and perhaps was not best positioned to produce a Rick Stein plate of food. So it was a fry-up of sausage, eggs, beans and fried bread. I had no need to ask, as it was lying in a heap on the carpet – directly below where it had struck the wall a few minutes before my arrival. The loud conversation centred on the quality of food, as far as I could make out. He was shouting; something like 'what kind of dinner is that to serve your man when he has been out working all day, while you are getting pished in the Ab?' I intervened at that point and asked if this was a new kind of art. The splat on the wall, with the colourful streaks leading vertically down to the plate on the carpet. They both looked at the wall, she called me a cheeky runt – I am sure that is what she said. Meanwhile, he fell silent and then burst out laughing, followed a short time later by her. I helped them clean it up, and we had a cup of tea. When I left, he was heading out to get a fish supper for both of them. I would see them later that night, in one establishment or another.

I relate both these stories to highlight, in my opinion, the complete nonsense of having a blanket approach to such incidents. What good would it have done at either locus, if I had simply arrested one or the other? It would have made no difference to either relationship, other than introduce more stress. Of course, people need to be arrested on some occasions and I do not deny that; perhaps there was a tendency in some areas for officers to do as little as possible and get out of there. However, a blanket directive to simply arrest one or the other, regardless of evidence, is oppressive. There was a project at the University of Stirling some years ago that engaged with the violent partner in order to change their behaviour. I think it was called the Change Project. Part of that was to look at assertiveness and try to help men – it was usually men – understand the difference between being aggressive and being assertive, the latter tending to reduce the need to simply hit out. It was showing good results, but – like a lot of other seemingly positive interventions – withered on the vine of the leafless money tree. Is that a mixed metaphor? I refer to domestic violence, and my despair at the new approach, in another section.

# CHAPTER 13

I FOUND the supervision in Central Scotland Police a bit more overbearing than in Northern Constabulary. In my view, unnecessarily.

I was attending to a routine road accident. Perhaps not that routine. A local councillor was involved. It was not serious, and no one was injured. Nonetheless, as my colleague and I dealt with it I spied the Inspector and Sergeant from Alloa standing a bit back from the accident, just watching. I approached and asked if there was a problem. They said no, and drove away. Seems it was always like that.

A silly wee story of no consequence and nothing to do with over supervision, but amusing nonetheless. In the early hours of one Sunday morning we came across two locals we knew well. Decent people; they had been at an event. They were leaving, and the lady was putting left over bits and pieces in her car. Her husband had obviously enjoyed his evening, and was grinning a lot and looking a wee bit happier than normal. We spoke for a couple of minutes and he decided to have a seat, so he opened the car door and sat on the passenger side. His wife was a lovely looking woman, which made her reaction to what he had done all the more amusing. She suddenly stopped speaking to us, jumped over to the car, threw the passenger door open and screamed at her husband

'Ronnie! You've sat on the fuckin' vol-au-vents!' And he had; a full tray of the little blighters. She dragged him out, too late. The seat of his suit trousers looked none too pretty. As we made our discreet withdrawal, we could still hear her protestations. Just another night in Dodge.

Another time, we gave a motorcyclist a bit of a fright. We had taken possession of a firearm: a point 22 calibre rifle, nothing criminal. On the way back to the office, we were flagged down by a motorcyclist looking for directions. There was also a pillion passenger; a witness to the following conversation. On seeing the rifle, propped up between the driver's and passenger seat, the motorcyclist asked if it was a firearm.

'Yes', came the reply.

'Do you always carry firearms?'

'Well, we are in Tullibody, and it is Friday night.'

He roared off to his destination. I have no idea who he was; maybe he remembered the armed officers in Tullibody.

Village policing can be varied, and our small corner of the country also had its 'ice cream war'. You may have read about such things in the west of Scotland. We had our version, sometimes vicious and always bitter. The usual practice would be muscling into the regular run of a rival. Not illegal. Often the opposition reported rivals for selling drugs from their vans. We would dutifully attend and carry out the required search. We never found proof. It actually took up a bit of police time. There were incidents involving getting third parties to intimidate rivals by throwing objects, bricks and/or stones, at vans. That not only caused damage; it could be dangerous. There was seldom evidence of the culprit, although we did manage to report two such incidents. One incident involved simply attacking a van with iron bars and wrecking it. That got to court. Two witnesses could name the accused and pointed them out at the trial. However, the defence was three other people – credible adults from another area who swore the accused could not have done it. They were both in their house having dinner. Not guilty was the verdict. That same night, I met the main accused – the owner of one ice cream company. A local businessman of some stature. He was completely unabashed when he said that the justice system is merely about balance. My lawyer finds out the balance of the evidence. We tip the balance away from them. It is not about truth, it is a balancing act: a game.

I dealt with my one and only train crash whilst serving there – in fact, while serving anywhere. A whisky-laden lorry was leaving Blackgrange bonded warehouses, just west of Tullibody, when it was struck by a train heading towards Alloa. The line was only freight then; it has since been upgraded to a full passenger service. The bonded warehouses had a lot of lorry traffic. There were no injuries. There were, however, a good many whisky barrels disgorged from the lorry. Not one burst open, to the annoyance of some locals who had gathered. The train company were adamant their signal system was foolproof. They backed up that claim with extremely detailed reports and explanations. Must be the lorry driver to blame. I duly reported the lorry driver. At the subsequent trial and after a very eloquent and extremely articulate and detailed explanation of the failsafe signal system, leaving the court in no doubt why the railway company could not shoulder any of the blame and how it could only be carelessness on the part of the lorry driver, the defence sprang into action. The driver said the traffic light was green, so he drove on. That was strongly contested: not possible, our system is failsafe. The defence then produced three hitherto-unknown witnesses, who had not been forthcoming during my enquiry. They gave identical versions of the lights being at green for road users. Despite an impassioned final speech by the Procurator Fiscal, the verdict was not guilty. *Hmm*, I thought.

My only real, long distance car chase happened whilst stationed at Tullibody. It was a classic, in every way; a 'follow that car' classic. It was late one dark Saturday evening when were told to be on the lookout for a 1600E Cortina, stolen in Dunfermline during the last hour. Then, a short time after that, a second call from a lone foot patrol officer in Alloa town centre. 'I am following the stolen car in a white taxi.' As we subsequently found out, the officer had spotted the stolen car parked in Alloa town centre and, as he approached the car, it roared off at speed. The officer was near the taxi rank, so he did what all the good film directors would expect – he jumped in a vacant taxi and told the driver to 'follow that car!' He did just that. Via a combination of police radio initially, then force radio as the police radio went out of signal, we were kept abreast of the position of the chase. In fact, the taxi driver was calling his depot and they kept an open line to police headquarters. We were soon involved as the unusual chase – now joined by the unmarked CID Ford Escort – sped into Tullibody, where we took up our position in the fast-moving procession. It went through the village, twisting and turning, before heading back east along King o Muir Road, past Glenochil prison, and out towards Fishcross and on and on along dark, twisty country roads at speeds in excess of 80 miles an hour. As we got near Rumbling Bridge and out onto the main road to Kinross, we were joined by a Traffic car that had sped over from Falkirk and a Support Unit car from Stirling. They must have 'flown'. The taxi and the unmarked CID car withdrew, leaving three vehicles – now seriously hurtling along in the wake of the red hot 1600E Cortina. We, in the Tullibody van, were right behind the stolen car and as we hit a straight part of the road (we, by the way – I was a passenger) attempted to overtake. We were right alongside and travelling about 80 miles an hour when he swerved towards us, forcing us off the road and along a wide verge. We bumped and were thrown all over the place, and in the headlights all I could see were trees. We managed to stay on all four wheels, and violently bumped off the verge right in behind him. Then on the long straight east of Drum and leading to Balado, we executed the perfect stopping manoeuvre at seriously high speed. This was not an exercise; it was for real. We, the Tullibody van, had dropped to three back. The Traffic car made two feints to pass, blocked each time. As the Traffic car pulled back in behind the stolen car after the second move, the Support car booted it past the Traffic car and the stolen car in one slick, daring movement. I think the driver of the stolen car was caught unawares. It was a perfect move, all worked out over the radio. The front car was now one of ours. The Cortina made an attempt to overtake, but failed and – as he edged back – the Traffic car pulled alongside him and we pulled tight behind, bumper to bumper, at speed. He was now trapped. However, we were still travelling at high speed, with one car on the wrong side of the road. As directed over the police radio by the lead car, we slowed down in convoy, eventually coming to a halt – perfectly synchronised – just short of the giant Golf Ball radar contraption at Balado (more famous for 'T in the Park', not that it was invented then). That was an adrenalin rush; over about 25 miles of narrow country roads, driven like a rally. I am not sure if the speed of our pursuit was the main adrenalin factor, or was it the shouting and swearing at each other in the police van during the chase? The taxi driver was recognised for his actions, and I bet he regaled many a party and taxi driver convention with his story. As it happened, the driver of the stolen Cortina 1600E was a resident of Tullibody.

Some months later, I charged our car thief with spying on his downstairs neighbours in the 'holes in the ceiling mystery'. It was a four-dwelling block of flats. He lived with his sister in one of the top flats. I was called out by the lady in the flat below his. She had been aware for some time of small round holes in the ceiling. They were above her bed and in her daughter's bedroom, also above her bed. She was puzzled, but had no idea what caused the holes. However, she was not alarmed. Well, not until she saw a long green narrow rod protruding through the ceiling from above; that was the morning she called me. She screamed, and it was pulled up. I was called and – on my own – headed upstairs to speak to the male occupant. His sister was out. After banging on the door and getting no answer, I opened it and went in. The sole male occupant was cooking breakfast with the radio on at full blast. He had not heard me at the door and, in fact, the first he knew I was in the flat was when I poked him with a section of his green fibreglass fishing rod. He got a scare. No, he really did. It was not long before he took me into his bedroom, pushed back a wardrobe, and rolled back the carpet to reveal wooden floor boards. I could see they had been cut into shorter lengths. He prised one up to reveal more evidence. He had removed all the insulation under the floorboards to give direct access to the plasterboard ceiling of the house underneath. Yes, there were the tell-tale holes through which he peeped into the bedrooms. They fitted his green fishing rod exactly. I arrested him. Another tale from the mystery tabloid of Tullibody.

Police management is hierarchical and, because of that, on occasion it can be quite overbearing. Some might even suggest bullying. I had passed my two police examinations and was qualified to be considered for promotion to any rank. I had not completed five years' police service. I was about to sign up for a course at the local college when a memo arrived at the office seeking applicants to study for a Higher National Certificate in Police Studies. I thought that more relevant to my police duties than what I had planned, so I applied. A few weeks later I received a memo telling me my application was successful and joining instructions would follow. I gave it no further thought, and got on with my job. The memo with my joining instructions triggered my first real, face-to-face encounter with small minded, repressive police management. I had never encountered it before. I would again. I was told I could not go on the course. The person telling me was a fellow Constable. My first response was to question why someone of my rank was involved. He did not want me to argue, as he had been given the task to tell me and dissuade me from taking up the opportunity. He should never have been put in that position. I took the joining instructions from him and headed off to see the boss in Alloa. He was adamant I was not going. 'Staff are thin on the ground, and I cannot afford to let you have one day off a week to go to college.' I pointed out that the memo telling me I had been selected had passed through his office with no adverse comment. My reply containing my acceptance had returned along the same route without comment. So why now? 'We cannot afford to give you the time off.' I argued it would have been fairer to raise his objections earlier, by commenting on my original application. Telling me now was simply bullying, and I would take it further – which I did. A couple of weeks later the Chief Constable, Ian Oliver, saw me. He listened for about a minute and told me it had been his decision, and I was going. He called in the Deputy Chief Constable and was giving him a hard time about it, stopped, and said to me: 'You do not need to hear this; just make arrangements to go on the course'. A week after that interview, the boss in Alloa stopped me in the corridor to tell me he had second thoughts and that I should go on the course. He said he would review his decision at the turn of the year. I heard no more. Are you detecting a pattern here? Decisions made on high that do not meet with the approval of intermediate officers. Solution: browbeat the Constable. Why? Because it will be easier than taking on the higher rank. That is not confined to the police service. It is cowardly and bullying behaviour, wherever it happens. I took it on myself to find a solution and, during the two years of the course, I did extra hours without payment to ensure my colleagues were not left working on their own. I did not run that past any senior officer; I just got on with it. I was successful, and gained my HNC.

Despite being run off our feet on occasion, and at other times not being flavour of the month with certain supervisors in Alloa, we – the team in Tullibody – stayed together and got on with things. Not everything was that serious, and there was the occasional light moment. A particularly awkward chap – a barrack room lawyer – lived in the village. Neighbours complained about him often; he could be quite antisocial. One complaint about his dog found us at his house, again. He claimed he did not own a dog. I pointed to a dog sleeping beside the fire. 'That dog? That is not my dog. It belongs to my son.' I pointed out his son was nine years of age. He quickly replied 'is there an age limit for owning a dog?' I then asked for the Dog Licence; yes, one was needed then. He shouted on his son and asked him if he had a licence for the dog. His son said he did not have one. Our choice was to charge the father or the son. We did neither, and told them to get one and we will check it the following week. He got rid of the dog.

Months later, the same male was at the District Court in Alloa, on trial for some minor thing he had been charged with. All citations instruct the witness or accused to be at court for ten o'clock in the morning. The court is always busy at that time. Everybody has to wait their turn. Just after midday, whilst the court was deep in session dealing with a totally unrelated case, the barrack room lawyer from Tullibody barged into court, walked straight to the bench, waved his citation in the face of the Justice and said he had an appointment for ten o'clock. He had been here in plenty of time, and had waited more than two hours; he was not prepared to wait any longer. The proceedings, which had been in full flow, were forced to a grinding halt. He was told to wait outside and he would be called in due course. However, he was just warming up. He refused to go and wait, going on: 'I have been waiting! I am a busy man. I have a business to run. I have waited long enough; if you cannot see me now, I am off'. He left the court and drove off, just like he said. After lunch his case was called. He was not present, obviously. A discussion then took place about issuing an arrest warrant. However, in the end it was decided that it was not in proportion to the minor offence. The case was dismissed, and our man got away with it. A public interest decision.

We disturbed a male breaking into a premises late one night. It was into the early hours of the morning, actually. He had headed out of the village and we lost sight of him when he got out of the area covered by street lights. Our chase eventually found us near the river Devon in the pitch black of a winter night. We got a police dog handler out. He let the dog off the leash and it bounded off in pursuit and was soon out of sight. The trouble was, it did not come back. We spent more time looking for the dog than we had looking for the thief. After a couple of hours we gave up, with a plan to resume in the morning. We did not have to bother. About seven o'clock that morning a male called at Alloa police office and asked if we had lost a police dog. He admitted that he had been chased by the police and had got away. He heard the dog barking as it got near him. He tried to get over a fence but couldn't. Then the dog was beside him. He faced the dog and spoke to it, whereupon it started to wag its tail and calm down. After a few minutes he walked back home with the police dog following. He gave it water and some food and it stayed in his house all that night.

Another dog handler, another shaggy dog story. The handler supported a football team from Edinburgh and definitely did not support a certain team from Glasgow. I happen to think the main attribute of a police dog is its ability to calm a noisy, threatening crowd. This dog was a real asset in such a situation. It was trained to growl, bark, and do scary dog things on command. It would only respond, however, to one word: 'Rangers'. Yes, on the word 'Rangers' the dog went berserk, and was very effective at bringing most threatening crowds to order.

I spent six months as an aide to the criminal investigation department, CID, whilst at Tullibody. It started out at the CID in Stirling – an interesting choice, as I did not know Stirling, had never lived there, and in fact had hardly ever spent any time there. My crime-catching skills were average and perhaps tipping the scales at not bad; however, my poli-

tics were well below par. My style in a world of macho com-
petitiveness left me a bit off the pace. I had not picked that up
early enough and honestly, if rather naïvely, assumed that
teamwork was the name of the game. Perhaps in certain pockets that might have been so. However, in the main there were
power cliques. My first mistake was in thinking I was there to
listen, learn the ropes, and – as time passed – develop my
skills. I soon learned that was not correct.

I was informed at a very interesting progress meeting
after a month in the job that this was not what they expected.
Seems I was too quiet and did not take the lead enough. The
message was not delivered quite as it appears on paper. The
Detective Inspector delivered his message at the top of his
voice with expletives and expressions like 'useless', 'waste of
space', and more. No matter how I tried to explain the crimes
I had detected, two of them historical and going nowhere till I
arrived, it was obvious that 'pep-talk' was the agenda, nothing
else. *Inspiring*, I thought.

He brought up an incident I will relate, because it
probably explains the whole flawed set up. I had only been in
the position just over a week, and was doing paperwork in the
main CID office. A young police officer, a probationary Constable as I later found out, came into the office and just stood,
obviously not sure who to talk to. I looked over and noticed
two or three experienced detectives completely ignoring him. I
asked if I could help. He was dealing with a minor theft: a
pair of jeans stolen from a washing line. He had a tip-off about
where they were and who had stolen them. He did not know
what to do next. I helped him fill a search warrant, explaining
he would have to get it signed by a Justice of the Peace. I then
advised how to handle the enquiry and the search. That included the advice not to use the search warrant if the house-

holder agrees to let you search without it. I told him to contact me on his return and I would help or advise with his interview of the suspect. He seemed confident, and off he went. My logic was simple. The crime was on the low end of seriousness, and perfect to cut his teeth and gain experience and confidence. He called to see me later. Jeans recovered and suspect admitting the theft. I helped with the wording of the charge and how to lay out his report. I congratulated him on his good work. My goodness, did I get that wrong. Later that day the Constable's shift Inspector called at the CID office and read the riot act about a young officer with no experience being left to carry out a search and interview a suspect. Soon I was in the firing line. Not from the shift Inspector, but from the detective Sergeant. 'Lazy', 'useless' and other expressions were used. However, more to the point, I had passed over a chance to get a detection on their books. That had been my mistake. I did not respond and, a few days later, got the inspirational pep-talk I mentioned. I did eventually speak to the young officer. He thanked me for what I had done and said he was embarrassed with how his boss had reacted.

There was other nonsense, not worth repeating.

I was soon shipped off to Alloa to continue my aideship. That was a totally different experience, and I learned so much and felt part of the team. At the end of my stint as an aide I was spoken to by my detective Sergeant. He recommended I be retained. His report came back suitably endorsed and supported by the Detective Inspector, the pep-talk giver. I was in the CID, and I was delighted. There is many a slip twixt cup and lip – or should it be counting chickens? Before the week was out, I was summoned to see the officer in charge of the Force CID. He went over my performance; it was better than average. I wondered where I was to be stationed. Nowhere, was his answer. I am bringing in another person, and you will return to your previous duties. Goodbye Yellow Brick Road, end of detective career. On reflection, all these years later, I cannot say I was particularly up or down about it. I had been led to believe I was to be selected, but life goes on and I went to my wardrobe and dusted down my tunic and bulled my boots. It was not sore.

# CHAPTER 14

S OCIETY has lots of 'wheeler-dealers'; some make it big, some not all. Communities have their share of those that did not make it big. However, they exist, and they pick away at the edges of our towns and cities. Alloa was no exception.

It was a Saturday morning, and two of us were on duty in the CID office when a call came in that a local wheeler-dealer was selling stolen property around the pubs. We wheeled him to the office and, as we explained our interest in him, his smile grew broader and broader. He asked if it was the watches we were asking about. It was. He opened his long black 'Crombie' style coat to reveal watches pinned down each side, with plenty spaces. The receipt for them was stuffed into his pocket. He had been in Glasgow the day before, and bought them at a warehouse for about £2.00 each. It was in the days when cheap, plastic digital watches could be obtained in filling stations and other places. He said if you want to sell these in Alloa, you need to make them look 'hooky' and the punters will pay a tenner for them. Trotter Enterprises came to mind.

Another day, and I was the only CID officer on duty in the Alloa area. A woman had been detained in the town trying to obtain drugs from a local apothecary, using a stolen prescription pad. The pad was not stolen in our area and, on investigation, she had used it that day all over the place – as far away as Peebles. I was in a bit of a fix. She was now arrested, and I had to put the custody report together for court the next day. I contacted the Procurator Fiscal and she took over. She was one of the best Fiscals it was my privilege to work with in all my service: Mary Robertson. And not just because of this case. We sat in her office and raked through the MIMS books. It was a book containing a comprehensive list of all prescription and generic drugs. My problem was that the offence is to be in unlawful possession of the specific regulated substance, not the generic drug. We eventually produced a list of the actual substances contained within the generic drugs and produced a charge sheet. The Fiscal did not want a summary; just a front sheet with the name and address of the accused, the locations of each crime, with the actual charge relating to that location and of course her previous record. Panic over. The accused pleaded guilty, and I heard no more.

I finish my life as a detective with an amusing tale. We were investigating a serious assault that took place half a mile or so on the Stirling side of Fallin, near a residential caravan park. Most of the caravans were owned by the same family or extended family, so when we arrived they all crammed into one caravan. My colleague explained why we were there and asked if anybody had seen or heard anything. Meanwhile, I had handed my warrant card to the old father of the group. The patriarchal boss. We drew a blank and, as we were leaving, I reached out for my warrant card. The old man was staring at it and, as he passed it back, he said: 'No son, I've never seen him about'.

I was next sent to Tillicoultry – not for long, as it turned out. I was back in Tullibody in a few months. It was nothing like Tullibody. However, I did get assaulted. Whilst dealing with a very serious assault, the suspects were being processed in the police office when, without warning, one of them lashed out and punched me on the mouth, chipping a tooth. My fault; I had lost concentration, and should have been on my toes. After the punch he flew at me, and we danced about for a while like dervishes before I settled the bout, winning on a technicality. My colleague did not interfere, but had a good chuckle. The risk assessment process for whether to handcuff a prisoner or not argues that the compliant prisoner is the most dangerous. Every day is a learning day. It hurt.

A mountain rescue incident got me in more trouble. A school teacher called in at Tillicoultry office, in a panic. He had been taking a group of schoolchildren hillwalking in the Ochils. One fell down a steep slope into a rough rocky section of the Daiglen Burn, near where it joins the Gannel Burn, just into the hills above Tillicoultry quarry. The teacher had run from the hill and, by luck, got a lift in a quarry lorry. The incident happened less than half an hour before. According to the teacher, the boy suffered a compound fracture of his leg and it was bleeding profusely. 'He is losing a lot of blood and will die if we do not act quickly.' We marked the location on the map and agreed a mountain rescue call-out would take too long. I telephoned the RAF Search and Rescue at Leuchars in Fife. I got straight through to the flight Sergeant. I explained the problem, the need for speed, and gave him the grid reference for the incident. We further agreed to rendezvous at the rugby ground in the village. He said he was getting airborne immediately, but that I needed to contact RAF Pitreavie who had responsibility for allocating assets for tasks. I contacted Pitreavie, and they allocated the Leuchars helicopter to my task. I summoned an ambulance and the police surgeon. The latter was my downfall; not his fault. That call alerted Police HQ to my situation. They despatched a uniform Inspector to take control. He was at the office within a few minutes. Taking control meant going over it all again with the ever frustrated teacher and deciding, over the protests of the teacher, to call out the mountain rescue team. He instructed I do that. I informed him there was not enough time and, in any case, that I had called a Rescue helicopter. 'No you haven't', he said, 'only a police Superintendent can do that'. I agreed that would normally be the case. However, because of the urgency of this case I have circumnavigated that route and done it myself. He was adamant that I could not do that. I assured him I had, and said if he put his head out the window he would hear the helicopter. We rushed to the rendezvous point as the Wessex Search and Rescue Helicopter swung overhead. The Inspector, taking charge I assume, dashed into the middle of the rugby field and held a handkerchief in the air. I looked on in disbelief as a flare from the helicopter bounced past him and rolled across the rugby field spewing out its bright orange smoke. He was obviously unaware that the waving handkerchief method of showing wind direction had gone out of fashion sometime before the Battle of Britain. I was just about to get into the helicopter when a voice on my radio asked for an update for the media. I declined to get involved, and was irately informed the media were on the telephone and needed an answer. I turned my radio off and got into the helicopter along with the police surgeon. In the event, I was not winched down to the casualty – the doctor was. He and the casualty were soon back on board, and in jig time we were back at the rugby field and getting the young ten year old into the waiting ambulance. From falling to getting to the hospital had taken less than two hours. He was badly hurt, and needed three or four dozen stitches to heal his gashes. He recovered well and, when I had been promoted to the town he lived a couple of years later, I was able to visit him at his home. The ambulance was no sooner away than my deconstruction began. First it was about the media. I asked, when did the media start running the police service, and whether getting to the casualty was a lower priority than feeding the press. We then moved on from the media angle to the 'who is responsible for calling out a helicopter?' angle. I was left in no doubt that it was not a Constable. Even reasoning with them about the urgency made no difference; I had stepped over a line, and it would be noted in my record. I have no idea if it was. My point was, and has always been, that there are systems and without doubt it is best to follow them. However, they are not a strait jacket, and on occasion there can – and will – be circumstances that require one to detour from the path. Such an action will require to be justified; that is reasonable.

The handkerchief Inspector, who incidentally was a really decent person, had – some time before – summoned a colleague and myself to his office in Alloa. For the life of me I cannot recall why we were there. Anyway, we were there. He was quite agitated and made us stand during our telling off. He addressed his final insult at my colleague, telling him – in no uncertain terms – that he had the brain of an idiot. As quick as a flash came the answering retort: 'Yes, sir. I know, sir. When do you think you will want it back, sir?' We were unceremoniously pitched out of his office.

Then I was back in Tullibody as the Area Constable. A slightly different role, and probably more of a support role to the team. Like being back in Fearn. I was working late one night with a colleague when we were asked to help out at an incident where someone had broken into a pub and was still inside. The building was surrounded when we got there. They had asked for a dog, but there was a delay. Someone suggested two officers go in and flush the intruders out. The Tullibody crew was picked. We went in; it was dark. We split up and searched systematically, one to the left and the other to the right – that was me. The unlucky side, as it turned out. Torch in hand, I set out. All clear so far. Then I went into a room with pool tables. Just as I entered, I bumped against the pool cue rack. I had not taken a step past it when a figure clad totally in black leapt up from under a pool table. He had a balaclava on, with only his eyes showing. The scene was a bit spooky, not made any better by the multi coloured swirling night-lights of a one-armed bandit in the background and the blood curdling yell he let out. I might have described the scene as surreal. However, the huge glinting blade of the knife he was carrying removed any surreal thoughts I might have harboured. He lunged straight at me, still yelling, with the knife held in front of him. I was calm, and my thought process made it feel like slow motion. It seemed obvious what I needed to do. Running or hiding did not even feature. I reached behind me, grabbed a pool cue, and as he lunged at me I stepped to one side, swung it – heavy end first – and hit him high on the side of his head. He collapsed as though pole-axed. The knife was not a kitchen knife; it was a nasty-looking, stabbing affair. It fell from his grasp. I kicked it away and handcuffed him. I took his hood off. He certainly was dazed. The locus was soon filled with officers, and the situation was under control. He had been alone, and was breaking into the one-armed bandits and anything else that carried cash. He was fine after a few minutes. If I had not bumped into the pool cue rack, I would have been stabbed. Sometimes you get lucky, and training has little to do with it.

A few years later we were issued with the PR 24, a long baton with a side handle. It was designed – so went the training – to be swung at an assailant, hitting them on the legs, body or arms. It replaced the old foot-long bit of wood we carried in a special truncheon pocket in our trousers. The police women were issued with an even shorter baton they carried in their handbag. Neither were quick-draw affairs. After that incident, the boss wanted to know why I had not used my standard baton. 'No time', was my reply.

I think it was in 1980 that Vietnamese refugees – 'Boat People' – arrived in Scotland; a few hundred. Two families were housed in Tullibody later that year, or perhaps 1981. As the area Constable, part of my job was to be aware of their presence and make contact. I am not clear that was an official order; it just seemed the right thing to do. It was not as easy as I imagined. Interestingly enough, the first contact was actually the other way round. One of the families got in touch with me. My impression was they had been a well-off, connected family and the male was quite assertive – not unpleasantly so; nothing like that. It was just that the whole family were always well-dressed and their general conversation and references, particularly to connections in London, I found interesting. My impression was they had been in politics at some level. I formed a reasonable relationship with them. Then they were gone; I did not find out to where. The second family presented a different challenge. They were not so sure of my intentions, unlike the first family. I suppose my unannounced visit to welcome them was clumsy and ill-thought through. After what they had endured, the sight of a uniformed police officer appearing at their door must have been terrifying. I apologised and backed off. Eventually their council liaison person contacted me and asked if I could help with a problem the family had. I happily sorted it out for them, and met them during the process. I did gain access to their house, and spent some time in their company. My wife produced baking for them. However, no matter how hard I tried they were never totally relaxed about a uniformed representative of the state being around them – and really, who could blame them? I did not get the opportunity to keep up with either family, so I can only hope things turned out well for them.

We would often participate in community activities, and even help organise some things. During the school Easter holidays, we organised and held a six-aside street football tournament. Sides were mixed and street-based, or a small cluster of streets. It had nothing to do with what school you attended. It went on all day for three-and-a-half days, and culminated with a big prize-giving in the Top Club. It was hugely popular, and reduced calls for police to attend the usual school holiday nonsense involving young people to almost zero. It was a good 'community' enterprise that did the police reputation no harm, and in fact it was time well spent. I have heard some claims that living and working, as a police officer, in the same community is not good practice and should be avoided. I totally disagree with that view, certainly in the areas I have worked. Today, however, as we lose the streets in some areas – as we surely have – perhaps the risk is too great. I contend that this situation, which appears to be growing, is partly down to surrendering our position in communities. Once the gap appears, getting it to reduce and regain some sort of control is near impossible. I lived and worked like that for about a third of my whole service, and any risks I ran were far outweighed by the advantages.

In all that time I can recount one incident directly related to the risk. I was finishing my shift at two o'clock one morning when I saw that my home's front living room window was smashed. It was a big plate glass window. The offending beer bottle was right in the middle of the room, and there was glass everywhere. It took us days to get rid of all the glass and make the room safe for the wee ones. My wife and children never even heard it being smashed and slept on. With community support, including the wife of the culprit, he was soon dealt with.

Then one day I got a telephone call from the Divisional Commander, who told me to report to the Chief Constable's office at two o'clock that afternoon. He did not say why. I attended in my best uniform. The Chief Constable was late; he had been playing badminton. As he arrived – still in his badminton gear, sweat dripping from him – he asked me to join him in his office. After wiping his hand on a towel he said 'Congratulations. I am promoting you'. He added: 'You are not being promoted to be King, just Sergeant. It is the first rung, no more. Enjoy it and learn. Remember: you are not one of the 'boys' any more. You are their first line in management. Keep a window between you and them'. He wished me good luck, and hardly heard me thanking him as he turned on his heel to go and get a shower. That was short and sweet; no big deal. I liked him, and not because he promoted me. No, because he treated management strategically and let his managers do their job.

I was then shuffled to the Deputy Chief Constable, who would tell me where I was posted. He telephoned the Falkirk Commander and, after some debate and changes of mind, it was Denny. I thanked him. He asked if I had a question. I did. 'When is it effective from, sir?' Expecting a week or two delay. 'Effective from this minute', he replied. I told him I had a shift tonight in Tullibody. He said: 'Well, do it if you want. But I would go out and buy my wife dinner'. So I worked my first promoted shift, as a Constable in Tullibody; I could not leave my colleague in the lurch.

Before moving on from Tullibody, I think I would like to mention something that always fascinated me. It is not a Tullibody phenomenon, and one can see what I describe in any town. It might just be more ingrained in my memory due to the hours spent patrolling around the streets late on at night, particularly the dark nights. Some houses, in particular the upstairs flats, did not draw their curtains. Late on, some would also have their living room lights on. As we slowly circled around the streets, one could see the décor, the wallpaper, the light shades, perhaps even the occasional person moving about in their own wee domain. It was not about being nosey. No, it was something else. It was about life, communities, families living cheek by jowl. I found it fascinating. There were never two colour schemes the same. It was not about the decoration; no, it was lives being played out. The tragedy, the joy, the family dynamics. Whatever. All just the depth of a dividing wall away from someone else's world. All different wee countries in their own right. There would be family connections all over the world. I used to marvel. Simple pleasure.

# CHAPTER 15

THEN it was Denny. I turned up at Denny police office for the backshift as a bright new Sergeant. Like the other strange developments in my policing life – getting into the service, driving test, single station officer – this was no different. I was a Sergeant and I was just about to brief a shift of officers, having never worked with a Sergeant, never having attended a shift briefing, never having worked a proper backshift. In fact, I did not understand the need for a briefing. I had self-briefed all my service; does everybody not do that? My next learning curve was getting used to being asked how to proceed with things that I thought were obvious. I honestly, for a while, thought they were asking me to catch me out. Yes, it was a learning curve – not helped by a couple of old stagers who were totally set in their ways and resented, quite openly, being told anything by me. In fact, that led to a woman being reported for something I might well have not reported myself. However, the two old stagers attended at the incident and – when asked about it – proceeded to prevaricate and miss out detail in their response. The more I asked, the more evasive they became. It culminated in them being ordered exactly how to deal with the incident and, to add insult to injury, to have the report on my desk in two days. It was. I may well not have reported her, and my decision would have been based on a variety of factors. However, there was only one factor in their mind: laziness.

I had got off to a difficult start. My second week in post happened to coincide with an office inspection. A strength of the police management system – certainly in my view – was the regular station inspection process. Woe betide any officer in charge of a station who ignored this. While many saw it as an inconvenience, a chore, even a threat, the more enlightened officer took a different view. They saw it as an opportunity, and made sure they carried out their own inspection some weeks prior to the official one carried out by a senior officer. If carried out properly, it was seen as support-ive and a good way of evidencing a well-run office. The in-spection covered just about every administrative function, including things like lost and found property, productions, foot patrol recording, and much more. It could take – certainly for a typical small town office – as much as two days to carry out. It did unearth the occasional issue. However, on the whole it was regarded as a very positive and useful exercise; it kept officers on their toes, and ensured they ran a tight ship.

There was, however, the occasional exception. I was in my second week in the rank and on day shift. The Inspector told me on the Tuesday, as he was leaving the office, that he would not be in over the next few days. It became crystal clear why in his next statement. The Superintendent was to carry out the annual station inspection over the next two days, starting the following morning. 'Don't worry,' he said, 'he knows where to find the books. Don't say much; just make him tea and keep him sweet.' The next morning dawned and I innocently, if somewhat naïvely, greeted the Superintendent with a smile and the offer of tea. He did not take long to put me in my place. He started by asking who I was and told me

he had no time for tea; if he found time he would tell me, adding that he suspected we spent too much time drinking tea.
He then told me to wait in the room while he inspected the
various books and keep quiet; he would expect me to answer
any queries he had. And boy did he inspect the books. He
studied each page and each entry as if he was searching for
hidden clues. I sat expectantly on the other side of the desk,
hardly breathing. To my shame, I was secretly wishing for
something serious to happen in order that I could make my
excuses and leave. No luck on that front; the good citizens
were on their best behaviour, and peace and tranquillity
reigned over the town. Every now and then he would, almost
with a smirk, probe some entry in a log or ask if I could account for some item or other. Bearing in mind this was only
my second week in the rank, and also my second week in this
particular office, I had no clever answers to any of his questions. In fact I had no answers, clever or otherwise. I certainly
was not impressing him. I am certain my uncertain responses
filled him with glee. Maybe it was rage, but I was struggling
to pick up the signs through my discomfort. I only knew that I
was in an uncomfortable place as the inquisition continued
unabated. It was then he hit me for his first six of the inspection. He asked me to get the fire alarm book. *The what?* my
brain screamed. The reader must understand something; in all
my nine years' service to date, I had never encountered a
dreaded fire alarm book. Since arriving at this billet no mention had ever been made of such an important piece of police
equipment. How important I was just about to find out.

'Well? Where is it?' he retorted. I use that word advisedly because, while he did not shout – nor scream for that
matter, although he might have considered it – his voice was
'demanding', as if barking an order. He obviously saw this fire

alarm book as important. No, very important – in fact, perhaps the most important document ever to grace the building we occupied at that time. I scurried off and found the office typist, come receptionist. If she did not know where it was, it would be back to plodding on the nightshift for me. Calmly she led me to the fire door and lo and behold the holy grail of books was hanging from a string tied to the accursed fire alarm at the side of the door. Its appearance belied its obvious importance. It was a red, soft-covered school exercise book, complete with multiplication tables on the outer back cover. As I retrieved it and headed back to the inquisition I snatched a glance inside. Argh! The last entry was about four months ago. Calm down; maybe they test the fire alarm every six months. I was soon disabused of that notion. He took the book and looked at the entries, then he pushed it across the table as if it had burned his fingers. 'What do you call this?' he barked. 'A fire alarm has to be carried out once a week and properly recorded in the official fire test book. This has not been filled in since Christ came to Kilmarnock. You are the senior officer on duty and you have responsibility for the safety of your staff. This is not good enough, and you will hear more about this. Call yourself a Sergeant?'

The only thought that jumped into my head at that point was 'no, you are the senior officer on duty'. I decided not to tell him. He got up and left the office, telling me he would be back early next morning and things had better improve. I never did make him tea. He had a bloody flask. The inspection went on another full day and, apart from being impressed by the 'record of foot patrol' book that I had completed the night before (three months' worth, all in my own handwriting, something he chose not to see), there was not a lot to write home about. With that, he collected his flask and headed back to the security of Falkirk. I experienced other station inspections during my service and, when carried out properly, they were usually a far better exercise than that had been.

I could get on and learn my trade. One of the first things I noticed was the knowledge of the beat. A Constable has a deeper insight than a Sergeant. The detail picked up by a Constable constantly working his or her beat is second to none. The Sergeant certainly picks up some, but it is not the same. Supervision requires one to get involved in other areas. The early shift commenced at seven o'clock in the morning. The first hour was bedlam. The preparation for the 'morning prayers' was underway. At nine every morning, in the Divisional Commander's office, various heads of areas and departments met to go over the previous twenty-four hour activity logs, crime returns, and any other important issue. It was power hour. Woe betide anyone at that meeting who could not answer the boss's question about anything that had happened in their area of responsibility over that period. Hence bedlam at my level. So the Sergeant had to be at work a fair bit before seven, to get up to speed. Once the morning muster and briefing was over, it was into the various document and logs, making sure you had all the answers – because sure as teats on a sow, there were going to be questions every morning. It started about half an hour in to the shift, and went on for another half-hour or so. First there was the CID Sergeant or Inspector, then there was your own Sub-divisional boss, usually a Chief Inspector. Your immediate boss, who was not an invitee to power hour, would pitch in somewhere with his questions that usually grilled you about what happened – what have you done, do you suspect anyone, what are your lines of enquiry, and things like that. They usually liked to throw in a suggestion. That was good for them, as they would drop that in at the meeting to show they were taking control. It usually went on until the Area Commander finally caught someone off guard who had no answer to a question. Game set and match to the boss.

While my references to 'morning prayers' and the activity surrounding it perhaps carry a touch of cynicism, I am using a bit of poetic licence. I did question the macho behaviour; however, I did not and do not question the actual model. It worked, and it worked well. Nothing was missed, and – I am not frightened to say – that style of immediate, at the coal face, hands-on accountable management would never have let injured persons lie in a car for three days. In short, I applaud the process but not always the style.

I worked hard to learn and develop a management style. It was important to me and, like anything I had done till then in my life, I took my responsibilities seriously. That winter we had a period when lot of snow fell. I was night shift and, just after I started, the call came out from HQ: all cars are grounded. Use for emergencies only. I got my troops working on reports, and I decided to have a walk round the beat with one of the Constables. The snow was deep. Not far from the office I saw the backshift van parked near a pub. The Constable opined 'they are probably on an enquiry'. They were on a staggered backshift, which meant they finished at two o'clock in the morning. I think President Obama would have called that shift arrangement 'a surge'. Anyway, the van was there and the officers were nowhere to be seen. We continued our ski patrol, and a while later returned to the office. The van remained static. I told the Constable to get the kettle on, as I had something to do. The side doors of the van were locked; however, the back doors were not. I got into the van, took the shovel – in winter, all the vans were so equipped – then proceeded to fill the front with snow. Right up to the bottom of the steering wheel; a lot of snow. I threw the shovel back in the van, locked it up, and went for my coffee. A couple of hours later, two hot and sweaty officers finished their shift, hung up their keys, completed their duty sheets and headed home. I was too busy to acknowledge them. About two days later, one of the said officers asked to speak to me in private. He apologised and assured me they had been way out of order and it would never happen again. I simply thanked him and said no more. Life rolled on. It did not happen again. The other officer never came near me; he had no character, and was in other people's sights for his behaviour. He did not complete his service.

On another occasion, the Inspector asked if I would take an officer onto my shift to see if I could get him motivated. He duly arrived and, for two days, I never mentioned anything about his switch of shift and Sergeant. On the third day I asked if we could catch up. I decided on a different approach. Often I let the officer talk, and we tried to reach an agreed outcome. Not this time. I asked him to sit, and I told him he was noted for being lazy, uncommitted, lacking in drive. It was also noted that he was first out the door at the end of his shift, never staying on to assist his fellow officers, and his time keeping was on the cusp. In these days we expected officers to be at the office at least fifteen minutes before their shift commenced. He never managed that. 'If you have a problem you can share, tell me. Otherwise listen.' I told him he had completed nearly nine years with over twenty left. That is a long time to hide. You might manage it, but why? What would be the point? It was going to be a long, boring stint. You have only one shot at life. To waste thirty years on something you abhor will make you ill. 'I know you are a fit, active person – certainly outwith the workplace – and I know you are intelligent; far more intelligent than many around you. You have choices in life. If you make the right choice I will be your biggest supporter, because I know you can do it and I know deep down you want to. So get some pride, get out, and let's get busy'. He simply agreed, shook my hand, and left the office. He hardly spoke. About three months later, the Inspector got me to his office and asked what I had done to him. He is a different person. And he was. I replied: 'Nothing much; I just asked him to believe again'. So I was learning, and making some kind of small mark. Was it the correct mark? Who really knows. Then the Miners went on strike, and a different learning curve arose.

There were three notable industrial disputes during my thirty years of police service. There were probably more; however, I mention these three simply because each was notable in its own right and – probably more importantly – I remember them. My participation in each involvement differed greatly. By relating that involvement, I hope to convey a little of the myriad incidents and situations my colleagues faced and the depth of experience gained as a result. The latter two disputes were UK-wide, and attracted wall to wall media attention. The first, however, was quite local and while it attracted a certain degree of media interest, it was nowhere near the scale of the other two. What did link them, however, was that each created a level of concern to the government of the day, for different reasons. The first had serious fiscal implications; the second, massive PR issues, and the third was about something way beyond the others: power. It was by far the most serious, and left a legacy that even today is still painfully raw for so many people.

I had hardly completed the first lap of my police service when an industrial dispute erupted at the yard of Highland Fabricators in Nigg, Easter Ross-shire. It was in the mid-1970s – I think 1975 – and not to be confused with the quaintly named 'Orange Juice' strike with which I had no involvement. Oil had been discovered off our shores, and the Labour government at that time – with Harold Wilson at the helm – saw it as the cornerstone of their economic strategy; some might argue, more than one cornerstone. The strike had the government a bit nervous, and they did not relish the prospect of it turning into a prolonged affair that would delay or damage their fiscal projections. My memory is sketchy as to the media angle in that respect. However, what I do remember was the view of locals and many of the workers. They were clear in their conviction that the strike had the government on the hop and that they, the government, wanted a quick settlement.

The yard of Brown and Root, Wimpey at Nigg boasted the biggest dry dock in Europe. They had not only sunk a big hole in the ground, but they had also sunk a lot of investment into the enterprise. Needless to say the company also wanted their staff back to work as soon as possible. At that time I was the single station officer based at Hill of Fearn in the centre of the Fearn peninsula. There were also police officers based on site. That had nothing to with the strike; it was because there were three or four thousand workers employed at the yard. Highland Fabricators paid the police board for the Ross and Sutherland police officers to work inside the complex.

The industrial conflict was pretty much confined within the large complex, and there was never any trouble. There were mass meetings and speeches – loud 'politically loaded' speeches from a few activists. Unlike the last of the three strikes I discuss, there was no real requirement for a large police presence. Not that the force had that many officers anyway. I was briefed by a senior officer at the commencement of the dispute. My task was simply to carry out my duties as normal, with the added responsibility of watching and listening for 'strike' talk. They wanted to hear any gossip about the strike, how it was progressing, and – most importantly – when was it likely to end. Many of the locals either worked at the yard or had friends and relatives working there. It was one of the biggest employers in the north. I took my radar ears out into the community, even once or twice into local hostelries, and reported back. Although not without suppressing the occasional grin. Did they imagine that I thought I was alone in seeking out information? I'm sure they had insiders far closer to the action than I ever got. Anyway, I just got on with it. I never did find out what happened to any of my information, or even if it was worth my efforts. What was worthwhile, however, was getting out and about amongst the community; that was worth every single minute. In any event, the dispute did not last too long; five weeks, if I remember correctly. Harold Wilson could stop worrying and get back to enjoying his pipe, and Newton could get his buses running again.

Two of the unintended consequences of the Nigg complex were suffered by the residents of Cromarty, directly across the water from it. I did not find this out until recently. Prior to the rig construction complex, it was possible to see the Northern Lights in the winter night sky occasionally. The massive illumination surrounding the site, however, brought that pleasure to an end. Then there were the thousands of empty, discarded plastic coffee cups, carried over from the complex on the tide and destined – for years – to despoil the foreshore at Cromarty.

Prior to the strike, and not long before I was trans-ferred to Hill of Fearn, I worked in Muir of Ord. In August 1974 the first oil rig 'jacket' was completed and floated out of the dry dock at Nigg to be barged to its final location in the Forties Oil Field in the North Sea. One step nearer to our oil exploration future. It would take a few days at sea before reaching the oil field, and then the 'jacket' – called Highland 1 – would be carefully tipped (if that is the word) from the barge into position to start life as an oil rig. That momentous event was captured on camera, and many national newspapers had a series of photographs showing the 'jacket' as it moved from the barge into the North Sea. On the day these photo-graphs appeared in our newspapers, I happened to be carrying out an enquiry at the home of one of our local Tinker families, just outside Muir of Ord on the Black Isle. Only the two sons were at home when I called. Both had worked at Highland Fabricators on said 'jacket'. Both had been dismissed, and had no love for their former employer. Unfortunately neither could read – in my opinion, an indictment on a society that could not care less about people outwith the normal circle. Whatever the case, they were illiterate. I had finished my en-quiry and was about to leave when one enquired of me, 'do you want to buy my horse?' A healthy enough looking black and white affair, tethered on the grass at the side of the house. I declined his fair offer but, before I could get back into the police car, the other brother emerged from the house wav-ing that day's newspaper under my nose. Both seemed amused and giggled. One asked if I had seen the pictures. I had not, and I had a look. It was the series of pictures of the 'jacket' being positioned at sea. I was puzzled, and asked what were they laughing at. Their reply took me aback. 'Can you no' see? It's fuckin' sunk!' They were quite happy. I drove off and never found the heart to tell them. One of the brothers was killed in a horrific road accident not many months after that. Police work in communities is like that. One moves from moments of laughter, via the normal to the bizarre and occasionally to the tragic, all involving people just trying to live their lives. The overwhelming role of the police is to work with people without fear or favour, trying where possible to help the ones who occasionally come unstuck. Yes, we can be involved in conflict, but each situation should be faced at all times with honesty, integrity and dignity.

In November 1977 Labour was still in power, and James Callaghan was Prime Minister. I had just arrived at Central Scotland Police, having transferred from the north. I was stationed in Tullibody. A senior officer, who had a warped sense of humour, told me it would just be like working in a Highland village and I would fit in well, based on my previous experience in the Highlands. I had hardly got settled when the second industrial dispute began. James Callaghan's main concern in this case was that the strike would turn into a PR disaster. The Fire Service had just withdrawn labour all over Britain, and it appeared they had overwhelming public support. They were demanding a reduction in their working week plus a 30% rise in wages. The government had decreed a cap on wage increases, and this would smash it. They could not afford to back down, PR disaster or not. The government response to this dispute, apart from overseeing negotiations, was to ensure a contingency strategy was in place to deal with serious outbreaks of fire. This was achieved by mobilising 10,000 members of the armed forces to take on firefighting duties. They were equipped with old Bedford RLHZ self-propelled pumps. These 'fire engines', based on the old troop-carrying lorries, were manufactured from 1953 to 1956 for the use of the Auxiliary Fire Service, or AFS. The AFS was part of the Civil Defence Service, and was established in 1938 under the Air Raids Precautions Act 1937. Its role was to support local Fire Services throughout Britain, particularly during World War Two. My mum was in the Civil Defence Service, although I always thought it was Corps not Service. No matter.

The livery of the Bedford RLHZ self-propelled pumps was green, hence the iconic nickname bestowed on them: Green Goddess. Each had a silver bell mounted on top of the cab, above the passenger side. History in action; a petrol-head's dream. Incidentally, one can still purchase a Green Goddess to this very day if you have about £5,000 to spare. Military units, each with their own Green Goddess, were stationed at strategic points throughout these islands. The police task was to liaise with, and support, the units billeted in their police area; in particular, to guide units to whatever emergency they had to attend. To achieve that, all police officers in the sub-division I worked were put onto twelve hour shifts until the end of the dispute. We alternated duties between our normal police work and 'fire support'. Two police officers were therefore constantly billeted with each Green Goddess crew. Attending a fire was always an exciting adventure. While one officer drove the leading police vehicle, the second officer sat, head craned, looking back to ensure contact with the following Green Goddess was maintained. Their crew had no idea where they were or where they were going. Losing visual contact could be serious in terms of a delay in getting to the fire. It would also be seriously embarrassing for the police 'guiders', who would never be allowed to forget.

An additional thrill – well, for me anyway – was the noise, the sound of the following Green Goddess. Well, its bell. A really distinctive noise. Not a peal, definitely not a toll, and most definitely not a tin tintinnabulation. No, none of these does it justice. It is a clang: a definite piercing, urgent clanging. Just as iconic as the Green Goddess itself. And not a Barney McGrew in sight.

The strike lasted nine weeks, into January 1978. Over one and a quarter million working days were lost nationally. Eventually the Fire Service Union settled for a ten percent pay rise, the top end of the government's cap. Nobody lost face, and the Green Goddess could be safely retired once more. Thankfully – in our area, anyway – there were no major incidents, although one police officer was hospitalised after running headlong into the leading edge of an open door, knocking himself out. As for the rest of us, constant twelve hour shifts did wear us down a bit. There were occasions involving serious fires with threat to life, a bit beyond the Green Goddesses' inexperienced crews. In these cases, the striking firemen stepped down from the pay dispute and responded to the incident. I saw no anger from the firemen; well, certainly not directed at the police or their emergency substitutes. They understood that whilst they were perfectly entitled to withdraw their labour, even though there were some who disagreed, the government also had a right to put measures in place to protect the public.

Every now and then in life and work, someone comes up with a good idea: a 'Blackadder moment'. That reference will no doubt resonate amongst those of a certain age and, dare I suggest, a certain humour. It was a cold, wet early morning at Bogside Pit in Fife sometime in 1984. The miners' strike was in full swing. I, along with ten other officers, had separated from our colleagues and weaved our way behind the throng of miners at the pit entrance. Our Inspector had his Blackadder moment. I was the Sergeant, in charge of ten officers. His idea was, if we were positioned behind the throng of striking miners on the wide verge areas at the entrance to the pit, we could prevent them pushing forward into their colleagues at the front and perhaps reduce the surge that always happened on arrival of the working miners' transport. That would ease the pressure on the police cordon. So far so good. We would achieve this objective by milling about amongst the potential pushers, blocking their progress or pulling them back.

The first problem we encountered was mud. There had been a fair amount of rain over the period and every day the striking miners had been tramping about the area, turning it into a quagmire. Undaunted, we took up position, spread out in a strategic manner, and waited on the offending transport to arrive. Our obvious clue was the noise and then, as if a goal had been scored, the crowd shoving forward. We sprang into action. To be more accurate, we slithered into action. We were not well received, and miner and police officer – in a death-defying series of sashays left and right, countered by dashing white sergeant-type manoeuvres – skittered, slipped and fell about, usually hanging on to a miner or two. By the time the buses were safely inside the pit area, we looked like we were the ones who had been down the bloody pit. Miner and police officer alike were covered in mud. It was mayhem. Funnily enough, the tactic worked, and the anticipated surge was reduced. Perhaps it was more about the utter shock the miners got when we started running about amongst them like people possessed. I have no idea if that ruse was ever employed again; if so, it did not include me. Incidentally, and for the *Blackadder* fans amongst you, the Inspector did not have his foot scythed off.

On 18<sup>th</sup> February 1984 the miners at Polmaise Colliery in Fallin downed tools. While their intention was to keep their pit open, as things turned out they were the first in the fight to keep the country's pits open. The ball was rolling and, shortly afterwards, the remainder of the Scottish coalfields joined Polmaise. We had a serious strike on our hands. In March the Yorkshire miners also came out, followed a few weeks later by most of the other English and Welsh coalfields. Nottinghamshire only partly struck and stayed divided. Whatever way you looked at it, by the end of March 1984, Margaret Thatcher and her Conservative government had a national coal strike to contend with. There is a certain arrogance in some accounts from the English press who say the strike started in mid-March, omitting to mention that the Scottish coalfields had already been out weeks before.

This strike was not an oil-based financial threat like the Nigg dispute, nor was it largely a PR threat like the firefighters' dispute – although a strike as divisive as this would always carry its own inherent PR threat. This was something else entirely. It was about raw power; a war of attrition around ideologies. Certainly that was how I saw the militants and the political activists on both sides approach it. But it was far more fundamental to the majority of hard-working miners. Yes, they might well dislike the Conservatives and perhaps hate Margaret Thatcher, but it was more than that, I think. Their jobs, their very livelihood, their communities, their whole way of life was at stake. The global economy was to kick in, and commodity markets would see coal arriving here from China, Poland, and wherever it could be sourced more cheaply. More and more of their pits would shut, become flooded, and never open again. The 1972 and 1974 miners' strikes, some say, brought down the Conservative government. Whether that was true or not, many miners and Conservatives believed it to be so. The miners were also clear in their belief that the Conservative government had not forgotten what happened a decade before, and were not about to forgive. Who knows? All I remember is that two very powerful people, Margaret Thatcher and Arthur Scargill, were about to have a duel to the death in public. In doing so, they would set miner against miner, set miner against the police service, and – in some cases – vice versa. Worse still, in some cases entire families were torn apart. I felt that as a serving police officer, from working class mining roots, I was being used as a pawn in a class war. This dispute was going to be epic, a watershed, and would likely be the last great workers' struggle, certainly of my lifetime.

As referred to earlier, the whole thing kicked off in the Central Scotland Police area at Fallin and quickly spread. I was a police Sergeant working in Denny, having been promoted the year before. Perhaps because we were a small force and because many of our officers, of all ranks, worked – and in many cases resided – in the same towns and villages as many of the miners and their leaders, it was not difficult for us to make contact with and begin a dialogue with them. At times in this book I will criticise some areas of police management. This is not one of those times. Senior officers acted quickly in recognising that closeness, and communicated with and met the strike leaders from the onset. I am convinced that was the key to keeping good relations between the police and the striking miners, certainly in our area. The police aim was, as far as was possible, to maintain peace and order by creating and maintaining positive and open dialogue, supporting lawful picketing, and working with the striking miners at all levels, to allow them to make their point within the confines of the law. Just to be clear, that was how I understood the way Central Scotland Police approached the dispute. I don't know if that was the universal approach of other police forces, and experienced a couple of instances which gave me rise to doubt it.

From a personal point of view, I was no stranger to the trade union movement. Prior to joining the police, I was a member of the Electrical Trade Union (ETU), both at Ferranti in Edinburgh and in Cosser Electronics in Essex, where in the late 1960s I was a shop steward. I was by no means an activist, but thought Trade Unions and their role to be important. The ETU under Frank Chapple had a reputation as a militant union. I found the parallels between my dad and Frank Chapple interesting. My father had been a cobbler and shoe maker and, while Frank Chapple was not, his dad was. Both my dad and Frank Chapple were born into a level of poverty. Both saw changes in their politics as a direct result of the Russian involvement in crushing the Hungarian Revolution in 1956. For different reasons. Whereas Frank Chapple rejected Communism because of the actions of Communist Russia, dad – who had already rejected Communism as a result of his experiences as a Prisoner of War – rejected both the trade union and the Socialist party for their refusal to support the Hungarian refugees fleeing the Russian army. Dad was an active member of his local trade union branch in Alexandria, Vale of Leven, and when they chose not to support a motion to have a collection for the Hungarian 'Fascists', as they called them, he quit. 'So much for Socialist ideals and man's humanity to man', he said at the time.

I was soon involved at the 'coal face', so to speak. My first taste of action was at Bogside pit, not far into Fife from Clackmannanshire on the A907 Alloa to Dunfermline road. We mustered at Alloa police office about four in the morning, grabbed a cup of tea, then headed off to the briefing. My duties in this respect were mostly split between Bogside and Solsgirth pits in Fife or at the open cast mine at Darnrig Moss near Slamannan, although I was once at Longannet power station and once at Frances Colliery, Dysart. Some of the striking miners I encountered at Bogside and Solsgirth were from Clackmannanshire, and I knew many of them. Some were from Tullibody, where I stayed and where I had policed for nearly five years. In fact, some of their children were school friends of my children. In terms of the Bogside and Solsgirth picketing, senior police would liaise with local trade union leaders daily and talk about codes of conduct for the day. By that, I mean codes of conduct on both sides. We, the police – and in particular the Sergeants and Inspectors in attendance – were quite clear as to the rules of engagement. I have no idea what was happening in other areas.

The law allowed eight official pickets. They were permitted to be at the entrance of premises, subject to the dispute, and were allowed to communicate with anyone entering or leaving, in a reasonable way. They were not allowed to use threatening, intimidating or abusive language or behaviour, nor were they allowed to block the entrance. In my experience that worked well, and I do not remember anything that could not be sorted by a quick word or even a look. If it was all going so well, you may ask, why did we need to send dozens of police officers? Well, as you might guess, the official picket was one thing; however, they pretty much always took a travelling support to all their gigs. These were the unofficial pickets. They had no role at the entrance, the law did not allow them to be there or to communicate like the official picket. One described their role to me like this. 'We are not pickets. We are not allowed to be. We are the "intimidators".' The main reason for a police presence, however, was that there were still some miners who had not joined the strike and who continued to work. It was these miners who attracted the anger of their striking colleagues. Many of the management and engineers, not in the same union, kept on working. They also had a role in keeping the pit from flooding. That was vital to the life of the pit, because – if left unchecked – the flooding could shut the pit for good. For that reason, striking miners were allowed to help out with this work on occasion. To striking miners, it was those who defied the union call to strike who were the devil incarnate; traitors to the cause. In short: 'scabs'. Hence the police presence at these locations.

The entrance at Bogside did not offer a lot of room for anyone other than the official picket. However, the 'intimidators' managed to find space for themselves. There was a limited grass verge opposite the entrance on the A907 road, with two wider grass areas flanking either side of the bell mouth entrance to the pit. Regularly, certainly in the early days of the conflict, two to three hundred unofficial pickets turned up and thronged these three vantage points. We de-bused and took our position, lined along the outer edge of these three areas – a human cordon, in effect, only one person deep. Our task was to corral the supporting cast of unofficial pickets, keep them on their grass verges, and not allow them onto the public highway. In no circumstances were we to allow them to obstruct the transport carrying the working miners. Thus the battle lines were drawn, morning after morning. Both police and pickets, unofficial and official, were in position in plenty of time, usually before six o'clock in the morning. Things were usually cordial, with the occasional verbal jousting and non-offensive name calling. Nothing too drastic and, in some cases, indicative of nerves. In the early days of the strike and again in the later stages, the early mornings were dark, cold and sometimes raining or even snowing. The area was eerily backlit from the lights inside the pit perimeter. On some mornings the early morning low ground mist would swirl, and in the lights would make the setting feel surreal, like a scene from a horror film. Our police radios gave us early warning of approach of the working miners' transport. I don't know if we thought that gave us some kind of edge. Well, I can tell you: it didn't. The pickets had just as much warning as we had.

Then the noise would start; it built and built as the anticipated devil transport approached. Initially it was a loud baying. Then the transport would materialise and the mood changed. The baying, as if by magic – as though there was a hidden conductor the police could not see – turned to something visceral and loud: 'SCAB, SCAB, SCAB, SCAB, SCAB' and on and on. There was something primal, primeval in the air; as if their very existence was at stake. At the same time came the surge, as the 'intimidators' tried to get at the transport and those being transported. The police cordon took the strain. We resisted and we better resisted, with all our strength. We were a team, a strong team, and despite their greater numbers and despite the intimidating noise and despite the bulging line we held them, we always held them. In addition to the pushing, the jostling and the noise, there were the expletives and the missiles. There were always missiles, aimed at the transport. Agincourt repeated. The buses had grilles welded over the windows so the projectiles just bounced off. No matter how well we performed, no matter how effective the grilles were, the transported – in their mobile cage – could hear it all, they could see it all. That miner who described his role as an 'intimidator' spoke wisely. And then the transport was inside, the gates were shut, and all went quiet and normal service was resumed. It was all over for another day. The mayhem had only lasted a few frenzied minutes, and then it was over. And for those of us who wanted to, we could hear the dawn chorus and with it a feeling of calmness and normality. Miners dispersed, senior police officers spoke to official pickets, then we all spirited away to return another day. The picket at the gate was a constant, twenty-four hour, seven days a week vigil. That meant a constant police presence. After my shift on those days I would head home to Tullibody and sometimes detour to the working man's club – as it was known locally, the Top Club. There I would be met by the same striking miners I had been jostling with a short time before. The Top Club was their strike headquarters. I did not go there to gain inside information; far from it. These people were my friends. I was always in uniform, as I had not got the length of my house by then. That always caused mirth when I walked in. I would have a bottle of beer and simply sit and chat. A couple of times I handed in prizes for the regular raffle they held to raise funds for the strike.

Back and forward, as the strike progressed, there would be a minor flare-up on occasion with a police officer perhaps getting pushed a bit more aggressively or maybe punched in the ribs during the 'action' moments. I remember one officer claiming to have been hit in the face. I certainly had no knowledge, whenever I was present at Bogside or Solsgirth, of anything too serious; nothing that could not be dealt with on the spot with a bit of diplomacy and a word in the right place. Personally, I saw no arrests. I was not, however, there all the time.

Then one morning at Solsgirth, something happened – an event that made me feel uneasy, and caused me to think: 'Is this how it is in other areas?' It was a cold, dark morning, and the low mist was swirling. Our contingent of officers was in position early. A senior officer from Lothian and Borders approached our local boss and asked if we required help. The Chief Inspector said he understood there was to be an increase in pickets that morning. I have no idea where that information came from, and even less understanding of why the Lothian and Borders presence was necessary. The senior officer said she had two serials of officers and would deploy them between the striking miners and our local officers. Off she went and, a few minutes later, about forty Lothian and Borders officers – complete in riot gear – marched down the hill through the swirling mist. It was a bit eerie, like a scene from a film and quite intimidating. We never wore such protective equipment; I never felt we needed to. We just turned up in normal 'street' uniforms. They took up position between us and the miners. Their senior officer addressed the miners in the following way, as I remember. 'I don't know how things are done here normally, but I am telling you how it will be today. My officers are now in position. If any of you touch them, push them, or otherwise interfere with their duty, you will be arrested.' I thought, 'my goodness; that is different – no cosy agreements, no local respect of each other's position'.

The day I found to be the most disturbing of all, perhaps not at the time but certainly on reflection, was the day I was at Frances Colliery, Dysart. A disturbingly adrenalin-invoking day. It was another early start at Alloa police office. There were more of us on duty that day. We were heading for Frances Colliery at Dysart, Fife. It seems intelligence sources suggested there was to be in excess of five hundred pickets there. I never learned where that number came from. The briefing at Alloa started the process. We travelled in Sherpa minibuses to a layby at Kincardine on Forth, and waited. Then we saw another convoy of dark blue Sherpa minibuses heading over the Kincardine Bridge to join us. Once the wagons were circled, so to speak, a senior officer from Lothian and Borders Constabulary addressed us. It was an interesting briefing. 'We should expect hundreds of pickets. We will be firm and take no nonsense. On no account will we allow our lines to be breached.' It was such a different briefing from our usual; more like a military rallying call. Designed to get our adrenaline flowing. I cannot recall how many officers were mustered; in excess of one hundred? Perhaps a lot more. There were a dozen or more minibuses, full of officers. We travelled in a tight convoy, each vehicle with its blue light flashing. Our route avoided the bigger towns like Dunfermline, and we headed to Dysart through smaller villages like Saline and the hamlet of Steeltown. My main memory, as we swept along on windy country roads through these tiny mining communities in the darkness at about five o'clock in the morning, was our flashing blue lights reflecting against sleepy houses and parked cars. I can only assume the choice of route and the illuminated blue lights of our convoy was a tactic designed to intimidate. I really do not know. I felt strangely unsettled, uncomfortable.

On arrival at Dysart we parked in the complex amongst some buildings. The whole area was floodlit. I will always remember the noise as we alighted from our vehicles. The pickets were ranked on an embankment near us and, when they saw us, they soon let us know. The crescendo of noise built and rolled down amongst us from their massed ranks; the jeering, booing, chanting and the insults, the expletives. The noise echoed around the buildings that early morning; it was more than a sound, you could feel it, touch it. The effect it had on me was strangely calming. I gathered my serial of ten officers, lined them up in two rows, and had them stand at attention. Then, as a unit, we marched smartly to our allotted position in front of the baying ranks of striking miners. Why did I do that? I am not really sure. Deep down, I thought that my officers needed to feel confident and that I knew what I was doing. I kept thinking: *If you are going to do it, do it right. Look the part; impress. We are police officers, we are trained for this and we are good at it.* The whole episode, all these years later, still fills me with emotion.

In thirty years of front line policing, that was not the only emotional incident. Years after the event, I related the incident and how I felt to a psychiatrist. He said I was 'taking control'. That is what leaders do. Then we were in our line, we were second from the front. There was another line of officers behind us and I think maybe a fourth. I cannot re-member exactly. The striking miners – and there must have been at least five hundred – were on a banking looking down on us. I remember for some reason thinking, 'we are occupying the low ground; I hope they haven't consulted Sun Tzu's *The Art of War*'. Things calmed down for a while, and striking miners and police officers stood lined up in opposition, staring at each other like a scrum waiting on the order to engage. The order came in the form of the approaching working miners' transport. Dawn had broken by then, and it was light. The banking became alive with screaming miners. Not only were they screaming and chanting 'Scab! Scab! Scab!', they were pushing forward: a living mass of angry men, trying to protect their jobs, their families, their whole lifestyle and – lined up against them, thwarting their efforts and keeping them away from their working colleagues and former friends – were the police, 'Maggie's Boys'. Suddenly one of the striking miners burst from his own lines, catapulted through the first police line, straight into me. I instinctively grabbed him, immediately supported by one of my own Constables. We quickly secured him and, in what looked like a well-rehearsed move – which was far from the truth – propelled him through the ranks behind us. The gap closed, and we were out in the open with our prisoner. He offered a very brief and unconvincing resistance and then calmed down. We were guided into the temporary custody area and committed his details, our details, and an account of what had happened, to paper. I think we were photographed with the prisoner. Then he was spirited off into the system: no bail, no summons; straight to court, as far as I recall. My colleague and I headed outside. It was all over until the next time. I saw groups of miners wandering out and back to their transport or cars. A hard core of pickets remained at the main gate. It had not been a good day.

The open cast mine at Darnrig in Falkirk was the scene of one or two of my other experiences during this strike. It was never as populated as the other sites I attended and, in some ways, was treated as being a bit more low-key. Many of the striking miners at that location travelled through from the Lothians and, in particular, the Dalkeith area. I only carried out duty a handful of times there. One incident probably said more about the attitude of some of my officers than it did the striking miners. No, that is wrong. It gives an insight into attitudes on both sides. We had arrived early at the main entrance gate to Darnrig. There was the usual brazier with several pickets seated around keeping warm. Parked in a layby on the opposite of the road was a converted ambulance – now a chuck wagon, property of the Dalkieth contingent of picketing miners. Fresh tea, coffee and various filled rolls were the order of the day, with black pudding, fried egg and sausage the usual healthy options. This was in the early days of the strike, and the police – who for the first few days were welcome to refresh in the nearby BP site canteen at Grangemouth – had been banned. In order to show solidarity and support for the miners, the union on site had liaised with the National Union of Miners and, as a result, we could not access the BP site canteen. Pretty predictable, I thought. As a result, we sat in our cold minibus for a full shift and munched on cold dry sandwiches put together in the police canteen. As the officer in charge of the serial, I spent very little time on the minibus and instead sat with the picket at their well-going fire. Officers from the minibus joined me in twos, then swapped over. Incidentally, while I was happily heating beside the picket's brazier, police in Yorkshire were refusing to allow pickets to have braziers and fires. I am not sure which 'power' was used to enforce that order. One of the pickets noticed my brown bag containing a meagre sandwich, a biscuit, a Mars Bar and a tin of Irn Bru. He asked if that was all we had to eat. I explained that it was; thanks to him and his union, we were barred from the BP works canteen. He was seriously taken aback. He did not know about that; I believed him. He thought for a moment, then went away and had a conversation with his fellow pickets. On his return, and given the circumstances and the positions we held, he made one of the kindest offers I ever received in all my years of service. He offered us free use of their chuck wagon, as long as only two officers used it at any one time. Seemed reasonable to me. I let my troops know of the offer. I was a bit taken aback at the response of some who refused the offer. One retorted 'they are the last people I will eat with; they can stick their rolls'. Some agreed with him. Some others were grateful, and graciously took up the offer. Later, I overheard one of these officers say to a colleague '...and the miners fed us'.

I recall one minor skirmish at Darnrig. The pickets got wind of coal lorries exiting the complex from a different gate. They were soon crowded around that exit. These were not official pickets. I was quickly at that location with my ten officers. Before long, a lorry trundled to the exit gate only to find it closed with about one hundred or more miners blocking the path. I was negotiating with the lead picket about letting the lorry leave. He was having none of it. I was joined by a police Superintendent who asked what was going on and why had I not moved the miners away from the gate. I tried to explain. He really was not interested, and ordered me to get them moved. I persuaded the pickets to ease back from the gate to allow my officers access. Eleven police officers lined up along the outside of the closed gate, faced by over one hundred pickets. They were not going to move or allow the gate to be opened. In the interest of officer safety, I spoke to the miners' leader and explained what my order was. He laughed and asked if I was serious, because they were not for moving. We came up with the following compromise, mostly to satisfy the eagle-eyed Superintendent who was looking on with a face like thunder. We would push them, and they would resist our efforts by leaning into us and not push. It was a farce. There were so many miners, they were spilling around the both sides of our line. I told them to get back on their side of the scrum as they were offside. Despite our best efforts, and despite the miners' agreement not to push, we were soon being pressed back against the gate. The uneven 'struggle' carried on for a few minutes until one of the police officers suddenly squealed and collapsed, clutching his back. The miners immediately eased back and helped move the officer out of the crush. One of their first aiders attended to him. An ambulance arrived, and the officer was removed from the scene. The miners did not take their eye off the ball, however, and the lorries did not get out. After a short conversation, the drivers withdrew and reversed back into the mine complex. The Superintendent left, and calm returned. He never spoke to me about the event again. The officer was not kept in hospital long, and was discharged with a few painkillers. He was off work for a few days.

I didn't personally witness anything like the events at Bilston Glen and Ravenscraig, and certainly nothing like the scenes I watched on numerous newsreels shot at Orgreave Colliery. I have heard about the alleged taunting and the waving of wage packets in the faces of striking miners. I never saw anything like that. Perhaps that day at Frances Colliery, and the day we were relieved by 'riot control officers' at Solsgirth, came nearest to making me feel a bit uncomfortable and to question such an approach. I have to conclude, however, they were in the minor league compared to what the media was portraying at Orgreave. Mind you, as I never carried out duty at any of the 'flashpoints', I should not offer comment. A lot of miners were arrested in Scotland throughout the duration of the strike. It does not make me proud to have contributed to that statistic. Nor is it any comfort to know that if I had not arrested that young striker at Dysart, someone in the next line of officers would have. He was a young man, not long married with a child. His less than serious behaviour was carried out in the anger that is brought about by hopelessness and fear. Not fear for his own physical safety; fear about his job, his livelihood, and his ability to provide for his family.

A postscript to that day at Dysart. A few months later, my colleague and I attended at Dunfermline Sheriff Court to give evidence as the arresting officers at his trial. He was found guilty and fined. The Sheriff commended both myself and my colleague for our clear, unembellished evidence and our fairness. When we were leaving court, both the accused and his lawyer spoke to us. They thanked us for our honesty and fairness, and the accused shook our hands. He lost his job; many arrested miners lost their job. On the day of his trial he was still looking for other employment. In my opinion, particularly considering the relatively minor violation, his punishment amounted to double jeopardy and was both draconian and unfair. To this day, I regret being anywhere near Dysart at that point. Two defence witnesses were called on his behalf – both, as I understood, union officials. I think they did not help his case, as they mostly spouted political dogma and offered no real defence. I think the Sheriff was less than impressed. I understand some of the miners dismissed as a result of being convicted for offences committed during picketing did get reinstated. I only hope he was among them.

To conclude, I will give some of the views expressed about the miners' strike by a few retired miners who took time out to speak to me.

To a man, they expressed anger at the Conservative government and the way they had been treated. They felt they were victimised – partly because of the ideological divide that existed between them and the government, and partly as retribution for the 1972 and 1974 miners' strikes that had, according to some, resulted in the Conservatives losing the election that year. One reflected on the whole change in global finances. In the mid-1970s, economists Jensen and Meckling resurrected Milton Friedman's original idea that the sole obligation of corporations was to maximise profits and, in doing so, maximise shareholders' value. At a stroke, he argued, all thoughts of employees, communities, and investment in their industries was a thing of the past. As soon as the Conservatives followed that model, which they did, the mines were finished. Why buy our coal when it could be shipped in far cheaper from other countries?

Miners I spoke with felt the police had been 'paid off', as Maggie Thatcher awarded them a considerable pay increase in return for their support. I debated this widely-held misunderstanding. The police pay rise, about 40%, had been agreed by a Labour government after an inquiry chaired by Edmund Davies in 1978. When the Conservatives took power in 1979, they implemented the pay rise a few months earlier than scheduled. Margaret Thatcher was the Prime Minister. My point being, it was not Margaret Thatcher who awarded the pay rise, it was proposed and sanctioned by the previous Labour government.

Some undoubtedly felt that Arthur Scargill's 'pigheadedness' helped prolong the dispute unnecessarily, and that they could have been back months before they actually were. They believed they had been misled. If the strike had been called off after three or four months, when many saw the writing on the wall, perhaps they would have been spared some degree of additional hardship – including the debt many got into to keep fighting and do the union's bidding. The legacy of debt that many were left to face might have been lessened, had they returned much earlier. In terms of the push for a national inquiry, only one miner I spoke to agreed whole-

heartedly that there should have been one, particularly covering the policing. Others were much more ambivalent and
ranged from no inquiry, to yes, but that it should be about the
political decisions. If it is about the police, it will miss the
point.

In general terms, they all talked passionately about the
hardships, the sacrifices, the camaraderie, and the bitterness.
One miner had saved for years to get a car. The £800 he had
saved didn't, in the end, buy a car. It was used instead simply
to feed his family. All had picketed at various locations, including the well-known trouble spots. They all talked about
police officers goading them by waving wage slips at them on
more than one occasion. These incidents happened at flash-
point locations in Lothians and at Ravenscraig in Strathclyde.
Two talked about the Army being used against them. Neither
had actually seen any military personnel. However, both were
aware of a story of one striking miner having seen a relative –
a soldier – amongst police ranks wearing a police uniform. I
had heard that story myself, but had always thought it an
apocryphal tale.

They spoke of picketing every second day and working
at their strike headquarters on alternative days. Amongst
other things, they spent hours roaming the country cutting
down trees and chopping them up into firewood. Mostly for
their families, but also for the pickets' fires. The women
worked hard behind the scenes, preparing meals, collecting
charity handouts, organising raffles, and simply supporting the
front line pickets and their families. Britain was importing
cheap coal from Poland; meanwhile, Polish miners were supplying food parcels to help support striking miners in Britain.

There were some who, from the beginning, did not join the strike and continued to work. They were despised. Families broke up, and some have never spoken to each other till this very day. Divorces happened. Some miners who had been on strike were starved back to work, in dribs and drabs. They were not appreciated, but they were not as hated or despised as the men who kept working throughout. I found no sympathy whatsoever for the latter, the scabs, but some degree of empathy for those forced to return. Perhaps not a lot. There were suicides.

All mentioned a police tactic of stopping them in early mornings en-route to picketing locations. They assumed that was as a result of government interference. I once read part of the diary of one miner, John Lowe, about his experiences as a Nottingham striker. He referred to an unpleasant incident when heading to picket and being prevented from doing so by a police patrol. He was a pensioner, and alone in his car. He was told to go home. When he refused, he claimed that the officers tried to pull him from his car and one called him a 'bastard'. He was injured, and was eventually taken to hospital. He claims that this was not an isolated incident. Reading that account and listening to the old miners made me recall being sent out on early morning patrols around some pits and told to stop all moving vehicles. If I judged the occupants to be miners, I was to turn them back. I only participated twice in that tactic and, while I did stop some vehicles, I did not turn them back. It was clearly not a lawful order, so I did not carry it out. I wasn't the only one who took that stance. Perhaps I was naïve. I had no idea where the 'order' originated. Had it come from somewhere much higher than my Chief Constable? At the time, I did not consider that possibility. I just assumed it was simply another local idea in action. Only when listening to the old miners and reading the diary did I ponder where the order might have originated.

I think it reasonable to conclude with a few quotes from a small book entitled *Coal Not Dole: Memories of the 1984/85 Miners' Strike* (2005) from the National Union of Mineworkers (Scotland Area) exhibition, *STRIKE: Fighting for our Communities*. Compiled by Guthrie Hutton and published by Stenlake Publishing Limited, who kindly gave permission for my foray into their domain. Thank you.

> 'At the beginning of the strike local police officers were on the picket line and the relationship was pretty good – a number of the police that were on the picket lines came from mining communities or mining backgrounds. That changed after a month or two, they started bringing in police from other regions, we had the Borders police up. Down south the Metropolitan police were ruthless... if you shouted at them the wrong way, you were arrested, if you looked at them the wrong way, you were arrested... everybody seemed to be six and a half feet, seven feet tall... they were vicious and they loved it – one policeman says, 'I hope this strike continues'... because they were earning more money.'
>
> David Hamilton MP, Midlothian

> 'The after-Christmas folk don't have the same stigma attached to them... because folk were on their knees, there's no two ways about it.'
>
> Liz Marshall, Ayrshire

'OK it was an organised return to work, but it was still a defeat; you could parcel it up any way you want, but it was a defeat and people were totally crushed by it. The women's committee went to the gate of Seafield... the men came round the corner in the bus and their body language was just as if they had been burst and every bit of life had been squeezed out of them. It was heartbreaking to see that.'

Cath Cunningham, Fife

I found policing the miners' strike a difficult period in my policing career, and save my final thoughts till now; I do not think it is, nor will I ever agree it to be, the job of Government to force thousands of their citizens – honest hard-working people and their families, just trying to save their livelihoods and protect their communities – to their knees, and crush the life from them.

This account of the three industrial actions I had the privilege to be involved in as a serving police officer is based on my own personal recollections, and those of some of the miners involved; honest, hard-working folk in the main, caught up in events beyond their control. It has allowed me to reflect on, and perhaps better understand, the motivations of those taking part – including my own.

After the strike, the pits across the British Isles continued to close and in 2015 the last deep mine at Kellingley shut down and they were no more. So Scargill was right all along, despite his methods. As I write this in July 2017, I have just read that one thousand six hundred coal-fired power stations are being built all over the world and I wonder, why did we take their hopes and dreams away from them?

# CHAPTER 16

THEN it was over, and I was back on normal duties and first line supervision. Some incidents have more of an effect on you than others. The trouble is that you do not have a crystal ball, so until you are involved you have no way of knowing. Policing is no different. Sometimes it is just the volume, year after year of the same stuff, and then you have had enough. I have experience of three who reached that buffer. Front line Constables all their service. One just could not deal with one more dead body, the other two had enough fighting and frolicking on a Friday night and did not want to deal with another alcohol-fuelled situation. Both of the latter, at different times, said they were at the end of their tether and if they had to deal with another angry, fighting, drunken person, they would not be held responsible for their actions. They had each completed twenty-nine years' service. In the first case the officer was transferred to the stores. In the case of the last two, they were dealt with locally, at their own office. Both, at different times, worked for me as my aide de camp and helping with the day-to-day running of the office, taking certain administration tasks away from the front line officers. The question arises: is it right to leave a police officer on front line duties for thirty years without a break?

Back to single incidents. The image of the young man who died in my arms has never left me. The Dunblane primary school tragedy had a real impact, although it was so enormous it felt almost unreal – and that is not to diminish the effect on the bereaved; for each of them, it was only too real. But to a professional with the task of working in that arena, it was so overwhelming, so unthinkable, it was almost unbelievable – and while it had a marked effect, sometimes the single incident, the one you get close to, the one that catches you off guard, gets into your psyche. That is the one that gets you.

I was in the office one mid-morning when the call came in. A shooting in our area. I immediately got on the road and called for the officer covering that area to join me. It was a normal house in a normal street, and inside was no different. In fact, it was pristine, with an infant in a cradle basket. A tranquil scene in a normal house. Except that it wasn't. The woman lying on the floor, bleeding from a wound to her head and the hysterical woman who let us in, attested to that. We immediately summoned an ambulance, and did what we could for the woman on the floor. A firearm was lying near the stricken woman. The ambulance arrived in a few minutes and, after their initial examination, they asked for a police escort. A traffic car was on the scene quickly, and in no time both vehicles are 'blue lighting' their way to the nearest Accident and Emergency. A radio message from the duty inspector asks for the land line telephone number at the house. By then the husband has arrived home, and he and the other lady are huddled in the kitchen. The house telephone rang, the Inspector gave me the worst news. I get my colleague to summon further assistance. Meanwhile, I gathered my thoughts and headed into the kitchen. There is no standard, textbook, best way to deliver terrible news. I had done it often; however, this felt worse. I can still see both as I went in. They probably expected bad news, but they still looked to have hope. It is the eyes. I shattered whatever hope that may have been lingering. I will not describe their response; their world had just collapsed. As they held each other, I put my arm round both. I am not sure if a cleverer officer than me would have found words; I could not. I felt so inadequate. After some time, things had subsided enough for me to be able to tell them what was going to happen and to answer their questions. Other officers and some other people had arrived by then and I was able to move out of the kitchen and catch up with progress. Then the land line telephone rung and I answered it. For an instant I just thought, 'oh – that Inspector must be looking for an update'. A woman, obviously on edge, asked who I was and what was I doing in her sister's house. It was now my turn to be shocked; I had been caught on the hop, suddenly I was not in control. For an instant I did not know what to say, my mind was racing. Was this really her sister? Where was she? How will she react? I told her I was a police officer. There was a gasp, and then nothing. The line was still open, but nobody was responding. Another woman's voice asked what had happened. I asked who she was. 'I am her manager', she said, referring to the lady who dropped the telephone. An instant to decide; I had no choice but to tell her who I was and what had happened. She kindly told me she would take control at her end, and she thanked me. It was a blur after that, as more and more people arrived: police photographer, and the CID who were taking over the enquiry. I spoke to the husband to make sure, as well as one can in such circumstances, that he had as much support as he needed. Later on, I am asked to attend at the mortuary to identify the body before the post mortem. None of the family were well enough to do that. Viewing and identifying the woman was my watershed. It was the actual moment I saw her; a beautiful woman, unblemished apart from an inconspicuous bandage round her head. I have never, in all the years that have come in between, been able to get rid of that vision.

For many years I could not speak about it. Even today it is difficult. I have tried to fathom it. Why that incident? I can only come up with questions. Was it the pristine condition of the house, the incongruous scene, the informing the next of kin, the unfortunate telephone incident, or simply that a beautiful woman had been so tormented, so ill, that she sought that way to deal with it? Only questions, no answers. There is not always an answer. That is not the only time I have said that.

I think I need, however, to put some perspective to this incident. If I found it difficult, my goodness, how did her poor family feel? I wrote this section after a lot of soul-searching. But I did commit it to paper, and not because I wanted to sensationalise anything about it – nothing like that. I included it to make the reader aware that in Scotland, in the UK, police officers are dealing with similar incidents every day – yes, every day – and they get up and they get on and get ready for the next one. Not one of them will ever be able to predict the one that gets through their armour, but they just keep doing their job and yes, every now and then one of them screws up and the media are on to it like a pack of dogs. So the next time you read about a screw-up, please remember all that goes on outwith the glare of publicity and the unflinching service these officers deliver, for us, without fear or favour, every hour of every day.

A Sergeant's duty meanders from the routine checking of reports to making sure there is enough shift cover to actual supervision of activity, and ensuring all situations are covered and being dealt with. That includes redirecting troops as required, listening to the radio chatter, and intervening as required. When I was a shift Inspector in Falkirk, I had two Sergeants. Every shift, after the muster and briefing, both came to my office. I got the coffee. It was usually a short get-together. I only wanted to know what they had planned, any issues I should be aware of, and any issues I had for them. I always left the same message with them, every shift. Take care out there; do not be frightened to ask for my assistance. And my final message: I will be listening, I will never interfere or interrupt or talk over you. If I have a concern, I will ask to meet you somewhere. Only then will I articulate my concern and, if necessary, suggest a different course of action. I will never countermand you over the open radio. It worked, and trust and mutual respect was built. I was learning team work and team building, and I was trying really hard to get it right.

\* \* \*

Back in my Sergeant's role, I had just started an early shift one day and the briefing was all about a trade fair that was taking place in the town. It was an annual event and was very popular, drawing several thousand visitors over the day. I had dealt with the policing of it before. I finished briefing, and all the Constables were out getting on with their allotted tasks. Sometime later, still early and when the event was still being organised, one of the Constables barged into the main office, threw his hat down and angrily shouted that 'the left hand doesn't know what the fuckin' right hand is doing!' I was in my office, adjacent to this outburst. He was not an officer taken to such language and outbursts. The duty Inspector, from another office, had appeared on the scene and started telling the officers to do things. Different tasks from the ones I had given out at the briefing. Just then, a second angry officer arrived back in the office with the same complaint. The radio crackled, and the self-same Inspector asked to meet me in the town centre. I was now as angry as my Constables. I asked what he was doing and why he had not called at the office to catch up with me. His line was: 'I am an Inspector; I have no need to catch up with a Sergeant'. I tried to explain that this was the third year we had policed this event, there was a detailed order issued, and that I had briefed the officers on the tasks each required to undertake. He was not impressed, and told me to accompany him into the area where the local organisers were putting the stalls up. I said I had been round earlier, adding that all that will happen is they will involve us in disputes about stall owners encroaching onto other stall owners' pitches. He soon learned, and we returned to the office where we had words about his lack of protocol and confusing the whole policing of the event. It was now his turn to be furious, and we did not resolve anything. He swept out soon afterwards with a warning that it had better go without a hitch or I would hear more about it. Assertive officers do not get caught up in such nonsense. They not only understand protocol; they have confidence in themselves and others, and have no need to micro-manage and over-reach their line of responsibility. It is not only de-skilling; it is dangerous.

I had plenty of run-ins with that officer. He left a message with our night shift once that he needed one of our two vehicles delivered to his office by eight o'clock one morning, for his own use. He was specific in identifying which vehicle he required. After briefing, I got two officers to sort that out and deliver it in plenty of time. They returned just before the crucial point to tell me they had been unable to start the engine. They had contacted the garage at HQ and a mechanic was being sent, to arrive about eight-thirty that morning. I did not get the chance to call the Inspector. He was on the blower at eight o'clock on the dot.

'Where is my vehicle?'

I explained the problem. He – obviously a bit miffed – asked if we had tried jump starting it?

'Yes', was my reply.

'Did you try shoving it?' was his next question.

We had tried that, to no avail; in fact, we even tried towing it.

Still annoyed, he asked, 'did you try taking out the spark plugs and cleaning them?' When I told him we had not tried that, he got quite irate and instructed I do so. I refused, and told him we were police officers and not motor mechanics. I informed him we expected the mechanic from HQ there any minute. He was still not happy. In the event, even the motor mechanic was unable to get it started, so it was taken away on a trailer. Right or wrong, reasonable or unreasonable, it made no difference; if you did not get things the way the boss wanted then it was personal and was never forgotten. A career destroyer.

A Sergeant's job was interesting. It probably did me no favours having worked in industry before joining the police and, in particular, doing the specific type of organisation and methods work I had been doing. On another occasion, different circumstances, I was in the company of a Superintendent and a Chief Superintendent. The latter was in a rage because some order he had issued a few weeks before seemed not to

have been a priority for some of his officers. The quick thinking Superintendent deferred to my knowledge on these matters. I gave him a look and thanked him for his confidence in
my opinion. I argued, reasonably in my opinion, that given the
constant stream of 'orders' that emerged from both Division
and from HQ annually – some ninety or so in total, every year
– it was no wonder the officers occasionally missed one. That
was the wrong answer. Being a police Sergeant, in my opinion, was – and perhaps still is – the most difficult position to
hold. One is working cheek by jowl with the Constables, yet
at the same time being driven by those above to oversee their
bright ideas in action being delivered.

Keeping track of all your officers is an obvious part of
being the first line of supervision. Each shift had a document
called a 'daily state'. It was a twenty-four hour record of all
those at work that day, when they started and finished, and a
lot more. It could be an important document in some internal
enquiries. I was on duty on a backshift, about six-thirty one
evening, when a Superintendent called at the office. He headed for the daily state, examined it, and – on selecting the officer working in the beat furthest from the office – asked
where he was and what was he doing? I explained he was on
his beat and that he had five different enquiries to be getting
on with. I did not know which particular enquiry he was dealing with at that precise moment. That was not good enough.
He wanted to know exactly where he was, and exactly what
he was doing at that moment. When I said I did not know
exactly, however, I did know what enquiries he had to deal
with. I also knew he has more service than me; he is a very
experienced officer, and I trust him. The next question was
about trust – how did I know to trust him, and what if he is
not doing what he was supposed to be doing? I was starting

to lose the will to live by then, and said that his work record would evidence whether or not he was doing as instructed. Still not satisfied, he came back with final straw of a question. 'You are not listening. I asked if you knew exactly your officer's location at this moment, and you obviously have no idea.' You know, he was correct; I had no idea, like I had no idea where any of my officers were at that precise time, other than on their allocated beats getting on with their work. However, he was looking for a response, and he got one. I picked up the police radio and called for the officer to respond. The Super asked me what I was doing, and I responded by telling him we pay PYE about £700 each for these radios; they are perfect for finding out the location of officers. Said officer responded. I asked him to tell me exactly where he was at that instant, and he did. I told the boss, who was less than impressed and – having placed a flea in my ear – headed off into the night to ask more stupid questions of some other despairing Sergeant. He was a regular early evening visitor, certainly when I was on duty, and our encounters often finished badly – for me, anyway. He always related these encounters to my Inspector, who always had me in his office for a pep talk. It was mostly nothing like that, and most were decent, level-headed, good people. However, there was a minority that seemed to proportionately cause more mischief than all the rest of the reasonable encounters put together.

One Sunday I was working with one of my officers on a break-in to a motor vehicle. We quickly traced the seventeen year old culprit and charged him. He was not held in custody. The next day my actions were subject to close scrutiny at 'morning prayers'. It seems I was not flavour of the month, as I had let one of the biggest criminals in our force area free. Not only that – there were multiple arrest warrants outstanding for him. I got the accusing telephone call when I got in for my backshift, along with a summons to attend at the Chief Inspector's office. He let rip. I asked him to explain who he was talking about, and how had they linked the young man I had dealt with to their 'most wanted'. He kept repeating that it was the man they were looking for, and I had let him free; no real explanation. He added my name was mud and I would hear more. Having put up with this assault on my integrity for a few minutes, I asked if I could explain what happened. The 'most wanted' was a person I knew well. He lived in Tullibody, and I had arrested and reported him in the past for 'Causing Death by Dangerous Driving'. I also knew that he was in his fifties. The young man I dealt with on Sunday had the same name, but a different date of birth and was only a teenager. He, in fact, was the nephew of the person the Chief Inspector was getting in a lather about. He asked for a short report with all that information. I did that, and I heard not another cheep. The trouble is, I don't even think they were interested; they had made their point. You will not be surprised that some decades later I still await an apology. Well not really, but you get my point.

I had a reputation for getting out and about to support the team as and when required. That led me into some interesting situations. I was at breakfast one Saturday early shift when one of the team asked if I could help at the front counter, where there was an awkward customer. My goodness, he was not wrong. I asked how I could help. The awkward customer thrust a letter in my face and said he wanted somebody from the Council charged with breaking into his house. The letter was a bit old, and he obviously had not been in the house for a while. He certainly would not be in it today, as the Council did what the letter intimated – changed the locks.

It seems he had not paid rent for a while and the Housing Department followed the legal process. They had tried to contact him, including leaving the letter at the address. He now had the letter, was no longer the tenant, and wanted something done about it. In addition, he was a rather unpleasant character, and his threats were not just about the Council. The more I explained this really was a civil issue, the more he got in a rage. His big disadvantage was I knew the address and that he was a suspect in criminal activity, involving stolen property. I said nothing and, as he again thrust the letter in my face and demanded action, that is exactly what he got. I took the letter and agreed to do something. What I did perplexed him, and more so my Constable. I ripped the letter up, threw it on the floor, reached over the counter, grabbed him by the front of his jacket, and pulled him over the counter and through the gap. My Constable might have been a bit shocked, but – give him his due – he trusted me and assisted in the 'arrest'. We took him, still protesting, to a detention cell and locked the door. I turned to the officer and said: 'Do not disturb me when I am eating again!' He was perturbed and, as I walked away, I could not suppress a grin. I asked him to look up the crime record book for our detainee's name and that address he had been so upset about. He soon found it, and realised he was a suspect in a crime. Obviously that had escaped my colleague's attention. We detained him and, after a while, he took us to a house – well outwith our police area – where we recovered the stolen items we had been looking for. My Constable had the honour of reporting the cheeky chap.

On another night, into the early morning, there had been a disturbance amongst some males and females who had over-indulged in alcohol and perhaps more. Two officers sorted it all out; however, not to everyone's satisfaction. A while after the incident, one of the officers said that two males from that night needed to speak to me. They were a bit drunk, loud, and pretty much out of order. One claimed that one of the officers had stolen a £5 note from his wallet. I asked how much was in the wallet now. Fifteen or twenty pounds. So how did he manage to get a fiver out and why, if he was about to ruin a good police career, did he not just take it all? And anyway, what was he doing with your wallet in the first place? His friend – the trustworthy, credible, gibbering drunk – said his pal had dropped it, and the officer had picked it up and handed it back. He must have done it then. The 'victim', however, had a different story; it seems the officer had asked to see his wallet to check his identity and had taken the five pound note. I pressed about why he would take just five pounds. He replied 'because he was trying to be clever'. I asked to see the officer's wallet. He had two ten pound notes and some loose change. I warned them that I was considering charging them with Wasting Police Time, but on reflection had decided to fling them out as I was not sure it would be in the public interest, wasting time on this nonsense. With that, I grabbed both, physically manhandled them outside, and told them to come back when they were sober. They got into the waiting taxi, and I never heard from them again. Just in case anybody is wondering, they picked on the most decent, mild mannered, honest officer in the office. These incidents and others went down with my officers as showing support and leadership. The higher echelons had other ideas.

# CHAPTER 17

**M**Y transfer from Denny to Bo'ness was another interesting chapter in my career; not just being in Bo'ness, but the actual way my move came about. There was a particular family whose behaviour was more bizarre than criminal; probably better labelled 'anti-social'. There had been several visits, with no real solution being reached. One of the Constables came back from that location and asked if I would help; it seemed they would take no heed of the Constables. My visit culminated in me telling the father off in front of his whole family. He complained about me – a long, rambling letter in which, among other things, he said I had humiliated him in front of his family by speaking like a headteacher would speak to a child. A few days after the letter was received, he stopped me in the street and said if I apologised to him in front of his family, he would withdraw his letter of complaint. Needless to say I did not agree, and it ran its course. I headed off on leave for three weeks, climbing in the Alps.

I got home the weekend before I was due to start back at work. One of my trusty Constables telephoned me at my house on the Sunday. He informed me I had been transferred in my absence to Bo'ness. I had not been informed, although that officer knew and had the decency to tell me. I turned up for duty as usual at Denny. Another person was at my desk. He asked what I was doing here. I told him, 'my job'. He had no other information. I headed home. Not one call did I receive until the Wednesday. The Bo'ness Inspector was wondering why I was not at my work. I asked when I was due to be there, and when was I to have been informed. In the event I started on the Thursday, and my first job was to visit the Area Commander in his office at Falkirk to ask what was going on. He said that these things happen, and the transfer was a just a consequence of circumstances. Whatever that meant. I asked how he would have felt if he had come back from holiday to find his office being used. He shrugged, and I headed back to another eventful three years of being a first line supervisor.

Bo'ness – or, to be correct, Borrowstounness – was where I had stayed for a short time many years before. 'Hamebider' is the name given to people from the town. What would I remember? Precious little, was the answer. During my first week I walked out the office one evening to do some familiarisation foot patrol about the town centre. I was no more the thirty yards from the back door, in Commissioner Street, when I came across a couple who looked to be in their early twenties. She was upset about something and quite distressed. I stepped forward, because I was the new police Sergeant and I cared. I asked if all was well and could I help? 'Fuck off', came her reply; 'it's got fuck-all to do with you'. With that, she stood up, took her gentleman's arm and turned on her heel. My 'I was only trying to help!' comment fell on deaf ears.

I continued my patrol, musing *my goodness, this will be interesting*. It was. There was something markedly different about Bo'ness – compared to Denny, that is. It was a com-

268

plete, compact, and very proud community – and still is. Before appearing on the books of Central Scotland Police, it had been firmly a Lothians police outpost. Some of the present officers had 'residential' privilege, because as previous Lothians officers they could not be transferred. I think that may well have been time limited; I'm not sure. Bo'ness's annexation from Lothians brought the occasional spat; nothing major. I was in the office one evening when a Detective Inspector from Leith called and instructed I arrest an individual and get him to Leith. I asked why, as obviously my officers will have to give him a reason and note it. Also, while I was happy to comply – given good reason – I would not be transporting him to Leith; the Detective Inspector could come and get him. He got a tad shirty at that point and, in no uncertain terms, told me to 'get him fuckin' lifted and I will sort out the reason once you get him through to Leith'. I calmly informed him that he was in contact with Central Scotland Police and that Bo'ness was no longer part of Lothians. He abruptly hung up, and I never heard back from him.

Such behaviour was not confined to Lothians. I only had one such irritation from them and, to be honest, it was not me who was irritated – it was the Leith Detective Inspector. Our relationship with Lothians was excellent, and travelling over the hill to help out Linlithgow and vice-versa was not uncommon. Maybe it was a CID thing. I recall three occasions whilst a Sergeant in Bo'ness where I had run-ins with the CID. If I am honest, most detectives were great officers; the issues I refer to can be narrowed down to a very particular, but powerful, few.

One called and instructed me to have a named person detained. I asked for the reason, a reasonable and lawful request. I was told not to be awkward; just get him in. I stuck to my guns, to be told that he was telling me to do it. I reminded him he was a Constable and ordering a Sergeant was not part of the master plan. He hung up. A short while after I heard one of my Constables on the telephone, agreeing to 'lift' said gentleman. I took the telephone from the officer and had words. I have no idea if the gentleman was ever detained or arrested. Please believe me, I was first in line to arrest or detain anyone the CID, or whoever else, wanted. My request for a reason was – to repeat – not only totally reasonable, it was a legal requirement.

My reluctance to dance to anyone else's ill-thought-out tune was born out of bitter experience. When a Sergeant in Denny I received a call one day to have a named person arrested for failure to appear at court. It was a CID officer who made the request. He had the full name, date of birth, the full current address, and an arrest warrant for the person. I duly noted all that detail in the log book and arranged for two officers to carry out the task and take the person directly to the CID office in Stirling. The CID would arrange for the court appearance. Job done, I got on with other things. Next day when I came on backshift duty I was met by a senior officer who was carrying out an internal enquiry. He asked why I had ordered the arrest the previous day. I was puzzled, and asked what the issue was. It seems we had arrested the wrong person. I gave my side of the story, in detail. My senior Constable, who actually arrested him, gave his statement. What became blindingly clear was that the CID had concocted a variation of the story, suggesting that we had only been given minimal information and that we then carried out our own enquiry and came up with the wrong person. The arrest was not their fault. Needless to say I was furious, as was my senior Constable, who had become the centre of the enquiry. At that point nobody had even looked at the log book. Next day, after my Constable had been taken in for questioning, I urged that the log book entry be inspected. It was exactly as I had related. I am not even sure they did not think I had added it later, after the enquiry started. What convinced them was that there were two other entries in the log book, entered soon after the 'suspect' entry. I couldn't have entered it later; the times did not support that. In the end, the CID officer admitted his mistake, the enquiry went silent and we heard no more. My senior Constable went on to be a Chief Inspector, and never forgave the CID officers involved. I also reached that rank, and my take was different. It was not about forgiveness; it was about remembering the experience and keeping evidence. Simple, really – it is what police officers are taught.

On another occasion there was a serious sexual assault in the town. We attended, did all of the early enquiry, made the scene and the victim safe, then – as required – informed the CID. Crimes of this nature, attempted rape (or, as it is properly termed, 'Assault with Intent to Ravish'), are serious and fall firmly into the province of the CID. I spoke to the Detective Sergeant and explained in full, even using the precise term to describe the crime. He informed me they were seriously stretched with other crimes and asked if I would just carry on with it. His reasoning was that we had previously worked together, he trusted my judgement and ability to carry out the enquiry, and thus would I get on and get it done. He was correct on all fronts; he was woefully weak on the internal politics, however. We had a victim and we had a serious enquiry, and time was marching on. So we got on with it – photographer, medical examination, and within an hour we had the two accused in detention. They eventually admitted it and signed statements in my notebook to that effect. We properly concluded our enquiry, left nothing out, got both accused charged and put into custody, and got the custody report completed and to the Procurator Fiscal. A good job, finished at about five o'clock in the morning. However, when internal politics intervene, doing a good job is no defence. Funny thing about working weekend backshift; you are often involved in the weekend frolics, and your decisions appear in front of the 'twenty-twenty vision' brigade on a Monday morning. So, as had happened often in the past, one signs on duty early Monday afternoon to 'face the music'. This particular piece of orchestral manoeuvres in the dark centred on the Assault with Intent to Ravish that I had dealt with over the weekend. The Detective Superintendent and the Area Commander did not visit each other's houses for port and lemon. They had a history, and their relationship was frosty. So any wee issue that could be used by one to poke the other was a godsend to their infantile feud. I was the patsy; the stick carrier. The Area Commander was raging at me. What possessed me to carry out such a serious crime enquiry without informing the CID? That was their job, and he was considering reporting me for neglect of duty. I calmly informed him that was not what happened. I had informed the Detective Sergeant and he declined to become involved; too busy, he said. That did not help. He told me the CID Sergeant did not know it was so serious; I had failed to explain properly. I asked how serious did he think Assault with Intent to Ravish was? This was going nowhere and, while I heard no more about it, my card was well and truly marked – in both camps. The detective Sergeant, with one eye (probably both eyes) on promotion, had to make a decision. He chose to favour himself over me. It happens, and is all too frequent when weaker individuals are faced with such circumstances. Do not be fooled; there are no winners amongst the lower ranks when involved in the power struggles of two managers. Yes, maybe if you amend the facts in support of one you think you win, and perhaps you do on one level. But you know, you are no better than the bully if you collude with him. I chose – and always chose – a different route. Was I any more a winner? In terms of my career, I definitely was not. But winning is about something else, and kowtowing to bullies is not the mark of a winner. By the way, both accused received prison sentences after a trial. So perhaps my enquiry and report were fine.

None of my shift, certainly in my earlier days in Bo'ness, would I describe as out-and-out crime catchers. They were, however, very conscientious and hard workers, and could be trusted with anything. A good shift. It was a busy corner of the world. I was amused – and sometimes irked – by some conterminous issues involving other services. When Bo'ness was annexed from West Lothian, did anybody consider how the services would meld? It appears not. For example, the ambulance service. Emergencies in the rest of the police area were taken to Stirling or Falkirk. In Bo'ness they were taken to Livingston. That creates a problem. From Grangemouth through to Denny, all emergencies head for Falkirk. Now that is neater. If an officer needs support or a lift, or if required another officer needs to attend, it is not a big drama. However, Bo'ness to Livingstone – that becomes a bit of an issue. The emergency 999 telephone system was not based in our area either, so such calls from Bo'ness through to Whitecross went to Livingston. That occasionally resulted in a mixup. The emergency operators would direct the call to Lothians HQ in Edinburgh. It often would take an age for them to sort out that in fact 'this is not our call'. Sometimes that never got sorted out until a second emergency call. A lady in our area had a brain haemorrhage. Her husband dialled 999, and the response went to Lothians. The emergency services spent ages trying to locate the address, unsuccessfully, and by the time it was recognised as being in our area, it was too late. The woman had died.

It was not unknown for an ambulance to turn out to an emergency, single-crewed. Solution: will an officer drive it back to Livingston? A second officer had to head out in the car to bring the other officer back. What a complete waste of police time. I see no bettering of that situation as Police Scotland steadfastly go down the route of closing local telephone service centres to centralise them in the Central Belt. I pity the poor person requiring police assistance somewhere like Tarbert.

Not all my issues were with other services, however. Some were right here on my front doorstep. I was in the police van one night, passing a well-known hostelry. There was a group of seven or eight males, in their forties and fifties. I recognised some. As we passed, one gentleman stepped onto roadway and bellowed – at me I guess, as I was in the passenger seat nearest the group – 'You are a fuckin' wanker!' Accurate or not, I could not allow the uniform to be subjected to such disrespect. Van stopped, I alighted and approached the group. I took hold of my admirer and informed him he was under arrest. He spouted the usual question, 'what for?' I told him that he knew perfectly well. Just then, the group crowded round and let me know that they would be at the court to say I made it up. One adding: 'So where's your pal?' My pal, as he put it, was hiding in the van. No corroboration was the defence being correctly offered. These guys had all been through the system and knew the drill. I know when to change tactics, and this was that 'when'. I told my opponent he had a point and suggested we sort our differences out some other way, just the two of us.

He looked at me for a moment and said: 'You are being serious!'

'You bet your life I am being serious.'

He then suggested this was getting too heavy for him and asked, 'what if I apologise?'

I replied, 'well, you started this nonsense; you make that call'.

He did apologise and offered his hand, which I took. Neither he nor any of that group ever passed me again without a pleasantry, and never again did any of them give me anything but my place. I might say, respect; perhaps that is going a bit far. As I went back to the van, a voice rang out, 'so much for your brave pal!' He had steadfastly stayed rooted to his seat. I got him to drive me back to the office, to get him out of my sight.

# CHAPTER 18

I N the background at this time of my service was mountain rescue. I had been approached by the Chief Inspector
in Alloa before being promoted to Sergeant and asked if I
would consider joining up with the Ochils Mountain Rescue
Team. I was a keen mountaineer, and I agreed to approach
them. They accepted me, and I served for several years during
my Sergeant stints in Denny, Bo'ness, and when in the Crime
Prevention Department. It will not surprise anyone to know
that it led to conflict with some senior officers.

I was called out during my rest days, my weekend off,
to a serious incident – a missing person in the mountains in
the Killin area. It was winter, and the weather was wild. I
was out for two full days, sleeping on the floor of a hall in
Killin. Unfortunately the male was found dead. I was back at
work, and had submitted a claim for overtime. The claim was
rejected. I queried this, and a Superintendent saw me. His
view was that mountain rescue was a hobby and not real police work. He actually said it was no different from playing for
the police football team. I reminded him that a missing person
was a police responsibility and that I had been engaged in
something I regarded as a duty. I also reminded him that it
was the police who asked me to get involved in the first place
and that I was a police officer in the team. He just got angry

and finished the dialogue with a definitive 'you are not getting paid'. He was true to his word, I never did get paid. I thought then, and I think now, it was unjust.

When Sergeant Lawrie was killed some time later, one hellish night high on the northern flank of Ben More, I wondered if the Superintendent told his next of kin he was just like a member of the police football team and taking part in his hobby? Anyway, that decision did not dampen my enthusiasm and I continued, eventually finishing up as team secretary. Serious camaraderie and team work. I spent many hours at incidents and in training to safely search and help people who had encountered difficulties in our mountains.

One Sunday a couple, armed with a torn page from a Sunday newspaper, set out from Menstrie to ascend Dumyat at the west end of the Ochil Hills. The south-facing flank of Dumyat is very steep, with several vertical rock bands interspersed with steep sloping grass. The Sunday paper had a weekly feature on easy walks, and included a route marked by a line on a sketch of the mountain that vaguely indicated to go along the steep south side. It showed a convenient car park and not a lot else. We arrived at the foot of the hill to see two people high on the steep south side, sitting on one of the horizontal grass ramps. The woman was waving a jacket to attract attention. When we got to the pair, the male was crag fast and the woman was fine. She acknowledged they were just out for a Sunday afternoon walk and were now well out of their depth, neither being mountaineers. Her husband would not even stand. It eventually took six of us to get them down. We fitted both with a climbing harness, with a rope 'tail' attached. The woman walked down with a team member walking beside her, securing her by holding the short length of 'security' rope we had attached to the harness. The man, however – tail or no tail – was not for moving. And so – in addition to the tail, with a team member holding it – we secured a full length of climbing rope to the front of his harness. Four of us then spaced out along the rope, walked it to its full length, and stopped. The man was then persuaded to walk by his 'tail' protector. As they reached each rescue team member in turn, that team member also walked with him, then the next, and the next, until all were clustered together. He stood still again, and the four rescue team members stretched the rope out once more. The man then walked again, and we repeated that concertina process all the way down. We did not go directly down the hill; there were several vertical rock bands, and we had to zig zag back and forward along the grass ramps, getting lower and lower. He was really terrified and, by the time we got him safely down, he was exhausted. He was a tall man, over six feet in height, whereas his wife was quite small. That really has no bearing on how one might be on a hill. However it was, if I can be cruel for a moment, quite amusing. I think he was not the one making the dinner that night.

Calls out could be anytime. Midwinter blizzard, scorching hot summer afternoon; it made no difference. I recall forcing my way through waist-deep wet snow as I tried to find a route into the mountain on steep ground, late one winter evening, snowflakes dazzling me as they reflected from the beam of my head torch. My thoughts were on the real possibility of an avalanche. The source of the light that had been reported flashing somewhere on the hill was never found. Another day I was the 'casualty' in a practice gorge rescue. The method being practised was a quaintly-named technique called a Tyrolean Traverse. I was strapped into a stretcher. I then trusted my life to the team as they fixed it to a pulley, then dragged it out – with me snuggled inside – one hundred feet in the air over the roaring river in the gorge. As I lay looking up at the single rope, the umbilical cord to which I owed my survival while the stretcher moved slowly along, it all went 'tits up', to use a military term. One of the pulley wheels jumped off the rope and jammed. Helplessly, strapped in a stretcher, I swayed and bounced about for what seemed an eternity as my team mates worked out what to do. I gazed at the dislodged pulley wheel, wondering how long it would take for the rope to snap. It is funny how a process of shouting, swearing and telling me to lie still and not panic, seems to be the universal method for sorting out these situations. I did not panic; no reason to. There was absolutely nothing I could do. In fact, I could not get my arms free anyway. Half an hour later I was unceremoniously dumped on the far banking, released from my 'mummy' outfit, and all was well. Tall tales in a Tillicoultry pub later was all that was left of the day.

I was on duty on the fifth of April 1990 when I was instructed to get my mountaineering kit and head for the village of Fintry. Just before nine o'clock that morning, a Cessna 210 plane, PH-EYE, had crashed into Dunbrach Hill, just over two kilometres directly south of the village. The plane caught fire, and the two occupants were killed instantly. While the general angle of the hill was 45°, the part they hit was a vertical rock outcrop and the site was in a difficult place to access. The pilot and co-pilot had flown over from the Netherlands in the early morning. They were fishing boat owners from the north of the Netherlands, heading to a conference in Scotland. The weather was not good; low cloud, visibility problems and cold sleet. The plane had suffered icing problems, and was lower than it should have been as it set up to land at Glasgow. At the rendezvous I was met by the police officer in charge of the incident. My task was to secure the crash site by staying beside it overnight and not letting anyone approach. I was accompanied by a member from the Killin Mountain Rescue Team. We were briefed, and supplied with food and a flask as well as waterproof bivouac bags. For the last couple of hundred feet or so, the site was steep and slippery. The bodies were being removed when we arrived on site. Then we were on our own. In the pitch black, we scrabbled and slithered about on the steep wet hillside, trying to find a suitable place near the wreckage to bed down. It was not easy. In the end, we settled for a sheep scrape. Not the best, but as near to horizontal as we could find. It was not a comfortable night. There were freezing sleet showers all night, and lying in such a precarious position with your arms zipped inside the bag was disconcerting. I felt like I was sliding, and all night I had a vision of me tobogganing to the bottom of the hill in the bivouac bag, adding a third casualty to the list. It was a sobering night as we looked onto the wreckage and contemplated the tragedy for two families. But life goes on, and nature has a way of bringing us back. As dawn broke we were awakened by the sound of a Blackcock Lek, coming from a gap in the forest below us to our right. It was early April, and I certainly was a bit surprised as I had always thought they were around a bit later. Reinforcements arrived within a couple of hours, and we moved out.

Two things happened in the years that followed. Ten years after the crash, a daughter of one of the occupants contacted Central Scotland Police to ask if we could take her to the site. A colleague had a brass commemorative plaque made, and we affixed it to the cliff. A few days later we took the daughter to the site. It was a moving experience, and I hoped it helped her come to terms with her dad's death in some way. In 2016, I flew in the opposite direction in a small four-seater plane. We landed at Lelystad in Netherlands, and stayed in Amersfoort. At dinner one night I was sitting beside a lady and gentleman. During dinner I was telling of the tragic incident all these years before in Scotland, involving the death of two fishermen from the north of their country. They looked astounded, as they informed me they knew both the people who had been killed and in fact he had been speaking to a relative of one of the deceased only a few days before the dinner. They were amazed that I had been so involved. It is an increasingly small world. What part of the experiences I have just related bear the slightest resemblance to playing football for the police football team?

On the subject of aircraft mishaps, I was called to an air crash near Blackness when the Local Unit Commander in Bo'ness. A group from a business organisation were spending the day on a team-building exercise. You know the kind of thing I mean. One of the tasks was an aerial treasure hunt. Participants were flown about the area, strapped into microlight aircraft clutching clues and probably the fuselage of the aircraft, whilst directing the pilot to whatever they were hoping to find. The type of microlights employed that day were also known as 'flexwings'. They have a hang glider-like wing with a seating unit suspended underneath the wing, like a pendulum. They are sometimes called 'flying motorbikes' and – like motorbikes – the 'rider', the pilot, is exposed to the wind and weather. Because of that, flying them can be an exhilarating experience. To the east of the field that they were using as an airstrip, there was an avenue of trees at right angles to their descent path. Landing from the east, the planes had to come over the trees. As they all flighted back to base after the treasure hunt phase of their day, the very last flexwing crashed into the line of trees and got caught in the branches, coming to rest suspended about twenty feet above the ground. The fire service used ladders to get the pilot and his passenger to terra firma. One had a broken leg; both were scraped, scratched and a bit shaken. I think being caught in the branches perhaps saved them from further injury. The pilot said they had 'hit a sink' just before the trees and the plane – unexpectedly and violently – dropped several feet in altitude and straight into the trees. By 'sink', he meant an air pocket. Aircraft enthusiasts have told me that air pockets do not actually exist. What the plane encountered was air turbulence. Flying through turbulence might well be bumpy, but one is rarely in danger. Unless of course you are about to pass closely over trees.

My last air mishap reference involves myself as the injured party. I fell – or to be correct, was pushed – out of an airborne aeroplane without a parachute and lived to tell the tale. It was another mountain rescue situation. I was team leader of a group toiling up through snow to an injured person high on a mountain. We were the stretcher party. Luckily an RAF Wessex Search and Rescue helicopter was free to attend and take us to the locus. Due to the steepness of the ground it could not land, and we were individually winched in to the helicopter. I was last, and there was not a seat for me. I simply sat at the door edge, still attached to the winch, with my feet dangling outside. We swung into the hill. Because of the gusty wind, coupled with the uneven, boulder-strewn slope, the helicopter could not land. They had no time to winch us all out, so a stark choice was offered. Go back down the hill, with the prospect of walking back up, or jump out. We chose the latter. We hovered about eight feet up. Technique: sit on the edge, push yourself forward, and drop feet-first into the deep snow. A dawdle. I was first to take the plunge under the swirling, noisy and buffeting blades. I had not factored in the detail that it was simply a big, well-used metal box with an engine. The door edge was a bit frayed and, as I pushed forward, the seat of my trousers became snagged on frayed metal. I was stuck and pitched forward, with the seat of my pants held fast, my upper body pulling me out to pitch me headfirst onto the boulders. The alert winch-man saved me from more injury by quickly and firmly pushing on the small of my back, thus breaking the helicopter's grasp on me and allowing me to stay relatively upright. It was still not controlled, and I fell on my side. I suffered minor bruising and major embarrassment, as well as a draught in my nether regions as the arse was ripped out of my trousers. The others evacuated without incident and avoided the stretcher that followed. Then we were left in the snow in a helicopter-induced blizzard.

# CHAPTER 19

B ACK in Bo'ness, however, mountain rescue could not
be further from the mind of the community as it anticipated the biggest annual event in their calendar: the
Bo'ness Fair. It is a huge occasion in the town and is, certainly
for many, bigger than Christmas. In terms of policing, it starts
months before, with planning both in terms of the police order but also in attending the 'Fair Committee' co-ordination
meetings. 'Kirkin' the Queen' the Sunday before the actual
Fair itself was the first event. Then it was the 'Fair En'e', the
night before, with the walking the Arches leading in to the
big day, the Fair itself. At eleven in the morning, Hamebiders
the world over get goosebumps. Why? Because it is time that
the Bo'ness Fair Queen is crowned, and it is a regal affair. It is
a big, complicated policing day. Several marches in the morning, the judging of the Floats, the Crowning Ceremony and
then the big parade: floats, children, bands... it is huge. Then
comes the big party and music at Douglas Park in the evening.
It is completely community-based, and it is good for local police to be involved. By evening the alcohol can get the better
of one or two, but it usually is under control. I return briefly
to the Fair later in my service and, therefore, later in the book.

Part of a Sergeant's duties involved checking the Constable's monthly claims for expenses. If an officer worked more

than one hour overtime, a refreshment allowance of £2.90 could be made. I am not sure the exact amount; it was a while back, but was not far off that amount. It was to compensate for having to buy a refreshment. If, however, an officer had to work away from their normal office for a day – a full shift – they could claim a larger amount. I think that was nearer £4, and was called subsistence allowance. My job was to check such claims. Did they do the hours? Had they worked away for the period claimed? In short, I needed to verify each claim and make sure the total claimed was correct. Not difficult, one would think.

Back to internal politics. I was summoned to the Inspector's office, where the Chief Inspector in charge of the sub-division was waiting to see me. He handed me a completed expenses form. I could see I had signed it. He asked me what it was? I replied, honestly, 'it is an expenses form'.

He said 'I know what it is. Why did you sign it?'

After having a look, I replied 'because it is correct'.

He then told me that we do not pay subsistence allowance. This was news to me. I told him I had not seen that order.

'It is not on an order. We just don't pay it; he can have refreshment allowance.'

Being as thick as a short plank, I continued my dialogue with 'but he worked away from the office for four days; he is entitled to claim subsistence allowance'.

'It doesn't matter what he worked. We do not pay it. Are you listening?' He went on: 'So you will have to get him to change his claim and re-submit it.'

I was now in full flow. 'I don't think so. I will not ask him to change a claim he is perfectly entitled to. If you want that, then you will have to ask him.'

He then got really annoyed and called me a Rebel. I asked the Inspector to give me the Statutory Instruments book. Policing in these days was regulated by the Police (Scotland) Act. Obviously certain things are reviewed and changes are made. Allowances, for example. Their changes are captured in the Statutory Instruments book, which – by definition – reflects the legal status of current conditions. He said he did not need to see the book; he was perfectly well aware of the regulation relative to allowances. I said that we were beyond that issue, and I asked if he could define a rebel. He was not for playing, so I suggested one might loosely define it as someone who usurps the law of the land. 'The Statutory Instruments are just that. Who is the rebel?' He asked me to leave. He did approach the officer concerned, who backed down and accepted the lesser allowance. So I not only wasted my time; I irked another boss.

I had another chance to irk him soon after that. I forgot to mention a quirk in staffing. Whilst stationed at Bo'ness, I also was Sergeant for Maddiston. So I hustled between both on a daily basis. An anonymous letter warned that a young boy was being neglected by being deliberately left in the family house on his own every Friday night. I instructed the troops to call at about ten in the evening and give me a call if they found anything. I duly got the call and joined them at the house. It was very clean and warm. There was a lit gas fire, protected by a suitable guard. There was a ten year old boy, in his night attire, watching a video with his supper on a tray. On the tray was a slip of paper with a telephone number. It was where his mum, dad and little brother were. Given the circumstances, I was totally relaxed in the knowledge he was in no danger and unlikely to come to any harm. I had no choice, however, than to get his parents here to explain why we were at their house. He called, and in less than five minutes they were home. I told them about the letter, and also that I would not be reporting them for anything as they had not committed an offence. I went on to explain about the Children and Young Persons Act and the relevant section about abandoning children, further clarifying that it was clear that any abandonment had to be coupled with the child coming to harm or likely coming to harm. This situation did not satisfy that section of the Act, and I would reflect that in the incident log. We left them with that assurance. They were a bit rattled, and worried about why anyone would report them.

Then it was the usual Monday backshift 'twenty-twenty vision' telling off. I was asked to explain my decision. I said the Act was not breached, as to be complete the two parts had to be there. Clearly they were not. I don't think he was even interested, and instructed me to have the parents charged and reported. I tried one more angle. I said the young lad had been out all night playing football with his pals. The garage site they were in was nearer the house his parents had been in than his own home. In fact, if he had stayed out another five minutes or so, he would have been out when the officers called. He knew exactly where his parents were: two streets over, and about one hundred yards as the crow flies. But it was all to no avail. Get them charged and reported. I refused, saying it was not lawful. He was making an internalised decision, based on how it would affect him. The fact he was going to traumatise a decent family was not even a consideration. Anyway, he got someone else to do the deed. The Procurator Fiscal returned the papers to the police with a question about relevance. No further action was taken.

Whilst heading out to go to Maddiston one evening, I was diverted to a male who intended to commit suicide by jumping from the old Kinneil Pit Winding Tower. He was at the very top and right at the edge, looking like he meant business. The Fire Service arrived soon after me, and we were working out how to get him down. It was going to be tricky. If he really was serious, there was no way we could get near enough in time to secure him in some way. Then I thought, *his mother will sort this out*. I was not confident and, may I say, I was not alone in thinking that. Anyway, I arranged that one of my officers got the guy's mother. She arrived soon after, and the whole thing was ended in five minutes. She adopted the direct approach. She shouted at him that he better come here right this minute or she would give him something to commit suicide about. She added: 'And I mean it! Get yourself down here right now; you are making a fool of yourself'. He came right down, and we got him home along with his mum and the family doctor.

That same week, we had a sudden death in the main street in Bo'ness. I was in the office when I got a call to say that the lady had identification: her Regional Council bus pass. A different animal from today's all-conquering variety. The officer asked me to call the Regional Council and get her address, as it was not on the pass. He gave me her name and the pass number. My conversation with the lady in the Regional Council was amusing, if dealing with the death of another can ever be amusing. I explained who I was, what had happened, and what we needed from her records. She was reluctant, but agreed to do it if she called back on the police number. She did that and, after listening to my request, she told me the old lady's address. Then she asked me, 'is she really dead?' I confirmed she was, indeed, really dead. The woman then said: 'Oh, good. We don't often get informed of a death. I can cancel her pass.' Small mercies, I thought.

Decisions in any walk of life are not made in isolation. They will likely include factors such as: what am I trying to achieve? What am I hoping will be the outcome? What evidence do I have, and what is happening – or has happened – that puts me in the position of having to make a decision? There are other factors and influences involved in decision-making; perhaps less tangible, even superlunary, but to my mind just as important as the more obvious tangible influences.

A book on policing cannot be complete without a reference to decision-making – in particular the less tangible, but no less real, influences. Underpinning all police activity and decision-making, at all levels, lurk the following: discretion, corruption, ethics, and perhaps I should also include, decisions made in the Public Interest. All can be contentious, and often they can overlap. In terms of discretion, Simon Bronitt and Philip Stenning, in a 2011 paper for the *Criminal Law Journal* entitled 'Understanding Discretion in Modern Policing', argue that discretion is a ubiquitous and legitimate aspect of modern policing. They go on to say that its scope and limits are poorly understood. The under-noted two paragraphs I have reproduced from the 'Police Manual', 1931 edition. In terms of this section, I thought them to be of interest:

An Address to Police Constables on Their Duties by The Late Right Hon., Lord Brampton. One of Her late Majesty's Judges from 1876 to 1898.

**Meddlesomeness:** Beware of being over zealous or meddlesome. These are dangerous faults. Let your anxiety be to your duty, but no more. A meddlesome constable who interferes unnecessarily upon every trifling occasion stirs up ill-feeling against the Force and does more harm than good. An over zealous man who is always thinking of himself and desiring to call attention to his own activity, is very likely to fall into a habit of exaggeration, which is a fatal fault, as I shall presently show you.

Discretion: Much power is invested in a police constable and many opportunities are given him to be hard and oppressive, especially to those in his custody. Pray avoid harshness and oppression; be firm but not brutal, make only discreet use of your powers. If one person wishes to give another into your custody for felony you are not absolutely bound to arrest. You ought to exercise your discretion, having regard to the nature of the crime, the surrounding circumstances and the condition and character of the accuser and the accused.

Be very careful to distinguish between cases of illness and drunkenness. Many very serious errors have been committed for want of care in this respect. Much discussion has on various occasions arisen touching the conduct of the police in listening to and repeating statements of, accused persons. I will try, therefore, to point out what I think is the proper course for a constable to take with regard to such statements.

Another way to look at this question might be gleaned from Officer Jim, a fictional character who appears in the 1999 film *Magnolia*:

> A lot of people think this is just a job that you go to take a lunch hour, job's over, something like that. But it's a twenty-four hour deal, no two ways about it. And what most people don't see, just how hard it is to do the right thing. People think that if I make a judgement call, that's a judgement on them. But that's not what I do and that's not what should be done. I have to take everything and play it as it lays. Sometimes people need a little help. Sometimes they need to be forgiven and some-times they need to go to gaol. Now, it's a very tricky thing on my part, making that call. The law is the law and heck if I'm gonna break it. You can forgive someone. Well, that's the tough part. What can we forgive? Tough part of the job, tough part of walking down the street.

Now tell me a police officer who would not agree with Officer Jim, and who has not walked that same street. Police discretion is a vague term that has an appropriately vague definition. There is one definition I will quote that supports Officer Jim's dialogue and it is: 'Discretion is defined as the decision making power afforded to police officers that allows them to decide if they want to pursue police procedure or let someone off with a warning'.

Lord Scarman, in his report after the Brixton Riots in 1981, makes an important observation when referring to the maxim 'let justice be done though the heavens fall'. He opines that while that may be apt for a Judge, if followed to the letter by a police officer it can lead to tactics that will be disruptive to the fabric of society. To wrap up the 'academia', I go back briefly to Bronitt and Stenning who further support the whole concept of sensible police discretion thus: 'It is necessary because limited resources make it impossible to enforce all laws against all offenders and strict enforcement would have harsh and intolerable results'.

I would also add that legislative process of common law and statute law – the latter conceived at the centre – is too cumbersome and unwieldy to fit neatly and appropriately to every circumstance encountered by every police officer. That is why we have courts, Judges, defence lawyers and stated cases, and – dare I say – discretion.

Having laid out my thoughts this way, I now confess. While every one of these issues are in themselves important concerns, what is not in question is that none of them featured very highly in my thinking as a front line police officer, certainly in my early years. Not that I was unaware of them or that I never gave a thought to them. No, it's just that there were more pressing needs. Surviving my probation was uppermost; getting the job done, learning, surviving, focusing on day-to-day tasks. It was that simple. Also, the notion of there being corrupt officers never actually crossed my mind in my Constable days as a police officer. Yes, there was the occasional mention of an officer somewhere who had crossed some line or other, but as none were in my area and I did not know them – coupled with the fact I never worked with any officer who displayed, directly or indirectly, any corrupt thought or behaviour – I never saw it as a problem. Perhaps I was naïve; they now have a department set up to do little else but investigate corrupt officers. If I can reassure the reader, or even myself, as to the standard of many police officers, I do so by using the words of the German philosopher Immanuel Kant, who said 'the starry heavens above me and the moral law within me'. So perhaps we are reassured by describing our local community officer as a person of integrity with his, or her, head in the clouds. Perhaps I go too far.

When I was on my Sergeant's course at the Scottish Police College at Tulliallan, one of the Superintendents running the course – an intelligent and decent man of vision, Iain McKie – chaired a session on ethics, standards and corruption. It was only one session, but I never forgot it. We discussed various scenarios. For example, you catch a young mother shoplifting some food. When speaking to her, she tearfully explains that she has is a single parent with two young children. She has nothing in the house to eat and has run out of money. Her allowance will not be due for two days. Question: 'Do you arrest her and report her, noting her plea in your notebook to use in your report as her confession?' A simple question, really. Our discussion ranged over ethics, discretion, and public interest. It might not surprise you to know that some officers were not 'taken in' by her tears, and were quite happy to say that their job was not to make such decisions on the basis of the circumstances. A crime had been committed, she gets charged and reported. It is up to others to consider her plea and make a decision. Not all had that view, and a 'healthy' debate ensued. One thing I found interesting was that the majority of the 'hang her and be damned' brigade came from the bigger, city forces. I was not convinced then – and I am still not convinced – that if each one of them had been exposed to a different police management regime, they would not necessarily have made that same decision. I think it was more about the way they had been 'brought up' in the service. Maybe they faced a harsher environment than their more rural cousins faced, and because of that their view was firmer. Who knows? Apart from anything else, it gives a flavour of how – when the single service centralisation emerged, dominated by the urban forces – decisions on styles of policing, insisted upon by the centre, caused tension in some of the remoter areas. Back to the hypothetical situation we debated. It was not so hypothetical. Many of us could relate similar scenarios.

I had not long been promoted and had still to go on the course. A woman was reported by the gas board, or whatever they were called back then, for having broken into the meter in her house and emptied it. The gas meter in her house operated by putting money in the meter, thus paying for an amount of gas. You had to pay before the product was released to you. The amount taken was about £37. Obviously she could not access her gas supply until the meter was repaired and until she paid what she had taken. I hesitate to say 'stolen'. When we spoke to her, she explained that she had no money and her three children were due to go back to school after the holiday. She needed the money to buy shoes for each of them and food for the rest of the weekend. She was desperate. There was money in her house; the problem was that it resided in the meter, right in front of her. A temptation. She asked what I would have done? She was cautioned, charged and reported. Should she have been? Did we have a choice? It further complicates the situation when you consider that not all the money belonged to the gas board. There was always a discount paid back when the meter box was emptied. One could argue, some of the £37 was to be given back to her, so in effect we reported her for stealing – in part – her own money. A further complication, in my view, was that some customers did not have cash meter boxes and paid by direct debit or some other non-cash method. If they failed to pay for gas used, it would be a civil, bad debt situation. No police involvement. So was there a 'public interest' consideration? None of these things crossed our mind; we simply reported her.

Speeding and parking are other thorny subjects. It is reasonable, in my view, for a police officer to stop a person speeding in his or her car and – assuming the circumstances merit it – administer a warning. I don't even think it need be recorded. That is discretion. However, where does discretion reach a threshold in terms of who applies the discretion? These two examples did not finish well for me, in terms of retaining friendships. I was approached, twice over the years, by different friends. Both had been stopped speeding and both wanted me to put a word in the right place to have their case disposed of. In both cases I refused to become involved. Why? As I explained to them, though not to their satisfaction, I will not become involved in the legitimate decision of another officer. His decision not to apply discretion is his decision. While I might well have warned both, it is not my place to impose 'discretion' as a third party.

Parking is another 'constant' – in terms of letters, telephone calls and whatever – to get the ticket scrubbed. As I never issued one, I did not get into that arena – until, that is, I became the Local Unit Commander in Bo'ness. A local Member of Parliament, now deceased, called at my office to remonstrate about his wife being issued with a parking ticket in the town. She had parked her car on double yellow lines. He was unhappy, and said it should not have been issued and that he wanted it scrubbed. I got the Traffic Warden to the office. The Traffic Warden and the MP were both local, were both in the same political party, and knew each other well. I started by asking if both were in agreement the car was indeed on the yellow lines at the times stated. Complete agreement. I asked the MP, on what basis do you suggest I withdraw the ticket? He did not have a good reason, other than suggesting his wife could not get parked anywhere else and the car had a Houses of Parliament parking permit. I let the Warden and the MP debate the issue. In the end, the MP left my office in a temper after the Warden came away with this logic: 'Tam, as I see it your car was just like the Belgrano – in the wrong place at the wrong time'. (A Falklands War reference to an Argentinian light cruiser which was sunk by a Royal Navy submarine.) I did not write off the ticket. Why? It was a matter of staff respect and trust. I respected his decisions.

Quite often 'discretion', in my opinion, is confused with not taking action because it would cause too much trouble. An example. In one area, the worshippers at a local church parked with gay abandon on double yellow lines outside the church, every Sunday. As many as twenty or more of them. They are never dealt with. Yet not one hundred yards away, tickets are issued. I expect the worshippers feel that it is trivial and, in any case, does not apply to them. When I see them I am reminded of a speeding case – a lot more serious than the double yellow line worshippers but, in terms of attitudes, not that different. It concerns Barrister Constance Briscoe, in the speeding points case of ex-Cabinet Minister Chris Huhne MP, when being sentenced at the Old Bailey to sixteen months' imprisonment for lying to the police. The judge said that she 'had considered respect for the law was for others'. I wonder if Socrates had people like these in mind when he wrote 'a system of morality which is based on relative emotional values is a mere illusion, a thoroughly vulgar conception which has nothing sound in it and nothing true'.

An interesting thought about the whole area: when does discretion or a public interest decision cross the line into corruption? When it results in a benefit to the officer. Is that cash, or goods, or simply to retain a friendship? All might be seen as a benefit. Whatever one fears, it is counterproductive to apply a blanket ban or to hog-tie a whole force to draw back from a perfectly acceptable police practice. I urge you to remember Kant and, if a problem does emerge – unless it swamps the whole service – deal with it on a case-by-case basis.

Lastly, one cannot apply discretion if an independent victim is involved. Public Interest decisions are also worth a minute or two of your time. One might ask, where is the line between 'in the interest of the public' and 'in the interest of the establishment', and are they the same thing? Does Aristotle have it nailed when pondering the notion that 'common interest' is the distinction between 'right' constitutions in the common interest and 'wrong' constitutions in the interest of the rulers? Where is the balance, or is there a balance?

The most obvious manifestation of such decisions, in the criminal justice world, lies with the Procurator Fiscal who will put his or her pen through a case, or desert a case and use 'public interest' as the reason. The whole concept of public interest lies deep in political philosophy. Thomas Aquinas would have you believe the common good would be the end of government and law, whereas Jean Jacques Rousseau suggests the common good to be the main object and purpose of government. However it is defined, one thing is certain: it can mean whatever the powers of the day want it to mean, and if not controlled it can mean different things to different people.

Whilst the officer in charge of an area and working closely with the community, I was overseeing a serious incident. It involved serious assaults and violent people. The officers investigating knew exactly what had happened and who was responsible. The trouble was that we could not get people to make statements and 'grass' on the culprits. It took weeks, and my intervention. I went round to see some of those involved. Each one more violent than the other. They were planning retaliation, and I feared a turf war. Anyway, for various reasons – not least because I had worked the area before in a lesser rank and they all knew me, and because I spent a long time persuading them that a turf war would not be good for anybody, particularly them – I managed to get enough corroborative evidence to arrest one of the alleged culprits. That was duly done, and he was reported. The suspect was detained on remand until his trial. By coincidence, whilst on remand he had a different crime to stand trial for. He was taken from prison, found guilty after the trial, received a custodial sentence and returned to prison. He now was in prison for two reasons. Then it was our day at court with him. We went round the doubting witnesses the night before, on a last minute reassurance and trust-building exercise. They dutifully turned up to give evidence. Over to the Procurator Fiscal, the criminal justice system, and decisions made in the public interest. The process of getting a suspect being held on remand from the prison to court involves paperwork. You will not be surprised to know that the paperwork to get someone out of remand status is different from the paperwork required to get a person serving a custodial sentence out. Well, what do you know? They arrived at the prison with the wrong paperwork. He could not be released. Decision of the Procurator Fiscal: do not sort out the paperwork and get him out for the trial – no, simply desert the case. Reason? 'In the public interest.' How does one explain that decision to a group who wanted to rip his head off, but were persuaded to trust the police, the system, and do the right thing? We informed them of the decision. They left us without a name. It took a long time to gain some respect in these circles again. How was that decision in the public interest?

In another situation, a Procurator Fiscal was giving a presentation to a community group. It was very busy, with a lot in attendance. There were various service leaders from the local council, including me. The Fiscal used a PowerPoint presentation; it was slick, and presented very professionally. When finished, the person chairing the meeting invited questions from the floor. A wise old gentleman, a retired local councillor, asked 'Mr Fiscal, is it right you walk on water?' Incredulous looks and a pregnant pause hit the hall. The Fiscal asked that the question be repeated as he had not heard it properly. I do not think one person in the hall believed him. The chair – in trepidation, I think – asked that the question be repeated. Same question came out, this time a bit louder. The Fiscal looked a bit unsure and said he really did not understand the question. The response from the retired local councillor was quite explicit and direct, and perhaps underlined the issue of an authority that cannot be easily challenged: 'You claim to make decisions in the public interest. When were you last in this town?' The Fiscal had never been. His tormentor then asked, 'if you have never been here and never met any of us, how can you make decisions in our interest?' The 'debate' continued, and covered drug warrants and how he and the criminal justice system were making things so much more difficult for the police to deal with local dealers because of the decision not to allow Justice of the Peace warrants. The whole thing got quite fractious. Then, to make matters worse, I was summoned to the floor to explain the local police difficulties since the search warrant changes. I said my piece under the glare of an obviously unhappy Fiscal. The whole thing ended, and tea and scones were ready for us all. The Fiscal rammed his documents into his 'important' pilot briefcase and headed out to his car without socialising. As he left, he accused me of setting him up and said he would be calling the Chief Constable. I don't know if he did; he had probably calmed by the morning. He was not set up. Procurators Fiscal are public servants; they are entitled to be questioned about their practices, stand cheek-by-jowl beside the people who pay their wages, and have an adult debate without getting angry. Coincidently, he was the same person who – when a Depute Procurator Fiscal at Stirling in 1991 – decided to take no criminal proceedings against Thomas Hamilton, taking the view that his conduct 'had approached but not crossed the border of criminality'. He marked the papers, no crime libelled, not in the public interest. A final thought: does the victim not have a voice in the process?

I will finish this whole section with a true story of compromise, discretion, and 'public interest'. It did not involve me, but did involve two well-respected officers and I tell their tale by way of paying tribute to them and a way of policing that is unfortunately vanishing. It happened a bit to the north of Tullibody, Denny or Bo'ness. Two resourceful police officers, getting on with their job, came across poaching on a big scale one evening. They got to the shore and secreted themselves in undergrowth as the offending craft came in from the water to disgorge the poached salmon. As the boat neared shore, a few local villagers appeared to greet it. In fact, there were a bit more than a few. One of the villagers roared out a warning in Gaelic. The senior of the two Constables – who also had the Gaelic – roared even louder that they had better come in or things would get worse. The boat landed. It had seven 'poachers' and a lot of fish aboard. A stand-off ensued. Our Gaelic-speaking officer was inventive as well as resourceful. He saw that one of the poachers was an officer in a branch of Her Majesty's armed forces. Their weak spot, and a bargaining tool. He – the military gentleman – was not himself local, but had a local friend. He stood a chance of being disgraced, and seeing his career ended. After discussion, a solution was reached. The police would arrest two poachers, and they would also take possession of a number of fish; less than ten. The remainder of the fish would stay with the other poachers, who would make a quick exit. And so it came to pass that in a Sheriff Court a few months later, two local men pleaded guilty to taking fish without a permit and catching them by illegal means. The fine was shared out amongst the whole of that night's crew, just as the remaining fish had been. Honours were even, reputations saved. The military officer continued his successful career. The police gained in terms of their reputation, and the community and the police continued to work in harmony. The Public Interest was served. Well, certainly to their satisfaction.

# CHAPTER 20

L IFE as Sergeant in my double station role was coming to an end. A new Area Commander seemed to have me low in his priorities and to quote himself, when speaking to me a few years later at the time of his retirement from the police service: 'When I started in the area I was briefed on all my supervisory staff. Your reputation was not high, and I was advised to get you moved from Bo'ness and the front line. Hence your transfer to Crime Prevention'. He had the grace and decency to say more, though. 'However, the more I got to know you, the more I understood you and realised that my early thoughts and briefings about you were wrong.'

So I was heading for a new experience, based on a misunderstanding. Nothing new there. I had been about six years as a front line Sergeant, and now I was heading for a really new adventure. Life is never dull in the modern police service. The next section is not about fighting and frolicking on a Friday night, a phrase I repeat. By definition, therefore, it will have fewer standalone tales of derring-do – or should that be 'front line follies'? However, it is no less important – perhaps more so – to the safety of the community. In that respect I will try to explain what I did by using examples, lessons learned, and doubts and opinions gleaned from my own experiences. The Crime Prevention and Community Involvement Department was based in a detached, standalone police office on the main street in Camelon. I had two Constables to manage. Two officers, in a run-down shack of an office – not the forefront of policing and, if left to some senior officers, never likely to be. My career has plunged from being trusted to run a single station, Hamish Macbeth style, whilst still in my probation, to a policing dead end.

The majority of policing rolls along from incident to incident, without much – if any – time being devoted to the causes of the incidents, the crimes. That is not a criticism of the officers on the front line; it is simply the reality of their job. Communities demand action on a whole range of issues; speeding, parking, dog fouling, anti-social behaviour, young people and alcohol – and in particular where they get it – and so much more. A lot of the activity has not a lot to do with what one might imagine as crime. Officers have little opportunity to dwell on the root causes of the things that create such demands on their time. In addition, there is always the pressure from local Councillors and letters of complaint from Members of the Scottish Parliament and Members of the UK Parliament. It is endless.

So who has time to understand the causes of crime and what might be put in place to deal with them? It can only be those in the ranks of the Crime Prevention Department. Or perhaps the Community Safety Department, as many are now titled. I started on a Monday. I had no idea what my officers did; I suppose that tells another tale. If I am to lambast other managers for their reaction to crime prevention, what have I been doing to find out about it? An early lesson; the department did not go in for a lot of self-promoting. I got the feeling I was swirling into a backwater. Well I, as sure as guns are made of iron, was not going to be swirled anywhere. We had to get into the mainstream. If Crime Prevention was important, it had to get on the police agenda. I made it my mission to do something about that. I have to say, brick wall and head came to mind.

Another historical perspective; this time, a statement from one of the early movers, referred to in an earlier chapter about the beginnings of policing as an organised force: Sir Robert Peel, MP:

It should be understood at the outset that the principal objective to be attained is the prevention of crime. To this great end, every effort of the Police will be directed. The security of persons and property will thus be better effected than by the detection and punishment of the offender after he has succeeded in committing the crime.

Even before that, in 1763, on the subject of crime and punishment, the Italian theorist Cesare Beccaria proposed the following: 'It is better to prevent crimes than to punish them'. So with such support for Crime Prevention, why did the police service relegate such a high, laudable ideal to a distant second place in their thinking? Why, despite evidence to the contrary, did the detection of crime take over as their key objective? And even if they understood that other services had more control over crime reduction than they did, why was so little effort made to move that agenda along? I think it was about ego, control, and the retention of power by certain senior managers in the police service over a good many years. It is also important when considering this issue to ask the question: why did the other services with influence over the causes of crime not step up to the plate and make their influence felt? I am sure I was not the first to realise all this. So, while I questioned the police role, I had even more questions about the role of Local Authorities, Health Boards, and more. One cannot lay all the blame at the door of Chief Constables.

While, to repeat, this is not a thesis on policing, I will spend some time exploring the things I unearthed and the behaviours I encountered during that term of my service. I spent time asking, reading, and trying to understand the ethos of the department and – importantly – its aims and objectives. What became clear, the harder I looked, was that it was not set up as expected; there was no clear direction. In the main, senior police management were not invested in it, nor did they show much interest. The fact that the top objective in the Police Act is to prevent the commission of offences had absolutely no impact. Catching is much more sexy.

The majority of police strategic direction takes it down the detection route. In short, the whole system was reactive, not proactive. However, I had a department to run and day-to-day issues to wrestle with. I sure was not going to build Rome in a day, if ever. So it was back to the basics of my earlier employment life and study of the workplace. Right back to organisation and methods; observe and learn. My first few days were spent simply shadowing, watching, and asking and occasionally doing the jobs myself. I was getting familiar with the 'how'. The 'why' questions were growing by the hour.

I was only in position two days when a woman contacted me. 'Which officer will be driving the minibus on Thursday?' she asked. I informed her that I was new to the position, and could she give me more information. I then said I would call back. On speaking to the troops I found that, for a long time now, this particular charity – the organiser being one of a previous boss's friends – relied on a police officer driving their minibus on a Thursday. Seems she had the rest of the week covered, but Thursday was a bad day for volunteers. I called back and agreed that it was short notice to stop the arrangement; however, this would be the last time we helped out in this way. She was not best pleased, and said she would go higher – and she did. I again found myself having to explain a decision. My response was about professionalism and that we were police officers. A senior officer argued that we were letting her down, and that she would think less of the service. My reply was along these lines: 'If it is so important, why don't we spread it out amongst the other officers, the CID, or the Traffic Department?' The reply was terse, asking if I was not seriously telling him that I thought the CID should be driving a community minibus. 'No', I replied, 'no more than my officers, who are professional officers like all the others. Are they somehow lesser officers?' He actually agreed with my argument, and challenged me to make a difference.

I moved on to the intruder alarm guru. His job was to record every single detail of every single alarm call the front line officers attended. There was a filing system of alarm activations going back years. He spent hours on that task. Needless to say I got to the why question, and amended the whole process including tweaking the annual return to the Scottish Office. An annual return asked how many alarm systems were in our police area and, of all the alarm activations, what percentage were false? After questioning my guru on the subject, it became clear that not every alarm installed was notified to the police. The bigger companies told us, but not the smaller companies and certainly not the scores of electricians who fitted alarms about the area. So we had no idea. In addition, nobody informed us when an alarm was taken out or when an organisation went out of business, leaving a dead alarm on the building. So we had even less idea. The annual return figure was therefore nonsense. We would just as well have been making it up. So that is what we did. We went over the last ten years of returns, worked out the percentage year-on-year rise in the number, then simply did it that way. The false alarm figure was treated in the same way. It was all mythical anyway. So I was making small changes, and freeing up time to get down to creating a department again. My biggest change was to ditch all the alarm files – years of useless history. It was so concise, one could go back several years and tell every time the alarm sounded in a particular location, including whether the activation was genuine or false and the reason. 'Why?' was the question. 'I don't really know', was the answer. Supplemental question: does it make any difference? The answer: no. The whole system was ripped out and replaced by a short-term dynamic process, reducing our input and – more importantly – that of the front line officers.

Another part of our job was speaking at schools and community groups, the latter usually about home security. The school talks were either focused on drug awareness or the consequences of crime. I would find out some disturbing – well, unsettling – information about both the school inputs some time later. I was an advisor on the board of a Regional Council establishment for young people. It was an alternative to being put in a residential school. For the young people – not me. I was at an open day in the company of some of them, and was speaking about the police input at schools. I asked if they had they been at any of the talks and, if so, did they have any thoughts or comments? One young man said the consequences of crime video and police input was really good. I asked if he could explain. He said that the police had no idea how to communicate with them. 'You do not understand how we think. My dad could not care less about me; he is more interested in his betting and the pub. I come in about nine at night and he shouts at me: "Where have you been? You will get in here before this in future! You have school in the morning! Your mother is sick of you!" I deliberately stay out even longer. He shouts at me every night. He never gets out his chair. He never puts his paper down. He cannot be bothered getting out of his chair. He does not love me enough to hit me. So, your message about "I will have no future if I don't get out of crime"? I have no future, so what are you telling me? It says I will embarrass my parents. Yes, I want to embarrass them; they don't care about me anyway. It talks about causing damage to the school, breaking the windows; it will cost money, and they will not be able to afford things like shirts for the football team. I hate school; good. You are telling me what I want to hear.' Some of the others agreed with him. I had no idea. These are national programmes. Did nobody check?

Drug awareness was a major part of our input to schoolchildren. The approach we followed was 'Just Say No to Drugs'. It was a national programme. The term was first penned – as far as I was aware – by Nancy Reagan in 1982, in the USA. The relationship between drugs and humans has been ongoing since we arrived out of whatever primeval swamp we emerged. In fact did we not enter a conflict with the Chinese in the 1800s about our right to trade in opium, conveniently called the Opium Wars? Many famous people, Royalty included, were able to purchase laudanum, or tincture of opium – an opium-based painkiller – freely at pharmacies during the Victorian era. It would appear it was, on occasion, spoon-fed to teething infants. As some do today with the prescription methadone. Women used it to ward off period pains. It was freely available, and popular. A Scottish Parliament Act of 1581 on drug use demonstrates that, even then, there was a struggle to control drug use amongst the population. The following is an extract of that document:

### Against superfluous banqueting and the inordinate use of confections and sweetmeats

Our sovereign lord and his three estates convened in this present parliament, understanding the great excess and superfluity used in bridles and other banquets among the mean subjects of this realm, as well within burgh as to landward, to the inordinate consumption not only of such stuff as grows within the realm, but also of sweetmeats, confections and spices brought from the parts beyond sea and sold at dear prices to many folk that are very unable to sustain that cost; for staunching of the which abuse and disorder, it is statute and ordained by our sovereign, with advice of his said three estates, that no manner of persons, his subjects, being under the degree of prelates, earls, lords, barons, landed gentlemen or others that [are] worth and may spend in yearly free rent 2,000 merks money or 50 chalders of victual, all charges deducted, shall presume to have at their bridles or other banquets, or at their tables in daily cheer, any sweetmeats or confections brought from the parts beyond sea, and that no banquets shall be at any upsittings after baptising of bairns in time coming, under the pain of £20 to be paid by every person doer in the contrary, as well of the master of the house where the effect of this act is contravened, as of all other persons that shall be found or tried partakers of such superfluous banqueting and escheating of the sweetmeats and confections apprehended, for which the provost and bailies within burgh and the sheriffs, stewarts, bailies, lords of regalities and their bailies to landward shall appoint searchers, to which searchers open doors shall be made of whatsoever house they come to search, under the pains to be esteemed culpable in the transgression of this act if they refuse; and the offenders being apprehended, to be taken and held in ward until they have paid the said pecuniary pains, to be employed the one half to the benefit of the ordinary officers and searchers and the other half to the poor of the parish.

No need for Justice of the Peace or even Sheriff warrants in those days. So it seems the use of drugs by the populace is frowned upon, and has been for a long time. Our contribution in Crime Prevention was to lecture school children. Our drug awareness input to schools involved a police officer taking the class for an hour, the teacher absenting her or himself. There was a set of photographs showing various drugs in different states of readiness to use and preparation. There were pictures of many of the organic drugs, including cannabis and heroin, in their plant states before processing into the drug. The aim was that if we made the pupils aware of the common drugs – what they looked like, describing the effects on the body and further explaining the danger involved in using such substances – that it should have the effect of stopping them using same. In fact, to put it the way one senior officer explained it, 'the only thing that works is to frighten them'. So we did just that. Was if effective? You know, at that time I had no evidence to say that it worked, or what did work.

A discussion with the Drugs Officer for the local health board suggested that we carry out a study. The idea was to take three secondary schools in the area, do what we had been doing in one, do nothing in the second, and try one of the newer, study-based methods we had read about in the third. We could then monitor a section of the pupils in each and periodically revisit them over the next twenty years or so. It would be a big exercise and take place over a long period. However, we thought it the only way to establish which approach worked – or if any approach worked. It was not a revolutionary approach; simply an adaptation of work ongoing in the Netherlands, studied and reported on by Willy de Haes. That study used three approaches, plus a control group where no input was given. The least successful was the 'scare' approach – the 'Just Say No' group – compared to the other methods. De Haes provided a copy of the findings to the Health Board in Scotland at the time. However, the Government in Westminster insisted on the harsh approach. Not just in the Netherlands was there disquiet about the 'Just Say No' method and about police officers delivering substance messages in schools. The approach of demonising drugs and the scare tactics involved was being widely questioned. Many teenagers treated it as a challenge to try it out, simply because of the message. Adults tended to exaggerate the effects and the dangers, and the young people soon found that out and distrusted the message. The claim about 'gateway' drugs was ridiculed by many young people. Julian Cohen, who was prolific in this area and wrote many study papers and drug education packages, was sceptical of the scaremongering approach being adopted. In fact, he claimed there was evidence it was counterproductive. It is no wonder that many young people rejected our methods. He was clear; police know about the law, so stick to that. Health specialists know about drugs and the effects; involve them more, and create a discussion programme.

There were other reasons why young people did not trust the message. Several celebrities from the pop world, from stage, screen and our television sets were reported as using drugs recreationally, and the 'system' gave a knowing smile. I confess that the drug awareness input had me puzzled after the foregoing and after reading some academic studies on the subject. I attended a National Drug Conference in these days, when one of the main speakers was a recovering user. She described a hellish young life with no dad and a hopelessly addicted mum. Then she addressed the audience and challenged them. She said they would listen attentively to her, sympathise, have their dinner with wine, then retire to the bar where – before the night was over – some would be worse for wear of a substance far more dangerous and prolific than the 'drugs' they lectured to young people about. Young people, she added, are not stupid. They see the adults and understand the hypocrisy. Why is it all right for a senior police officer to get drunk? Why is it alright for pop stars, some who knowingly take drugs, to perform in front of the Royal Family and get everyone's adulation? Yet if you are unemployed and living in the less well-off parts of our towns and cities, you get treated like scum. Isn't it no wonder that the message has failed? A thought on education: 'To truly know a thing, one must experience it.

> To understand other people, one must come into contact with their lives and see their deepest needs. Then one can teach with true sympathy and what one has to give is well received
>
> *I. Ching*

I finish with a view of the USA's War on Drugs:

> Prisons bursting at the seams, mostly black, non-violent offenders. On release the majority will back in court, if not in prison in three years. What is outside to prevent their return? They have a record and even if there was a job, how many would get one? How is life inside going to improve the War on Drugs? Unintended consequences of tough politicians, making tough laws. Thousands of young persons, mostly men, rotting in prisons, at our expense. The prisons are full, the streets are full, of drugs. Who is winning what? We are insane.
>
> John Grisham,
> from his book *Rogue Lawyer* (2015)

Anyway, my plea to rethink fell on deaf ears. 'We cannot do nothing; we have to be seen to be doing something.' That was the order from on high, based on the assumption that our credibility would be damaged if we did nothing. So we soldiered on. Of course, substance input to vulnerable people is important; we just need to devise a programme that works. Intervention with 'at risk' families, when the children are toddlers, has been shown to work. In such programmes the approach is not about drugs; it is about life skills and development.

As I write, I see that the 2016 drug and alcohol deaths in Scotland have both increased.

# CHAPTER 21

A VERY successful crime prevention programme emerged from the United States of America in the early 1960s, from the State of Wisconsin. It was not labelled 'crime prevention', because that was not one of its aims. I suspect, however, that the psychologists and others – when planning it – may well have had that hope. It was initially designed to address educational failure, and involved working on the conscious mental process of the participants in the social environment and the health development of the children. It involved working with children of 'at risk' families from pre-school age. There were similar other programmes, as I understood it. However, the most-quoted was, and is, the High Scope Perry Preschool Programme. It dealt with the association of early intervention and its effect on later behaviour; in this case, apart from education and health issues it included anti-social behaviour. Among the factors required to ensure a level of success were things like robust staff development, meeting developmental needs, child-initiated learning, having small numbers in each class, and continuity with infant and other primary timetables. Important elements were that the children took responsibility for activities and, through that approach, learned to take responsibility for decisions made and their behaviour, their actions. It taught both the children and the parents to have boundaries for their behaviour, and a lot more. Subsequent evaluations have found it to be successful on many fronts. For example, results have included increased educational achievement, higher rates of employment, lower crime rates, lower rates of teenage pregnancy, and generally better health. A 1993 follow-up study on 27 year olds who had participated, conducted by Lawrence J. Schweinhart, H.V. Barnes and D.P. Weikart, evidences fiscal benefits; because a significant number of the participants stayed healthier, stayed out of prison and sustained longer term employment and earned more, they were less of a drain on the economy. They paid more tax, cost less in health care issues and in the criminal justice system. In fact, the study states the financial returns – in terms of taxes paid – significantly outweighed the initial programme cost. They specify by about 12.5 to 1. Another study, conducted by Clive Belfield, Milagros Nores, Steve Barnett and Lawrence Schweinhart when participants were aged 40 years, replicated that success by observing lower criminal justice costs, lower welfare costs, and more paid in taxes. That study followed the High Scope Perry Preschool Programme. It is reported in the Winter 2006 edition of the *Journal of Human Resources*, University of Wisconsin. Though that later study was not published until well after my Crime Prevention travails, I was fully aware of the programme and of earlier evaluations and of its success.

Another part of our routine day job involved giving crime prevention advice, mostly to householders and sometimes to businesses. That required specialised training. I first went to the course run by Strathclyde police at their training school at Oxford Street, Glasgow. It lasted a month, and was for Scottish officers. Later on, I was selected for the course at Stafford. That was at the internationally-recognised Home

Office Crime Prevention Centre. Again, it was a month-long course; I followed that up by attending the Home Office Architectural Liaison Course. It was all very intensive; however, I was learning new skills. Among much else, it covered designing out crime, the private space versus public space concept of reducing crime, zero tolerance, and a skill I found really useful in understanding how criminals operate – crime pattern analysis. When it was over, the Principal said we were trained to the very highest level, perhaps in the world, and that we should go back to our respective forces and assertively make our presence felt and make a difference. He added another thought, and it was that no matter how well you are trained, there is one area in which you will not be allowed to participate – that is terrorism prevention and advice on protecting economic key points, and more. The CID will not let you in that door. They will not be nearly as well trained or have half your knowledge, but it is about power and credibility and we have neither. In any case, they do not understand what your training entails and they confuse Criminal Pattern Analysis with Crime Pattern Analysis. In short, they only want analysis that shows them 'who did it'; they are less interested in analysis that prevents it being done in the first place. He was correct.

Back at force some months later, I broached the subject and was left in no doubt that was not an area a Crime Prevention Officer would be considered for. I might well be trained, but it did not compare with a CID officer's training or knowledge. By the way, he said that in a senior detective officers' meeting, so I was in no doubt about the high regard in which Crime Prevention was held. Reputation had to be earned, and we soldiered on undaunted. High regard from our communities was important; the rest was unimportant.

The department in Falkirk continued to change and be-come more dynamic, in terms of trying to get ahead of the game, getting onto the policing agenda, and – importantly – in making a difference in communities. Part of that involved giv-ing basic crime prevention advice training to Area Constables. The logic being that they are on the ground; why not invest in them by equipping them with the basic skills to be able to advise householders in their areas? We were genuinely busy, and attending public meetings in communities two and three nights a week. The staff was increased to four Constables, and still we were busy. A new Superintendent was on the scene, and he was totally committed to this approach. He reported regularly to the Chief Constable. It was during this fertile time in the development of the department that the notion of merging with the Criminal Investigation Department emerged. The joined-up entity would be called Crime Man-agement Services and, in that form, would deal with crime holistically. On reflection it was a reasonable idea; however, I am not sure enough work was done in preparation, and not all the parties were committed to the same extent. A comment early on probably was truer than the tongue-in-cheek way it was uttered: 'We [Crime Prevention] have got on the ladder without them [the CID] noticing. Better hang on, because when they do we will get pushed back off'. So despite the rhetoric, there was a road to travel. The main interaction was at the management end, and the front line troops got on with their respective duties largely unaffected. Some within the CID were really not happy with the merger, with one opining 'we are seriously highly trained specialists; you are not'. An-other development, just prior to that, was the work going on with the Central Regional Council to embed a police officer in their Policy Department for three years to develop a strategy to make communities safer. While some councils in Scotland had police officers linking in to their systems, this was different. A senior officer was to be completely seconded, embedded, in the Chief Executive's Policy Unit, working and being supervised by their management system. However, these were ideas and had not yet come to fruition, and would not for some time.

So, back to where I was: developing the staff, the department and myself, I hoped. I had undergone a serious amount of training, and I was getting to grips with the whole concept – and, importantly, gaining confidence. Liaison with the local authority at Falkirk and linking in to community groups was happening. The increased liaison with Falkirk Council offered an opportunity that eventually led to the development of a new national approach to giving safety advice for women. Without our close ties to Falkirk Council and the mutual trust that developed, what I next describe – and many other opportunities to help people in communities be safer – would not have emerged.

I was speaking about personal safety to a group of women in Falkirk one night. I was using the video provided; something that had been compiled by the Metropolitan Police and used in forces up and down the country. It was the first time I had done this particular talk. That was the domain of my troops. I was simply 'walking the walk'. I was not long into the video and answering a question when I realised I had picked the wrong audience. 'Walking the walk' looked like it was going to be walking the plank. A voice from the gloom shouted out 'do you show this rubbish to all the women's groups?' There was a murmur of support. I stopped the video and had the lights turned on. 'Why do you say that?' I asked. I was rounded upon by some very motivated women, who took no time to let rip and tell me it was totally out of context with their lifestyles. One pointed out that the woman in the video was telling her to park under a street light. 'What do I do if I don't have a car? What do I do if there are no street lights?' Another member of the group added: 'Where I get off the bus, I have to walk down a lane with no street lights.' They concurred that the video and advice was not only aimed at middle-class women, it did worse than that; it instructed them what to do. The assumption being that if they did not follow the instructions and they come to harm, it would be assumed it was their own fault; they were to blame. My talk was in ruins, but the night was just beginning. A long discussion took place, and I scribbled lots of notes. I got safely off the plank. My head was filled with hope and ideas. I was back on the shop floor in Cossor Electronics and I was listening, asking, learning and being invigorated. Back to the drawing board. I reported the incident and asked that we work with these women to produce our own guidance on their safety. Back to reality. There are dozens of these books; why do you think you could write a better one? No, there is no budget. I withdrew, but retained that dream and waited for my chance. It would take nearly a year, but it came along. But first, the other things that were happening.

My awakening continued, and I read a few back copies of the British Crime Survey and compared their crime rates with Police Recorded Crime. It was not a well-circulated or widely read document in Central Scotland Police. While I understood the gathering protocols to be greatly different, I still was taken aback at the difference in the respective crime rates. The police figures are restricted to a subset of notifiable crimes or offences that have been reported to, and recorded by, the police. A crime might be classed in this system as notifiable; that does not mean a victim has to tell the police. There is also a discrepancy in what is reported and what is recorded. Not all crimes or offences reported are necessarily recorded. What also can further complicate the police figures is that the recording protocol can and does change, and police activity that can give rise to crimes being uncovered and recorded is not consistent over every area. In addition, there can be changing behaviours in the public reporting. One report published in a British Crime Survey noted that figures based on police recorded crime were not considered statistically reliable for most crime types. The British Crime Survey is based on a series of questionnaires and interviews. It is not fettered by notifiable crimes. It is therefore argued that it gets a lot nearer to the actual reality of criminal activity. I will leave that to the statisticians, the mathematics and the criminologists to debate. What is not in doubt is that they consistently differ. When I studied the differences in the late 1980s and early 1990s, I saw the differences to be quite large. Sometimes the police rates were a half, and less than half, of those published in the British Crime Survey. Jon Bright, who was Director of Operations for Crime Concern at that time, is quoted as putting the difference much more starkly. He says that only about one quarter of all crime is actually reported to the police. He also states that the clear-up rates – detection rates, as the police tend to call them – are about 35% of what is recorded. In short, the Criminal Justice System is responding to less than 10% of all the crime that is committed. Coupled with that, I was also aware of the recording procedures in Central Scotland Police and the actual detection rates in force and throughout Scotland, and I realised he was not that far-fetched in his observations.

In terms of crime recorded, I can give a snippet of evidence from my own experience as a victim. Five cars in the street where I lived were deeply scored, to the metal, along the whole length of the nearside. It appeared that a person had come down the street and gouged a deep score in each one. Cost of repair to each was estimated at one thousand pounds; five thousand in total. It was recorded by the police as a single incident: same time, single culprit and same method. The officer referred to it as a series. So five victims, and one recorded crime. Is it any wonder the recorded crime rate is so different from the British Crime Survey crime rate? I mused, if that night there were no cars in the street – only five residents having a conversation, and the same person had stabbed all the residents – how would that have been recorded? A single crime? I don't think so. The recording system, designed by the criminal justice system, is flawed and disingenuous. It is not about victims, it is about the system.

The foregoing is not about police bashing. On the contrary; I believe in the police service, and I think they do an impossible job extraordinarily well. I do question some management practises and decisions, but these are a flea-bite compared to the selfless work carried every day by the police service. I just wish they would not become embroiled in politics. No, my point is about the need to recognise the important role other services have in reducing criminal behaviour and keeping communities safe. The police service should not be seen as the only solution, and they must not be left to carry on alone. The police service has little, if any, real long-term lasting influence over the causes of crime and things that make people unsafe or, in fact, safe in their communities. What have they to do with long-term unemployment rates, a factor well recognised to have an influence in criminality? What do the police have to do with cutting people's benefit to a level where some of them resort to petty theft just in order to survive? We were not involved in decision-making about housing policy, schooling, staff in housing projects, design of new build, and much more. In latter years we did get asked about one or two of these things. However, it was a relatively minor input.

The following is a small local example of that flawed process. In the early 1990s, Central Regional Council and Stirling District Council were working on a joint plan to change the face of Stirling Town Centre. Part of that included a pedestrianisation scheme incorporating restrictions of vehicle access at certain times and to certain areas. A lot of local businesses, 'influential' people and organisations were rounded up for discussions and attended meetings about the plans, where their voices were heard. The plans were to include enforcement issues. The police were not invited. An example of where decisions that may create offences were being made, yet the organisation which would be left to enforce the legislation – the bye-laws – was not included in the planning. D.J. Smith, in *Police and Policing in London* (London: Policy Studies Institute, 1983), puts it well: 'The police are not for the main part the prime movers, the initiators of the processes that control deviant behaviour. On the contrary, they work at the margins where the usual processes of control have broken down, they act as a continuation of more general efforts by the mass of people and institutions to maintain order, control and coherence. In other words, they are a small but extremely important element within a much larger complex of interrelated systems of control'.

Detecting crimes and presenting suspects to the Criminal Justice System is another area worthy of comment. In particular, the notion that the Criminal Justice System will be able to reduce crime. The percentage of crimes detected is under 50% of those recorded. I have said that crimes recorded by the police fall well below the real crime rates published by the British Crime Survey, over and over. Couple that with the low detection rates and with the low number of guilty perpetrators who actually get sentenced. My question in this area concerns those who regularly appear at court, many of whom return to prison on multiple occasions. If being caught, convicted and imprisoned was such a deterrent, why do we have so many repeat offenders? So why do the police seek to restrict crime figures? I believe it is about detection rates. Whether one agrees or not, the police service – in the main – is driven by catching offenders, and their detection rate is seen by them as the most important measurement of their success. I think they do believe that detecting offenders does reduce crime. Whether it does or not, it definitely is more satisfying to detect an offender, finish the report, and tie a bow round it. Preventing crimes that you did not actually know were going to happen is almost nebulous. All the more reason to involve methods, practices that other services would be responsible for. However, whenever crime is mentioned the other services think 'police'. It is a never-ending circle that is getting us nowhere. Whatever way it falls, detecting crime is important and front line officers are entitled to get job satisfaction and believe they are making a difference. It is, after all, what they are best at, and that is their contribution to making people safer. It is no fault of theirs that the whole system is not joined up; it never has been. Nor is it their fault that other services – the ones who can make a real difference, the ones who work with young people, those who carry out planning functions, those who design the built environment, and develop employment opportunities – have no responsibility for crime rates. They have as much, if not more responsibility to reduce crime than the police service. Perhaps if Local Authorities had the main responsibility for reducing crime rates, it might shift the focus from the police service. There is a danger in that thought, however. As I have to be convinced that Local Authorities and politicians understand more about causes of crime than the police service, which I doubt, they would simply embroil police services in politics and that would not work either. Whatever, something has to change. I used to wonder and did ask – to be treated like a fool – why fatal road accidents fall into the police indicator process. The police did not design or build the road, had no role in dealing with the roadside obstructions – such as trees and bushes that obscured visibility – and they certainly did not train people how to drive and use the road. It was becoming obvious that we needed to seek a new direction.

In the meantime, back at the ranch, we'd keep on keeping on, and we further developed our partnership with communities and the council. Neighbourhood Watch was the big thing, and my staff – which had doubled in size to four officers – were really hard at it attending launches of Neighbourhood Watch all over the Area Command. I forget the actual number, but in less than a year we had set up more than one hundred. Another change was to join the old Crime Prevention Panel with Neighbourhood Watch, and the Neighbourhood Watch and Crime Prevention District Committee. There were over two hundred people at the first Annual General Meeting of the new group. It was really successful.

One of our ventures was, in partnership with Falkirk Council, to hire Falkirk Town Hall and have a Crime Prevention Trade Fair. We invited lock companies, CCTV companies, alarm companies, safe companies, and lots more. We had in excess of thirty stalls as well as speakers, and on the day it was attended by well over a thousand people. A success. We were getting more calls from officers within the Council to advise on security issues, during new build, during renovation, and with existing problem areas. We worked with the Council to establish one of the first town centre CCTV systems in Scotland. It was a small system in Falkirk Town Centre. A rod for our own back. I say that tongue-in-cheek. We soon had demands from towns all over the area for systems. Crime Prevention was on the map and, from that first week in Camelon, a journey had been embarked upon. It was turned around, and it was creating sustainable safety partnerships. It was slowly gaining credibility; not with everyone, but it was moving. We still had to withstand the occasional jibe – 'sausage sizzlers' being the favourite. 'Hold your head up' was our watchword.

The work with Falkirk Council grew, and we increasingly were asked to examine and comment on troublesome community problems involving anti-social behaviour or just looking to enhance community safety involving design and layout. It was enjoyable, satisfying, and always challenging. Our recommendations did not always meet with universal approval, particularly the position of footpaths in housing estates. But that was fine; the important and positive thing was we were on board, contributing, and learning.

In terms of our approach, a fundamental cornerstone of our advice concerned public versus private space, and a thing called 'defensible space'. None of these things were new. The concept had been around for centuries. I have already made mention of some police history. Here is a minute snippet of some environmental safety examples, mostly near where I policed. However, you will not have to travel far to unearth similar examples near where you live. The principle is using natural landscape, or creating landscape, to create a barrier – a defensive barrier. The deep moats surrounding some castles is a perfect example of created defences. Both Hadrian's and Antonine's Roman walls being two more. In the case of the latter, the Romans adapted the landscape to create earth walls and ditches to mark and protect the extent of their Empire in Britain. Some ancient armies used heavy afforested areas, particularly Blackthorn or other naturally thorny species of plant life, to protect an exposed flank. Bringing that thinking forward, it can be preferable, cheaper and more environmentally acceptable – rather than constructing a large ugly fence – to create embankments, ditches and slopes around the perimeter of an industrial estate, then surmount the bank with hawthorn or blackthorn planting, further strengthened by intertwining them with bramble bushes. Using the same principle, it is possible to protect ground floor windows with aggressive shrubbery. A famous whisky distillery in Scotland 'employs' a flock of geese as an environmentally-friendly alarm system around the distillery.

These two case studies give a flavour of the public versus private space approach to helping reduce anti-social behaviour and vandalism. The public library in Larbert had been the subject of much concern and disputes between the police service, local people and local councillors, principally because it was constantly subject to large numbers of young people hanging about and many acts of vandalism being committed. Members of the public were, certainly in the evenings, afraid to use the car park behind it. Examination revealed a design feature that made it a favourite gathering place for young people. It was overhung on three sides, and there was a ledge under the overhang. A great place to gather and sit. Young people did just that. It had been ongoing for twenty years. Police attendance had little or no sustainable impact. It is also worth noting that the optimum age of people reported for offences was about 15 years. Examination of that statistic revealed that when the trouble started some twenty years before, they were not even born. Yet the trouble was a constant. The solution had to involve breaking the habit, reducing the 'gang hut' model. In short, turn what had been seen for years as public space into private space. A report containing that and other information, along with design recommendations, was submitted to Falkirk Council. Work was carried out on the design and the problem reduced markedly.

A typical street in Falkirk. There was a wide grass area halfway down the street on one side; it split the line of houses on that side of the street. At the grass area, four houses had been built at right angle to the street, forming an 'L'-shape with the other houses. A public footpath ran from the street across the grass area, right along the front of the four houses on the angle. The access gates to these houses were on the footpath. In addition, the house in the block of four – furthest from the street – had its gable end facing directly on to the grass area, with no barrier. In other words, the public grass area butted directly against the gable wall of the house. The residents in these four terraced dwellings had been suffering from inordinate amounts of anti-social behaviour for many years. Particularly the house furthest from the roadway; the one with the gable end unprotected. The council had a huge file on the issue, as did the police. The blame was passed about like a parcel at a children's party. No lasting solution was found, despite the inordinate amount of time and effort expended over the years. The residents were at their wit's end, and many had moved out over the years. I went through the same procedure as just described with the library. It was principally the same problem, requiring a similar solution. Create a private area around the houses and reduce the public area, and in doing so also create defensible space. Reroute the pathway away from the four houses, to the other side of the grass area. Leave the section giving access to the houses and block with a barrier of some sort – a wall and or fence – thus creating a 'private' area. In terms of the gable end, exposed to the grass and constant games of football and more, create a garden area and plant it with thorny, aggressive shrubbery to create a barrier. It all had a positive effect.

My last word on that approach and where one might see it used to this day. At the entrance to some new housing estates, pillars are positioned on either side of the entrance, sometimes with a short section of decorated wall. The road surface at the entrance is made of red tar. All of this gives the appearance of a 'private' area. Can I go in there? Obviously you can; however, it causes you to think twice. Another example might be at a drive leading up to a dwelling; in the country, most likely. You see a 'private' or 'private: access only' sign. Are you allowed to go past the sign? Well, there is nothing illegal if you do, nor is there a physical barrier. However, many will not enter. Both the latter are psychological barriers turning public space to private space. Both have been shown to be effective. I included these to demonstrate that there is more to preventing crime or anti-social behaviour than police patrols and arrests. If we don't look about and embrace new ideas in this arena, we will be chasing the same problems round the same corners for ever; the only thing that will change will be the actors.

# CHAPTER 22

BACK at the ranch, I was challenged by a doubting detective supervisor to demonstrate Crime Pattern Analysis. The way he broached the matter showed it was a challenge. He said 'I've heard you going on about the Crime Pattern Analysis stuff. Well, we have a problem with cars being stolen from a the municipal buildings car park. So show me how it works'. He really was not convinced. I examined a full year of reported crimes in the car parks surrounding the location. There were actually four car parks. One at the front of the buildings, one at the back, and a third to the west side. The fourth was also to the front; however, it was the Town Hall car park. I examined every detail. Exact location, time, the day, what had been stolen, the method of committing the crime (MO), where property was recovered, who – assuming arrests – had committed the crimes, and a bit more. I was able to demonstrate that stolen cars were not the problem. There had been five. All of them during the daytime on a Friday or a Saturday, and from the car park immediately in front of the Municipal Buildings. There was not really a useable pattern beyond that. The major problem, accounting for the vast majority of incidents, was thefts from parked cars in the Town Hall car park. I also established that these crimes were mostly on the nights when there was something on at the venue, and that they happened between seven o'clock and ten o'clock on these evenings. There was more; however, that was the main thrust of my report, and I told him that if he wished to mount an operation, he should stick to the nights there was an event on in the Town Hall and stick to the times highlighted. His answer was to destine my report to a pile of papers on his desk. In fact, I am not convinced he bothered to read it. He then ran an operation and had one officer looking onto the front car park and one looking onto the rear car park for a week during office hours, between ten o'clock in the morning and four o'clock in the evening. They saw nothing. So we might have been making progress, but not in every corner.

In addition to our work, there were external clues and pressures. Central Government was getting in on the act, and urging police services and local authorities to get their act together and work together. There were several high-level reports indicating that we, the police service, should be doing more to develop partnership working, on the basis that the key to preventing crime lay with other services. A Police (cc) Circular No. 6/1984 identified this, and urged work to engage with partners. It was also circulated to Chief Executives of Local Authorities. It fell on stony ground. A further Police (cc) Circular No 5/1990 on the partnership approach to crime prevention reminded recipients of the 1984 circular and asked what had been done? Not a lot, was the answer. This was supplemented by the widely heralded Morgan Report and the Scottish Office 'Crime Prevention Strategy for the 1990s'. The heat was being turned up. While we would take advantage of such reports, things still moved like the Moine Thrust: slowly. Our strategy was to keep developing the department and looking for opportunities to move the agenda. We set out to take advantage of these reports, and assertively approached our local partners with a view to get things moving.

Then we got our big breakthrough. It was an exciting chapter, and had taken shape over the previous months through discussion and negotiating between the Chief Constable, William Wilson; Superintendent Muir; The Chief Executive of Central Regional Council, Douglas Sinclair, and his Depute, Keith Yates. Their discussion culminated in a report to the full council meeting on 11 November 1992. Among the recommendations were that the Council should establish a Community Safety Unit to be located in the Chief Executive's office, which would include a seconded police officer and another officer (not police) who would be expected to have a wide experience of community development. The unit would be guided by a Community Safety Steering Group, chaired by the Chief Constable and including high-level representation from major council departments and the voluntary sector. It would also have a budget of £70, 000 per annum. The project was approved, and would commence in the March of 1993. I agreed to take up the challenge and was convinced this was the first step on the road to moving the focus for preventing crime from the police service and actually convincing the other services they had a role and could positively contribute in creating sustainable safety in communities. I believed it then, and I firmly believe it today. It was not just my belief; it had all been laid out in the Morgan Report and the other documents. The Moine Thrust had jumped forward.

Before long, my partner in the two-person team was recruited and our journey began. It was uncharted territory; it was the first time in Scotland that a Regional Council had adopted this model to develop and implement a Community Safety Strategy for a Region, and the first time a senior police officer had participated in such a model. It was not the first time police officers had been seconded to councils, however, and in fact we had Constables embedded in the three District councils conterminous with Central Scotland Police. We would soon have one officer with the Forth Valley Health Board. We were convinced that the Criminal Justice System – important though it was – is, could not, cannot and never would be the sole answer to reducing and preventing crime. How often has a politician said that if we are hard on the criminal it will reduce crime? How often have you heard a Chief Constable ask for more police officers and more powers, with the argument 'if we have that, we can be more effective in reducing crime?' It is a myth. I am a real believer and supporter of the police service; I think we did, and do, carry out a seriously important function in keeping people safe, and I also believe that offenders need to be brought to the Criminal Justice System to be judged and – if appropriate – punished. I just do not believe that can be the only approach. While working to change the direction of the department, I was – apart from the training courses that opened my eyes to these issues – studying, and having a real think about the police function and the causes of criminal and anti-social behaviour. There were so many signals telling me there was more to it than a uniformed police officer on patrol, supported by a detective and a Traffic Officer. The Regional Council partnership would be the principal project.

I had run my course in the department and in 1993, ten years after gaining my Sergeant's stripes, I moved up another management rung to that of a police Inspector. I had earned my Bath Stars, and was susceptible to being referred to as such. It was, as many of my police moves, not without some controversy and interest. Crime Prevention had not yet

336

merged with the CID into Crime Management Services, although that would not be long in happening. So all my talk about the real causes of crime, and where much of the responsibility lay, had come home to roost. I was embedded in Central Regional Council. We got started and set up the Community Safety Steering Group. We then selected champions from each of the main services and formed them into a subgroup. A cornerstone in our plan was to involve and listen to our communities. That was a mammoth task, and we did it the only way possible: we got out and amongst as many as we could, all over the Region. Not only geographic communities, but also special interest communities from single mothers to people with disabilities and many more. We used a technique called Priority Search for this, starting with focus groups, and then taking the questionnaire developed from their input to bigger groups to complete the questionnaires. It took months and we wore out shoes, but it was the only legitimate way to listen and learn. That consultation exercise – better to call it a participation exercise, because that is what it was – involved well over one thousand residents. That ensured our strategy was firmly rooted in reality. The following were among the concerns raised, and this is only a small selection: Policing at a local level, action to reduce speeding in communities, effective drug and alcohol programmes, support for Neighbourhood Watch teams, affordable recreation facilities as well as employment opportunities, safer play areas for young people, and action on obstruction of footpaths (e.g. wheelie bins). In one community, a woman said she was frightened to use the ATM in her village as the footpath was wide and car drivers came onto the footpath and used it like a drive-in bank. She had nearly been knocked down twice. The Council dealt with that in a few weeks and installed bollards to prevent vehicles accessing the footpath. A simple and quick solution.

At another level, we held many meetings with service heads to discuss where their services could make a difference. Some did not see what their service had to do with making people safer. We soon explained their responsibility. Part of our mission was to find out the main vehicle the council used to deliver its services. The engine room, as we liked to call it, was the service planning process – that was the only sustainable way to ensure delivery of Community Safety. It was our job to get the outcomes from our community participation exercise into that system, where it would get delivered. The following is a summary of what we achieved through this partnership approach. It is by no means all we achieved, but it gives an indication that a lot of positive things happened, all for the benefit of our communities:

- **Multi Agency Strategy on Racial Attacks and Harassment** was a successful approach to dealing with, and raising awareness of, these issues.

- **Closed Circuit Television (CCTV).** The project resulted in systems in Alloa, Grangemouth, Stirling and Falkirk, which were monitored by people with disabilities.

- *Talking Sense* and *Seeing Sense.* A new approach to safety of women. I had never let the women's safety issue go; the one I had been 'hung, drawn and quartered' for by the 'radical' – but correct – women's group some months previously. My opportunity came at a meeting with members of a community group, where my boss and I broached the subject of a brand new approach to women's safety. We got approval, and the snowball was rolling. A paper was prepared and presented to the Crime Prevention Unit at the Scottish Office. Not only did they agree to us writing a book that they would fully finance; they also had £50,000 to produce a video. Full steam ahead. I selected one of the female police officers in the department and, together with women from Rape Crisis, Woman's Aid and Victim Support, we got to work.

It was exhilarating, enjoyable, hard work, and rewarding. We prepared rules and guidelines. The whole approach would be advisory; we would give information, describe scenarios and choices. No blame would be attached. The booklet was entitled *Talking Sense*, and it became the preferred document for delivering lectures on women's safety and for handing out. It opened with this statement: 'You have the freedom to do as you please, and the choice about what to do and how to do it. If something does happen, you are not to blame'. We wanted to start with the correct message. There was a lot of discussion and thought about that statement before the form of words was agreed.

In the end, the printed book *Talking Sense* covered the following areas: At Home, At Work, Doorstep Callers, Unwanted Telephone Calls, Out and About, In the Car, Violence Within the Family, Sexual and Child Abuse, and it concluded with a section explaining what a victim should expect of the police and other services if becoming a victim. It was well-received, and my credibility with the group in Falkirk moved up a notch. Not a lot, but a notch. My point being: ask, listen, involve, and turn uncomfortable criticism to positive outcomes.

The booklet was supplemented by a video entitled *Seeing Sense*. In terms of the video, it would involve five scenes, each cut off before the end. That would allow for the audience to discuss possible actions they might consider. When the discussion was over, the video would be run to the end of the scenario. All were positive; there was no danger. The actors included Blythe Duff and Elaine C. Smith. It again was a success, and came to be used extensively throughout Scotland.

The only annoying issue, in my view, was the national launch. It was in 1993 at St Andrews House, Edinburgh. I had been away mountaineering in the European Alps the two weeks before, participating in my hobby. The day before the launch, I learned that a policewoman would be the main figure to present the book and video and speak to the media. I had no issue with it being a policewoman; none at all. But I did have an issue – a big issue – with who it was. Not the person, because she had been instructed by her senior officer to do the launch. No, my issue was: who is this person? She was a Strathclyde officer who had not been involved in any way, shape or form with the project at any stage. So why her, and why not the policewoman who had actually worked on the project from start to finish? What was going on? My protests were greeted with the usual banality that equates to: What is your problem? It is none of your business.

It was launched, and neither the Central Scotland policewoman nor I got near a member of the press. I watched the questions being asked about the thinking behind the approach and winced as the answers came nowhere near the truth. The poor Strathclyde officer was not to blame. No, this was a power game way above our heads and Strathclyde – incidentally the present-day drivers of the shambles that is Police Scotland – were flexing their muscles. I had been made aware of this the day previously, as I said, and had told my boss I would not be attending. I was then ordered to attend, which I did – under protest.

- **Initiative to Promote Women's Safety**. This was delivered as follows:
  - An education worker in schools to incorporate the issue of violence against women into the curriculum. A civilian support worker was based in the police for women who report domestic violence: the first of its kind in Scotland.
  - Open Secret: a counselling service for adult survivors of childhood sexual abuse, which was based in a voluntary centre.
  - Funding a worker to develop Rape Crisis in our area.
  - Funding Women's Aid to provide training on domestic violence to agencies.

- o Funding the first person in Victim Support to work with minority ethnic victims.

- **Planning Referral Scheme**. Aimed at developers to engage with police Design Out Crime officers.

- **Domestic Security Programme**. Work with council housing to address problem crime areas, using Crime Pattern Analysis to articulate the exact programme and seek solutions.

- **The Magpie Youth Cafe**. In recognising that young people had a right to gather in their communities, we got a local Public House to open their Lounge Bar two nights a week when it was normally closed. That approach reduced the instances of calls to young people hanging about and causing disturbances in the area.

- **MECS Alarm System to Combat Domestic Violence**. This was an extension to the long-running system for usually elderly vulnerable people. In this variation, it was a service offered to women identified to be most at risk of domestic violence.

- **Pedestrian Crossing Facilities**. A locally-developed crossing criteria was developed. It varied from the standard government formula, and brought other considerations into the decision-making with a view to making crossing roads safer. It was that approach that identified a particular problem at one crossing, where the junction was busier than normal and the road was wider than normal. The engineers altered the switching on of the lights to allow a longer time to get over the road, after the invitation to cross light had gone out (the green man) and the vehicle green 'GO' light came on.

- **Crosstalk: Intergenerational Community Media-tion Scheme.** It was developed by Falkirk Communi-ty Safety Group, Falkirk District Neighbourhood Watch, the Regional Community Safety Unit, and 7:84 Theatre Company. It is aimed at a concentrated local level, where young people gather in communities and cause fear, anger and anxiety to local residents. It is drama-based and only the people directly affected, the actual young people and the actual householders are involved in the process. It has been very success-ful.

- **Freagarrach.** Social Work, Education, the Reporter to the Children's Panel and the police work with Barnardo's on this project, aimed at breaking re-offending patterns in some young people.

Evaluation was tricky. However, these figures might indicate progress:

- A reduction in crime rates over four years, with a 20% drop over the last two years. That, coupled with a higher detection rate than most of the rest of Scot-land – 50% – is indicative of the close work with communities and their growing confidence. A reduc-tion in vehicle crime, a reduction in serious assaults,

and the lowest injury road accidents since records began in 1926.

- Over the period we were able to report an increase in
  Community Safety spending from £1 million to £7
  million.

The strategy was entitled 'Switched Onto Safety'. The whole
approach could be summed up by saying that everybody has a
shared aim and acts in concert for the benefit of the community. One might call it 'Local Solutions to Local Problems', and
is a good example of a corporate approach to safety in our
communities. The specific Central Regional Council project
was recognised both nationally and internationally in the following ways:

- Habitat II: a world conference called by the United
  Nations General Assembly, entitled the UN Conference on Human Settlements – more commonly referred to as City Summit. It was held in Istanbul in
  June 1996, with the aim of making world cities, towns
  and villages healthy, safe, equitable and sustainable.
  'Switched Onto Safety' was published in a book on
  UK Good Practice – 'Living in the Future: 24 Sustainable Development Ideas from the UK' – written
  for, and presented to, that UN Summit Conference.
  At the time I was out of favour, and the police refused to allow me to go and present the paper. A Stirling Local Councillor attended and did that. He was
  furious with the police and, to this day, we discuss
  the small-minded police management who thought

that was a reasonable decision, in a show of uncalled-for power.

- The strategy was also published in a UK Government White Paper by the Department of the Environment, featuring twelve local, sustainable development projects. I was allowed to go to London, Birmingham and Preston to speak at conferences on that document.

Interestingly, and taking you to my last two months of service, I had applied for a position and was not supported on the grounds I was not a strategic thinker. Not only had I been deeply involved in 'Switched Onto Safety', I had also been the author in the Forces Drug Strategy as well as the national police strategy on young people – not that the latter, as I will articulate later, was much of a success.

During that period I was asked to advise the Scottish Office Environment Department on the issue of planning out crime. I involved our current Central Scotland Police Architectural Liaison Officer in the exercise. Along with two officers from the Scottish Office, we headed to the Newcastle area and were shown around some seriously deprived areas where the design and layout of the housing increased the 'fear of crime' felt by most residents, and actually contributed to actual crime suffered by many. At a place called Byker – just to the east of Newcastle City centre – under one high rise block of residential dwellings there was a parking area. It was directly below the building and one drove down a slope to enter this black, unlit cave in the bowels of the high-rise. In the gloom, one could make out a handful of cars. Two were burned out. It was a big enough area; however, it was not used to park cars. It was intimidating. Two local police offic-

345

ers accompanied us. After a day in the Newcastle area, we were introduced to the good, the bad and the ugly of urban design. Even the Senior Planner said: 'We would not design areas like that for ourselves to reside; why do we allow such areas to be designed for other people? We plan in deprivation.' Our advice and deliberations resulted in the first major Scottish Office advice to planners to reduce crime. It was entitled 'Planning for Crime Prevention', and was one of the library of Planning Advice Notes, PAN 46, issued by the Scottish Office to Planning Departments in Scotland. It will still exist today.

The point about that whole section was to evidence that working together was, and still is, the only real way forward in creating safer communities, and to show what could be achieved when we got our act together and did so. It was just a tragedy that whole piece of work was to disappear because of politics. We had no sooner completed the work and got all these things running – not to mention the accolades – when the 1995 new shape of local government in Scotland came into being. Central Regional Council was no more, and was replaced by Clackmannan, Stirling and Falkirk Councils. They hitherto had been smaller District Councils, but their new form was that they continued with the functions they already had, along with taking on the additional Regional functions. They were too busy playing power games and internalising decisions to bother with anything good that the Region had produced. 'Switched Onto Safety' was destined for the bin. After the Cullen report into the Dunblane shooting, the Education Services of the new Stirling Council seconded a police officer to help develop and deliver a Community Safety Strategy. There was a perfectly good one lying in the bin. The wheel goes round.

# CHAPTER 23

A YEAR or so later I was working as the Local Unit Commander, and was attending a meeting about the new Private Finance Initiative/Public Private Partnership (PFI/PPP) Bo'ness Academy. The Director of Education was addressing the meeting, laying out the justification for the new school and the demolition of the old one. Part of the justification, he said, was that the old school had been neglected by the Regional Council and they – Falkirk Council – were having to make good that neglect. Probably very true, and a reasonable case I thought. The fact that his job in Central Regional Council had been educational buildings and stock, and in effect he was criticising himself, seemed to pass unnoticed. Or if not, it was not mentioned and I certainly kept my mouth shut.

The statement – 'Local Solutions to Local Problems' – that appeared in several documents on safer communities through the 1990s until fairly recently, reflected a direction that had brought success and a closeness to the people we serve. It was directed not only through local police commanders and officers based in communities, but by a close working relationship with other services and local councillors – the latter not only through local contact and dialogue, but through the Council-based police committees. We were hardly into the new single force when the Chief Constable, Sir Stephen House, informed us – in his speech at the annual Apex Lecture in September 2013 – that the days of the police solving the community's problems were over. His new direction for his police was about enforcement and control. 'We are not a solutions agency', he said. Was that change of direction based on listening to the communities he serves? I don't think so. I have no doubt he was saying exactly what his masters at the Parliament at Holyrood directed. He could hardly say anything else.

When changing to central control, one cannot listen to communities and one cannot have a policy directed by local problems. At a stroke, he took the service from an approach that had worked in communities for years – including an agenda to enforce when required, but based on local solutions to local problems – to a more distant, may I suggest, less caring policy: Enforcement and Control. That direction was not an obvious agenda item in the lead-up to a single force. If it had been, perhaps communities and local councillors, through police boards, might have had a chance to participate in the debate. Now that the process is centralised with a professional control mechanism, overseen by the national political process, we see the next step on the way to a police state. All in place without proper scrutiny. Lest you forget, the majority of councils, Chief Executives, COSLA and more, were against a single force. House did articulate an arguable point about other services and organisations having more influence on behaviour than the police service, and I have argued the same and asked why these other services have not been more visible in the whole area of reducing criminal and/or anti-social behaviour. However, I think he has gone too far and too fast in stepping down from that arena. Simply locking people up and handing them over to others cannot be the answer. Abrogating your responsibility to not only keep communities safer but make them feel safer will not happen by simple throwing your dummy out the pram and saying 'hey, it has nothing to do with me: I only enforce and control'. Yes, the other services have more to offer in this area. However, two wrongs don't make a right, and communities have been given no say in this. Officers now routinely arrest and commit to custody at least one person from every domestic violence incident they attend. Evidence is not the deciding factor. No, it is a directive from the centre. Some victims now think twice about calling for help. They simply cannot afford to. The Chief Constable was on television speaking about that 'policy'; he said that he checked every day and, if his officers fail to apprehend a person after having been called to a domestic violence incident, he will want to know why. Trust me: if a Chief Constable says that, the Constables will simply lock somebody up every time. I think it was Confucius who said that 'the best judge cannot settle domestic quarrels'.

Recently a pensioner was arrested and committed into custody for a hate crime. He used the word 'Tink' in a neighbour dispute and, such was the seriousness of the offence, it was four days after the incident before the police attended and arrested the pensioner. The three elements one would normally consider before deciding to bring a person before a court on the next lawful day are as follows:

- Seriousness of crime. (The fact that it was four days after the event when the arrest took place, with no other incident in the intervening time, suggests it was not serious.)

349

- Continuing threat/danger to the public. (The four day gap before the police acted, with no other incident, negates the need to arrest.)
- Finally, the likelihood of avoiding justice by absconding. (The accused was 71 years of age, and had resided at his house for in excess of forty years.)

That is oppressive policing, driven by politics.

Then there is breath-testing *en-masse* during various campaigns that appear from a policy unit, like the Christmas campaign. A family friend was driving to work one morning when she came upon just such an operation. There was, in effect, a road block. She, like other motorists, was waved into a queue of cars and crept forward until she reached two police officers. They stopped her and asked for her driving documents. That is perfectly within police powers. She was then asked to provide a breath test. That is not a power that is bestowed on the police in these circumstances. The power to demand a breath test comes when there is suspicion the driver has been drinking and is above the legal limit. There are a number of ways to arouse such suspicion. One involves smelling alcohol on the breath of a driver, and another involves seeing the car being driven in a way that might raise suspicion. As she had not been drinking and as the officers did not see her driving the car on the highway, they could not have been suspicious. Yet they demanded the breath test anyway. It was negative; in fact, it did not register as she had not touched alcohol for days before being stopped. You might raise a the pedantic point about a demand and a request. Trust me; when the police request a law-abiding citizen, it is a demand.

Finally there is the disgrace of the stop and search 'policy'. Although it was not a policy, it was a verbal directive from the centre. In my service days we utilised stop and search on occasion. It is a necessary and useful power, if used properly and correctly. One has to have a suspicion that the person has, about her or his person, something that it is illegal. For example, it could be illegal drugs, stolen property, or perhaps a weapon. It is an effective tool in the fight against crime. Some areas have more need to use it than others. For example, some areas of our inner cities have serious problems with gangs carrying weapons. It is an ongoing problem. In such circumstances it is only sensible and reasonable to have a robust search policy in place. Apart from anything else, the law-abiding community would expect no less. I would call that reasonable and proportionate. I would also call it a local solution to a local problem. My issue with the national stop and search 'directive' is that it was disproportionate and took absolutely no cognisance of local issues. One ex-colleague, who is still in the service, told me he despaired. He worked in a small village and was regularly directed by his Inspector to carry out at least four stop searches every weekend. It was not articulated what particular offence he was searching for; was it weapons, drugs, or what? He was simply instructed to get four searches carried out. So what was the local issue? Well, over any weekend there were very few local young people about. So he was searching the same young people more than once. The *Glasgow Herald* of 21 August 2013 has a report referring to a memorandum seen by them, purported to be from a police Inspector in which he authorises overtime solely for the purpose of targeting stop and search activity and finishing; nil returns are not acceptable under any circumstances. What this stupid directive has done is to take what was a very useful crime fighting tool, if used properly, and tainted it. When I policed, if an officer were to conduct random searches with no good reason and without suspicion of any wrongdoing, he may well have faced a disciplinary enquiry. So how does that work if they are 'obeying orders'? It is oppressive policing. It does not stop there, and it is based on dogma – not evidence. Ross Deuchers, Professor of Criminology and Criminal Justice at the University of the West of Scotland, said this about the practice: 'Using stop and search in a random way, driven only by police targets, is ethically wrong'.

It is very reminiscent of how Stalin ruled the Communist Party. Strong central control, supported by a strong bureaucratic process. Presently, the new service has hundreds of guidance documents and Standard Operating Procedures in place. One even explains how to wear your uniform. Centralised, remote Standard Operating Procedures (SOP) create a divide by stifling officers' ability to think for themselves and respond appropriately to local needs. They are about central control. They are not about protecting the community or the officer; they are about protecting the organisation. Modern-day management is often cowardice masked by cleverness, leadership by poll and symbolic gestures.

Oscar Wilde had a view I thought informative and relevant: 'Consistency is the last resort of the unimaginative'. Policing is easy. Train an officer, provide his or her power through the warrant card, and then allow the officer to get on with the job. It is so simple. There is a requirement to have some guidance documents. Not to tell the officer how to do the job or how to act in a given situation. No. A guidance document should provide information that is not about the law or power; it should simply give guidance on whom to contact, who to inform, things like that.

To be honest, however, such unhelpful search tactics did not simply emerge at the birth of Police Scotland. While I was in the job and a Chief Inspector, I was asked by a Principal Director of Education about the legality of searching children, school pupils, on a school bus. The circumstances she described were thus. The morning bus to a secondary school was stopped by the police and a police drug search dog, complete with handler, was deployed. It was directed to search between all the seats, sniff school bags and round about the pupils. At the back of the bus it hit pay-dirt. It got a positive scent. A young male was detained and removed from the school bus. The concern was that in order to get to the source of the police suspicion, a number of school children had been 'searched'. Complaints had been received at the Education Service head office. Was that legal? My answer was simple. It was not illegal, in terms of the law. However, it was a search conducted – several searches, in fact – all beyond the power invested in a police officer. The majority of searches were carried out whilst no suspicion was present. They should have gone straight to the person they were suspicious of and simply searched him. That answer got back to the Chief Constable, and again I was 'keel-hauled'. There was no counter argument; only the comment 'we have always done it that way'.

Back to my own circumstance as a police officer. I explained what my intentions were when moved into the Crime Prevention Department, and perhaps have evidenced I was involved to some extent in changing its direction and its status – not, however, without some personal cost. I referred earlier to the idea of merging the Crime Prevention and the CID into Crime Management Services. Well, it happened when I was embedded in the Regional Council. It was a disaster for me personally. The dust had hardly settled on the merger before I was in the sights of the CID management – or, to be correct, the new Crime Management Services management. I will describe them as unscrupulous. Prior to the merger, there was a vacancy for a new head of Community Safety. I applied and was invited for interview. I might well have been the person with most experience in the field, and I was certainly in with a chance. However, at the eleventh hour a Detective Inspector appeared on the short leet. There was also another surprise. His boss in the CID insisted on being on the interview panel. Do you know what it feels like to be headed off at the pass? Well it was happening to me, and I felt a bit helpless. There were six or seven for interview. I did what I could, but felt *why did we have this farce?* After it was over, we were informed that the Detective Inspector and I had been so close that they could not decide. We were to be interviewed the next day by the Chief Constable and the Deputy Chief Constable. That night I was at a community meeting in Falkirk. A Chief Superintendent, who had been on the interview panel that day, told me I had a mountain to climb and that I had little chance of getting the job. 'You were the best today at interview. However, one of the panel insisted it should not be you.' The interview the next day was bizarre. It was all very friendly; comfy seats, tea and biscuits. I was told not to worry; they just want to go over a couple of things to help them make up their minds. After a couple of non-event questions, the Deputy asked me if I was not getting tired of the job and running out of ideas. I knew he could not ask the other person that question and, as I already knew I was not getting the job, I had a bit of fun. I said that it was not like a scientist sitting in a laboratory and rushing out shouting 'eureka!' with his hair straight up and soot all over his face. It was not like that. If you have experience and know the job, ideas emerge based on developments and opportunities that you come across, because you knew enough to make the connections. No, I do not feel tired and running out of ideas. I did not get the job.

Two or three weeks later, the new boss got all the Crime Prevention Officers to a meeting. After laying down the new way it would be and reminding us we were now in the CID, he turned to me and said we need to get you to move on from the Regional Council project. He then dismissed the rest and ordered me to stay behind. Then, in no uncertain terms, he told me to get myself out the project. I said it was a contract, three years in length, fully budgeted through a full council agreement. And in any case, the unit has a civilian in it – there are two of us. He would have none of it, and said 'that is an order; get yourself out'. I suggested he speak to the Chief Constable, who was responsible for setting it up. I was dismissed.

To put this into perspective, the project was not quite two years in, with one full year remaining. We were also in the middle of the important stages. A few weeks later, he telephoned me at my office in the Chief Executive's unit and told me to be outside in ten minutes; he was picking me up to go to a meeting in Perth with him. Seems he knew nothing about the agenda and I did. It was a ruse. I did not realise at that moment, although I caught on. This was the start of an intensive bullying campaign to get me out of my position within the Chief Executive's Policy Unit at Central Regional Council. The management of the CID had no interest in the Crime Prevention Department. The boss was looking to move up a rank, and to do so he needed justification. An extra Detective Inspector would help his case. Simple plan; get me back over to police headquarters, then replace me with... whoever. The impediment was me. We pulled into a layby and stopped.

He asked if I had made any attempt to get out of the Region. I said I hadn't, and that I had no intention of doing so. He got a bit heavy and told me this was not a request and my career was at stake. There were another two such private conversations in his car, always away from prying eyes and ears. The latter two being in the hills near North Third Reservoir. The conversation in each case was pretty similar. My career was now not under threat: it was finished. That was the last message. There were other bits about me 'bursting' to the boss, apologising, and – wait for it – 'why don't you invite him out for a game of golf?' He finished by telling me the boss would be furious by my refusal to do as he wanted. I retorted by letting him know that it was not my problem who was furious. My last comments brought all of the 'secret squirrel' stuff in his car to an end. I suggested he would never understand what I was about to tell him, which was as follows: 'I tried so hard to get into the police service; it meant so much to me. I had tears in my eyes when I signed my first report after being confirmed. I doubt if you can understand that. I had no notion of career when I joined; being a police Constable was all I ever wanted. Yes, I suppose you can stop me ever being promoted again, but you cannot take away my right to be a police officer. Only I can do that. So your threats are worthless. Now get me back to the office'. He did not understand, and I doubted he ever would. One cannot be bullied or intimidated if one is not afraid, or if one has nothing to lose. It is important to remember that some managers misuse their power and, to help, they surround themselves with weak-minded sycophants. Classic sociopathic behaviour. Why remember that? Because they are no threat to you. We headed back to the office. However, there would be one more trip to the same isolated part of our police area. I will talk about that later. He was correct by the way. Any chance of a career had been binned.

Life was going on, and I was heading to Ottawa in Canada to an International Conference entitled 'Management Challenges in 21$^{st}$ Century Policing'. It was through Stafford-shire University, and the Local Authority approved and paid for it. At that time I was having to brief my new boss weekly. I let him know about the conference. He was not best pleased, and asked why I was going. I said it was to do with my project in the Council. He took the leaflet from me and said that he would be going and I would not; he was in charge. My response was calm and measured. I told him that was correct; he was the boss, and I asked him to let me know the outcome. I heard no more.

On the first morning of the conference in Ottawa who did I meet at the first coffee break? You are ahead of me; the officer in charge of the CID, and my taxi driver to cosy places for a chat where my career could be discussed. I went to sit down beside him, a reasonable thing to do. He snarled at me 'how did you get here?' I responded, quite correctly: 'I flew; how did you get here?' I did not sit at his table. The reader will wonder how infantile senior police officers are. Well, some are more infantile than others. There was another Cen-tral Scotland Police officer at the event; he was there because of his job at the Scottish Office. The conference lasted for a week. During that week, he and I attended the office of Daw-son Hovey, Assistant Commissioner of the Royal Canadian Mounted Police, to speak about our approach to police in communities. We were also treated to lunch at the world fa-mous Royal Canadian Mounted Police Musical Ride Centre. It was a bit humbling to be invited, and that such a high-ranking officer in a world famous, iconic police service was even remotely interested in my view on anything. But he really was. It was a magical week in my police service. At no time during the week, apart from that first coffee break on the first morning, did I or my 'Scottish Office' colleague see either of our Central Scotland Police colleagues again; not once. I have to assume they were in Ottawa for another meeting.

A few years later, whilst a Chief Inspector in Police HQ, I was invited by the Rt. Hon the Lord Graham of Edmonton to attend a Reception on The Terrace, House of Lords. I was to be in full uniform. I sent the invitation along to the Chief Constable, for his information, as a courtesy and just in case he was also invited and we bumped into each other at the event. How embarrassing would that be? Two days later, my memorandum was returned with a 'NO' penned in red on it. The invitation was not returned. I queried this with his secretary. He was the Chief Constable; he was going in my place. I nodded and went back to my mundane life and thought no more about it. Many weeks later, and about a week before the event, my invitation was returned by the Chief Constable's secretary with the message 'I have booked your flights and a hotel'. I asked why the Chief Constable was not going to attend, and she told me he had an invitation to something else. I remember thinking 'how childish'. The allure of one toy only lasts till a shinier toy comes along. In reality, as I discovered later, the invitation was personal and it had not been addressed to the Chief Constable.

# CHAPTER 24

ON the 13<sup>th</sup> day of March 1996 I was on the cusp of completing my twenty-second year of police service. A service probably not that different from many other officers. I had seen death and tragedy, and so many magic moments – inspirational moments that restored one's belief in people. I had also enjoyed serious camaraderie. It had been a rollercoaster, and it had been all the more enjoyable and fulfilling because of that. It was just another Wednesday, but this time it was not.

A 'mutant' had walked into Dunblane Primary School and taken out his deranged anger on a class of five year old children, shooting and killing seventeen of them, including their teacher. He shot and wounded another seventeen children and adults. He was lots of things – he was devious, manipulative and probably very controlling – but mostly, Thomas Hamilton was a coward.

I had been at my desk in the Regional Council, since about eight-fifteen that morning, working on another urgent report on something or other. All reports in the Chief Executive's Policy Team seemed important and urgent; my secondment was nearing its conclusion, three eventful and successful years nearly up. The telephone on my desk trills. I think twice before answering it; I was doing something really important. I succumbed to the hypnotic melody of the ringing telephone. I picked up the receiver, and the caller transmits urgency even before speaking. Then the voice simply says 'Ian, something terrible has happened. There has been a shooting at Dunblane Primary School. Some children have been shot'. I am not sure how I responded. He continued, 'the situation is still unclear, but there are six or seven children dead'. I ask if there were instructions for me. He said: 'Not yet, Ian. I am just letting you know before things start to escalate'. I thanked him and asked him to keep me posted, and then hung up.

I did nothing for a few moments, trying to stop my brain spinning, trying to make sense of what I had just heard. What I did next was unforgivable, really; probably the most selfish few moments of my whole career. I slumped onto my desk and cried. I remember thinking: *What was all that about, three years of strategy building to make people safe? What a fucking joke. International awards? What for? We cannot even keep our children safe in our own schools.* The accursed telephone was ringing again. I wiped my eyes and answered. It was more news. 'Ian, the latest from the school is that there are fourteen or fifteen Primary One children dead, and their teacher. Others are injured. I think there will be more'.

I asked: 'Who did it?'

'Thomas Hamilton. And I think he has shot himself. I have no more at the moment; things are chaos up there. The Chief Constable wants you to tell the Chief Executive, but don't say who we think was responsible. I will update you as I hear more. Good luck.'

I composed myself, and I remember thinking: *Don't be so pathetic. It is not your tragedy; put yourself in the shoes of the parents. Get a grip. You are a professional police officer, this is what you do. So get it done.* I calmly briefed the Assistant Chief Executive and, in doing so, defied my instruction. I told him who we believed was responsible. I did think about that, and reasoned that there had been a long history between Thomas Hamilton and the Regional Council; the media would soon learn that. So it will be better if the Council knew, to enable them to get the file out and be prepared. Years later, the Assistant Chief Executive – since retired – thanked me for that decision. I spent that day with the Regional Council strategic team, and kept them abreast of developments and advised when or if I was able. One early decision was whether or not to release the class photograph. It was a difficult decision, involving a lot of debate. Decision reached, the class photograph was released. The logic that swung the decision was simple: if we do not release, we will lose control and the media will get images from whence it can.

It was an emotional day. The teacher who was killed was known to all in the Education Service. By late afternoon my role was finished in terms of advising and briefing the Regional Strategy team, and I was summoned to police headquarters. The mood was tense and business-like. I was to join up with a Chief Inspector, a Sergeant and a member of the civilian support staff to organise and run the close family support teams that were to be pulled together. The logic was that each affected family would have a police officer, partnered by a social worker with children and families experience, assigned to offer support. On the day of the shooting, while things were chaotic and order was being restored, two police officers had been assigned to each of the affected families; they were later joined by a social worker. Our involvement would kick in on day two. That meant we needed to get an office for the teams, transport, communications, as well as somehow furnishing the office, even sparsely. That work started in the early evening, with the invaluable assistance of senior personnel from the Council. By the morning we had everything in place.

It was a long night; a few hours' sleep, a cool shower, and back at the coal face. We started with a briefing at eight in the morning. The social workers were intrigued by this new concept – well, new to most of them, anyway. The biggest shock was that it started when it said it would. Then there was the debrief at the end of the day, at five in the evening. After getting accustomed to this structure, some found it supportive and very organised; in fact, one or two were quite impressed, even if they might not have said as much.

As each team had met their assigned family on the day of the shooting, all that was required was for them to meet up again and explain their role. That was mostly advice and explanation about what was going on, and why this or that was required. Among the tasks included were transport to hospital, accompanying parents to the Procurator Fiscal's office, post-mortems, registering the death, and whatever else seemed necessary to assist the family. Not all families required or even wanted the same levels of help, and some were reluctant to take any help at all. It was never forced on people, but it was available. It was an emotive and stressful time, and there were tears shed on all sides.

I was in my office on maybe the third day when I received a telephone call I cannot forget. It was a woman's voice, and she was upset. She did not identify herself at first, and all she said was: 'You have forgotten about us'. I was puzzled, and asked who we had forgotten. Her answer rocked me. She was the mother of one of the children in the fatal class who had not been at school that morning. Two children were ill and had not gone in that morning. She said the other mum was also upset. She said they felt guilty, and that she was really upset. I assured her it would be taken care of, and I apologised for our omission. I said that through my own tears. We were wrecked. A policewoman was sent to liaise with both families. That was a lesson learned; a lesson I hoped I would never have to remember, ever again.

The mood behind the scene was sombre. Our team worked out of police headquarters. A number of incidents sort of evidenced the mood and exposed the characters of some. The Chief Constable received a letter of complaint during the first week after the shooting. It was from a bereaved mother. She was angry about a mix-up on the fateful day, and had written her displeasure to the Chief Constable. He appeared in our office with the letter, and asked that we compose a reply for him to sign. He wanted to apologise and added, 'I will go and speak to her and apologise in person'. He was upset. He was a seriously decent person, and he meant what he said. A while later, the head of the CID – an unpleasant individual, in my opinion – arrived at the office to see what 'Billy Liar' had wanted. Yes, he referred to the Chief in these terms. He was briefed about the letter and how the Chief wanted it answered. The response was that 'we are apologising to nobody; leave this to me'. He took the letter, and I never heard any more about it.

A second incident of note took place. I cannot recall if that was the same night or the next day; it was in the same office, involving the same two people. The Chief Inspector produced a memorandum he had written some years before, in 1991. It was about an investigation the Chief Inspector had carried out, when he was a Detective Sergeant, into the behaviour of Thomas Hamilton. It concerned how Hamilton

had behaved at a boys' camp some years before, including assaulting one boy and other behaviour tantamount to a breach
of the peace. It questioned his suitability to possess a firearm
certificate. It had gone to senior officers and the Procurator
Fiscal at the time it was written in 1991. That night, however,
the Chief Inspector was instructed to lock it away in a drawer
and only produce it if told. As with the letter of complaint, I
never saw that report again and never heard it discussed.
Well, certainly not at that time or by these two officers.

The content of the memorandum, however, did re-
emerge – some months later, in very public circumstances,
when the Chief Inspector talked about it during his evidence
to the Cullen Inquiry into the Dunblane shooting. It was also
the subject of questions at Westminster, and is referred to in
Hansard. I have absolutely no idea why the memorandum was
referred to at the Inquiry, nor do I know why it was so secret
or why it had to be locked away in the first place. I also know
it was the subject of intense discussion the day the Chief Inspector was due to give evidence at the Inquiry. Two senior
officers, one being the Detective Superintendent, went over
the evidence and coached the Chief Inspector on what he
would say in relation to the memorandum. For some reason it
seemed to have them running scared. In the event, under
questioning the party line seems not to have been followed. I
do remember the newspaper headlines the next day, however.
One had a photograph of the Chief Inspector leaving the
hearing after his evidence. As I recall, that publication had
him as a hero. He was not, however, any kind of hero within
the ranks of his immediate supervisors. I take you back to the
'bullying fields' of North Third Reservoir. Some weeks after
the Cullen Inquiry, the Chief Inspector – yes, the same one –
transported me there in his car. To my surprise, he had no

threats for me that day. On the contrary; he asked for my help. He explained about the serious fall-out between him and the head of the CID and another officer, over his evidence at the hearing – and, in particular, his reference to the memorandum. He said he was being bullied, and that they had ostracised him and not spoken to him. In fact, he said they were refusing to even acknowledge him.

Many years later I met a senior colleague from those days, who told me that the Chief Inspector had met with a lot of resistance from other officers at the time. This apparently included an anonymous note being left in his office with the clear intention of causing him distress. The only way for me to know the full story would have meant speaking to the Chief Inspector himself, though after the way he had treated me back then I would – for obvious reasons – have no desire to get in contact with him.

Back to North Third and the final car meeting. After telling me about the massive fall-out and the way he was being treated, he asked me to talk to the Chief Constable and get him transferred away from them. He said that the Chief Constable listened to me. In short, he was asking me to get him out of the CID. I told him I would not approach the Chief Constable, adding: 'You have followed the Superintendent though your service in his coat tails. Whatever position he got, he took you along behind him. Right through the ranks. Everybody in the force knows that; you have no respect. This is your chance to stand up for yourself. You do it'. He eventually did move on, and I really had little more direct or meaningful contact with him. Thinking back to that day in his car, I did not need to reject his plea for help. I am not proud of that. That is not how I was brought up.

In researching this book I found said memorandum and additional notes, in open view on the Internet. Perhaps they have helped me understand the eagerness by certain officers to keep the memorandum in a drawer. I include one short part of the notes, not the memorandum:

A Procurator Fiscal Depute prepared a note indicating that, in his view, there was not a great deal to substantiate many of the charges proposed by the police, with the possible exception of the charges of assault and a breach of the peace based on Thomas Hamilton shouting and swearing at the boys. When the precognitions were obtained it was noted that none of the parents had anything to add to their statements and some had shown concern at the thought that Thomas Hamilton was being suspected of anything untoward. They had not stopped their children going to his clubs. On 18 November 1991, having considered all the material, the Procurator Fiscal Depute, decided that no criminal proceedings should be taken, marking the papers, 'no pro: no crime libelled: not in the public interest'.

There is that expression, 'in the public interest', again.

The view within the Fiscal's service in Stirling, having discussed it internally on several occasions, was that the conduct – while troubling – had approached but not crossed the border of criminality. At the hearing, one view was that proceedings could have been taken against Hamilton, while another view was the child struck by Hamilton had obviously been behaving in a violent and bullying manner. Lord Cullen was of the opinion that there was no basis for entertaining criticism of the decision taken by the Procurator Fiscal.

Make of that what you will.

A day or two after the shooting, the Secretary of State for Scotland wanted the names, addresses, as well as the ages and dates of birth, of every sibling of the deceased children. He also wanted the same information about the injured children and their siblings. I explained to the senior officer making the demand on behalf of Michael Forsyth that the teams were all out, and it might not be possible to get all the information that day.

'The Secretary of State needs the information today, so just get it', was the command.

'This is delicate', I replied. 'Some will be at mortuaries identifying their dead children before post mortems, and others will be at hospitals. Some are just trying to gain the confidence of the families. We will get the information, but perhaps not today. The Secretary of State will understand; the last thing he will want to do is upset any of these families. He only wants to write to them. He will understand if there is a delay.'

My reasoning fell on deaf ears. 'Just get the information.'

Later in the day, I am shouted at along a corridor: 'Have you got that information yet?' It took three days to get all the information. I handed it over, and never heard another thing. A braver officer would have explained the delicate position to the Secretary of State's staff, and they would have understood. Some have their career to the fore; bravery is not an option. After ten or eleven days, we withdrew the police officer element from the close support team, leaving the social worker to continue with the support if required. As I said, some had less need of it than others. After the debriefing on that last night we closed off a section of the canteen in police headquarters and had a buffet, with refreshments, for all the close support teams. The logic was – which I agreed with – after ten days of such intense and emotional work, it was reasonable to allow the teams to wind down. That decision did not meet with universal approval, particularly with some officers, none of whom had been involved in the teams. Some expressed disgust that we could 'party' at such a time. They were not slow to make their feelings known.

On a positive note, some months later Lord Cullen made reference in his report about the support teams. He praised the work which was done by Central Scotland Police and, in particular, he made mention of the expressions of gratitude received in respect of help, the support professionalism of the force, and the sensitivity and support provided to relatives by members of the liaison teams. He was quite right; these teams put so much into the task and did it, even when emotionally struggling, with complete disregard for themselves and whilst displaying the utmost professionalism. They had been plunged into the unknown, and they acted like the compassionate professionals they were. I was proud to have been associated with them, even at a distance.

I got something that has stayed with me since then. I never did get a commendation or award during my service. Never deserved one. However, I did get something after our work at Dunblane. It was a card, addressed to me – but it was about more than me. It was handwritten, and had a few simple words:

Det. Insp. McNeish and the team (Dunblane);
Thank you all very much for what you are doing!
We appreciate your work and support for the public.

It was dated May '96, and was not signed. Better than a commendation, and more cherished. The three years of strategy work within Central Regional Council was not for nothing, however, despite my outburst and display of selfish despair. A single person – a mutant – cannot be allowed to derail something that is good. In the years that followed, two of my grandchildren were pupils at Dunblane Primary School. Every year, on the anniversary of that terrible day, the school held a service involving all the pupils. My grandson was always distressed after that day, and was for a few days. He was scared that a man would come back and shoot them, and he worried he would have to protect his younger sister. Out of the mouths of babes. I had not realised. I am now clear, however: the annual, all-school service should stop. Perhaps it has? Of course we should not forget, but we must find different ways to remember. We should not make children, who were not even born in 1996, have to relive that terrible day. It is abusive. We must not allow Thomas Hamilton to define us.

It didn't matter, in the end; the politics of local authority boundaries derailed our good work, and it had nothing to do with Hamilton. I continued for a few months working between the emerging Stirling Council, linking in to their Dunblane strategy team which consisted of the directors of the new authority and the new Chief Executive. He had been the Assistant Chief Executive of Central Regional Council, and I had worked directly under him for three years. Again, it was interesting work, if sometimes a bit beyond me. I refer to the budget discussions. There were grants and budgets concerning the Dunblane community to consider and take decisions on. Donations and gifts were coming in from far and wide. They had to be distributed. I really had little input to that. However, there were other things that I had more opportunity to voice an opinion about.

There was still a liaison role for me with the remaining social work support teams. I attended all their meetings, and contributed in many ways. I was in limbo for a while about then, circulating between the new council and police headquarters. I took part in creating the new drug policy for the police. I was summoned by the Detective Superintendent, who had my annual appraisal in front of him. I had not worked in the police for three years. The Assistant Chief Executive of the council was responsible for my annual appraisal, as he was effectively my line manager during my secondment. In the same way, an officer seconded to work at the Scottish Police College as an instructor received his or her annual appraisal from an officer at the college, not a Central Scotland police officer. I asked the Detective Superintendent who had compiled it. He said 'we did'. It did not make good reading, and had me marked down on most areas. I asked how he could do that, as I had not worked in the police during the period it covered. He did not comment on that. However, he did finish by telling me I would have to prove myself as a police officer again. I asked if the last three years did not count. He agreed that it did not, and I would not be considered for promotion for a while. I objected, to no avail. I asked to speak to the Chief Constable. He would not see me, though the Deputy Chief Constable saw me. He was not in the least supportive, and agreed with the comments. I argued that I had not chosen to work on the secondment. The police had sent me, and I was there at their behest. It did not matter what I said; it fell on deaf ears. Meeting over, stitched up.

So I was sent out of force, at their behest, to find it had no bearing on my service and certainly not my career. I told the Chief Executive of Stirling Council. He was angry and compiled a stinker of a letter to the Chief Constable, challenging the whole approach and referring to the police actions as insidious. A few days later the Chief Constable did see me. He waved the two-page letter about and asked if I knew about it. Obviously I did not. He was angry about the tone of the letter and told me the senior officers it referred to were furious, and that I should keep my head down. That did not work, and a few days later the Chief caught up with me in headquarters, put his arm round my shoulder, and said he had a plan to protect me from them. 'I am transferring you back to uniform duties. You start at Falkirk as a shift Inspector next week.' So my crime prevention days were behind me. One day I was dining with the Assistant Commissioner of the Royal Canadian Mounted Police in Ottawa while he asked me about our approach to policing in communities, then I was grabbing a coffee from a vending machine whilst working nightshift in Falkirk. Funny old world. But then, I had been warned.

# CHAPTER 25

FALKIRK was good. It was like a breath of fresh air to be back working on the front line with decent, hard-working officers who had no agenda and whose only interest was working and doing their duty. I cannot praise them enough. At a stroke I became a 'commander' at some football matches at Brockville. There was a small control box at the south-east corner of the terracing, giving a complete, uninterrupted view of the ground. Manna from heaven for a Bairn. Well, there was the small matter of being in charge of the policing, and some clubs did bring troublesome hordes to support them. One of the duties of the match commander was to speak to the referee before the match. At Brockville the 'enclosure' in front of the main stand was not a big area. Maybe ten or so steps from front to back. It was right on top of the pitch. Supporters could lean over and almost touch the linesman. Or today, that would be assistant referee. (What is that all about?) Anyway, the discussion was always the same. The evacuation signals and procedure were always first. Then then it was about the home support in the south enclosure. They were notorious amongst match officials, across Scotland. 'Will you have an officer in the home enclosure? The abuse they hurl at me and the linesman is vile and really abusive.' Same thing, every game. The big secret after the final whistle was to get the away support to the train station or to their buses as quickly as possible. We allocated officers to shepherd them away from the stadium. Sometimes a few of the train travellers were intent on having a few beers in Falkirk. Depending on their team, we might allow that or not. Some supporters came with a reputation, so the shepherding was a bit closer and no one was allowed to sneak away to slake their thirst in the town. I am too much of a gentleman to name and shame; however, they were not necessarily who you might think. One particular 'gang' would leave us with spittle on our backs. Scottish football? It was a case of getting them onto the train and getting them out of town.

Away from the football, my Falkirk Burgh shift consisted of two Sergeants and a shift of six to ten Constables – depending on sickness, courses, leave, and so on. Weekend nights were usually spirited and lively. It was worse once we got out of the office and onto the street. My style was to wait till after the full shift briefing, taken by one of my Sergeants with an input from me if required, then retreat to my office with the two Sergeants, grab a quick coffee, go over the issues and anything important that needed addressing, and then on with the show. I left them with the same message every time: if I feel there is an issue I have to pick up with you, I will call on the radio and arrange to meet you. I would never question or change a Sergeant's decision over the live airways. We met and had that discussion face to face. There was a different scale of supervision from my days of policing in the north to the Central Belt; I have previously alluded to that.

Here is another example. I was in the Superintendent's office in Falkirk to discuss some future policing event. We both carried police radios. As we spoke, one could hear the chatter about a road accident on the outskirts of town. There were two injuries – not too serious, but requiring an ambulance. As the radio chatter continued I could sense the Superintendent getting uneasy. He could contain himself no longer.

'Do you hear that?'

I said I could.

'Why are you still here?'

'We are having a meeting. You called it.'

'Yes, but there is a road accident. Should you not be there?'

'There is a cast of thousands at the accident. I have the shift Sergeant and two Constables. In addition, there are two fully-crewed Traffic cars and an ambulance. They all know what they are doing. I trust them. If I was needed, my Sergeant would have called me.'

He shook his head and said: 'Well, it's your shift'.

We got on with the meeting. My officers dealt with the accident perfectly well, and had no need of my interference.

One night shift, about five in the morning, the CCTV staff reported seeing a man sitting on a seat in the town centre. They thought there was something strange about his movements. We located him and got him back to the office. He was shaking and spoke very little English. After getting him a coffee, we tried to find out more. He told us a really strange tale. He said he was from India. He had paid Russians, he thought, to get him to England. He had been put on a train and, after two days, was then moved by lorry as he got nearer the West. He could not be more specific. He was bundled into the boot of a car and had travelled like that for days. He was allowed out every few hours, but bundled back in for the travelling. The car dropped him off on the outskirts of Falkirk about an hour before, he said. We got no more than that. He had no papers. We eventually handed him over to the Immigration Service and heard no more. That was in the mid-1990s. To be honest, the tale was a bit far-fetched and we did not believe him. Knowing what I know now and being aware of similar stories since that time, I am not so sure that maybe he wasn't actually telling the truth.

I make a plea to be known as the caring service. I do it deliberately, with the words of Sir Stephen House still in my ears: 'We do not solve community problems'. Well, Sir Stephen, we used to, and we were respected for that. An old man had spent three full days on a bench near the Falkirk Police Office. He had not moved, and his bodily functions took place where he sat. Three days' worth. We did offer to help, but he would not budge. So we made sure he had something to drink and eat. We tried other services, but to no avail. We even tried the hospital, with the suggestion that he had mental health difficulties. It made no difference. Not one service could find the box to tick that would enable them to do something. Trust me, it is getting worse. Nobody will make a decision, and certainly not if it does not fit a criteria. After three days of wasting our time, we did something. It was not my shift, and I give credit to the Inspector who took the bull by the horns. He went out with two officers and lifted the old man from the seat and half-carried, half-supported him into the police office. Then two young officers removed his clothing and gave him a hot bath. In fact, they needed to give him three hot baths to get him clean. He was covered in human excrement and urine. His clothes could not be used again, so we got him clean clothing and we fed him. Once we got him sorted out, we played our next card. We arrested him and brought him before the court the next day. The Sheriff has more power in these matters than the police. We knew that, and had done it before. The Sheriff ordered that the hospital take him in for assessment. We did not see him again. Would that happen now? I do not know. What I do know is that many of the front line officers would do the same as we did if given the opportunity. However, they would be forced to consult a higher rank, who in turn would have to consult the relevant Standard Operating Procedure. They would not have one, and would be stymied.

About that time I became quite ill, and collapsed a few times in serious internal pain. Luckily a few of these incidents were while working, and one of my Sergeants would take me to hospital. I had a few episodes, culminating in a couple of longer periods in hospital and an operation. I got back into harness on restricted duties, and was put on office duties whilst I recovered. That was about to change. Coincidently, I had another ailment about that same time. A few years earlier I had been a Sergeant in the Public Order team. That required lots of intensive training. Line-up facing an angry mob who are throwing missiles at you. Bottles, Molotov cocktails, bricks... whatever they could get their hands on. It was usually in serials of thirteen. Ten Constables with joined shields at the front, two Sergeants with shields behind them, and an Inspector with a smaller shield behind, making up the 'Baker's Dozen' and shouting the instructions. A target was picked and, on the shout of 'Go!' we rumbled forward, keeping the line and keeping the shields closely overlapping to prevent missiles getting through. We would rumble right into the crowd to reach our target, our objective. That could be anything; perhaps a lamp post, or some other piece of street furniture. On one occasion that we were lined up, we had our objective and we were being bombarded as we waited on the 'Go!' Time was passing, the angry crowd were closing in on

377

us, and we were being well and truly battered. Still no 'Go!' Then the 'Go!', and off we went. Unfortunately for the Inspector, he did not issue the order. So he was standing still while his team rumbled off, creating a deadly gap. The missiles were bouncing off our full length shields. Meanwhile, his small round 'targe' offered him scant protection from the 'Agincourt'-style rain of missiles that passed over our heads to connect with him. After we had attained our objective, we stopped to review our performance. On this occasion, there was only one thing to review. Who shouted 'Go!'? The Inspector dragged his battered frame along the line of Constables, asking each one in turn: 'Did you shout "Go!"?' We never found the name of our new leader.

Another exercise was a suicidal manoeuvre involving two Constables with shields to the fore, protected by a Sergeant who pushed in close behind them with a long shield held over the trio, overlapping the top of the other two shields like a makeshift roof. The Romans called this way of holding shields above their heads *Terstudo* (tortoise); meanwhile the Greeks referred to the manoeuvre as *Chelon*, later to be *Foulkon*. We were not so imaginative, and simply called it a three man entry. It was the method we used to enter buildings. The 'roof' being required to protect from missiles being hurled from above; sounds the very dab. I was the roof carrier one day when a 'gung-ho' instructor, with his brains kept safely in his locker, projected a lorry tyre on top of us. Totally unexpected, my arms buckled and the 'roof' and the tyre struck me right on top of my helmet. I was seriously stunned and in pain. I thought my back was broken. However, I did the stupid thing; I just took it as part of a learning curve and moved on. I did not even record the injury. Because injured I was. Over the weeks the pain eased off and I got on with life. However, my real problems were lurking, and emerged during my spell in the Regional Council. They got worse when in Falkirk. The pain in my left arm was getting so bad, I would do some shifts with it held in my tunic belt. If I tried running, my whole arm would be alive with pins and needles. I honestly thought I would have to take early retirement. I went to the Scottish police convalescence home for two weeks and got intensive treatment, twice a day, along with an exercise regime. They saved my career and, whilst alleviating the symptoms to a degree, warned me that it would never be completely right and that I must never jog or run any distance ever again.

While at Falkirk, my wife and I separated. I had to purchase a place to live from my hospital bed, with a bag full of ten pence pieces and the hospital telephone that the nurses rolled to my bed. Catheter to one side, intravenous drip to the other and telephone in hand, I was a fine sight. But I got it all done. After the operation, I had to get my stitches taken out by my local District Nurse. I knew her well. That morning I stuck a plastic keyhole decal over each site on my stomach, where stitches were to be removed: four in total. I was horrified to see that I had never seen the nurse before.

'Where is Helen?' I asked.

'Oh, she had to take time off.' She told me to take my shirt off.

I hesitated, then said: 'This is embarrassing'.

'Have you never taken your shirt off in front of a woman before?'

I took my shirt off. A pregnant pause, then: 'What on earth is that?'

I looked down, waited a second, and then said – as though puzzled – 'Eh, I had keyhole surgery'.

Silence. Then, 'I don't think that is funny. Take them off.'

After having the stitches removed and being dabbed with blue-coloured, nippy liquid, I put my shirt on and stuck the offending decals in my pocket. I was halfway out the door when the nurse said: 'In case you are interested, I thought it was really funny'. Last laugh on me.

I was not long back at work on restricted duties when I was offered the post as Local Unit Commander, in charge of my own area: Bo'ness and Blackness. I had lived there in the early 1960s, I had been a Sergeant there in the mid-1980s, and now in 1997 I was going back to being a Hamebider. The move was very quick and, although still on restricted duties, I started in Bo'ness the following Monday. I will say this now: I regarded my service in Bo'ness to be one of the high points of my service, almost equalling the experience of my single officer years in Fearn. My briefing on the first day covered all the usual 'hand-over' stuff. It also included a very detailed section on the local politicians – who to trust, who to be wary of, and – in a section of his own – the local MP. It appeared the person I was replacing had difficulties with the MP, and he warned me about him. Then I was off, on my own again and loving it – just what policing should be like.

* * *

It was not long before my first brush with the local MP slid across my desk. It was a full-on, challenging, no-punches-pulled kind of letter. I read it, and the first thing I noticed was that it did not contain a question. It simply railed on and on about how the police handled a particular problem. I brought it to the attention of the officers concerned and, after listening to their version of events, responded. My letter was very brief, merely acknowledging his comments and saying that I had brought his concerns to the attention of my staff. His response was terse, and asked what my answer was. I reminded him that he had merely drawn my attention to a situation as recalled by one of his constituents, and as promised I had discussed the content with my staff. Nowhere in the letter was there a question posed. Our relationship was kind of like that for a while. Then we met up and, after discussion, we reached an understanding and things moved on. If one is to be in charge of a policing area, being challenged in that way is healthy and necessary. Letters from MPs, MSPs and local Councillors are all an important part of community policing, and a crucial part of keeping you abreast of local concerns – particularly if you treat them seriously and continue the written dialogue with verbal communication. They are also a gauge for the community as to your commitment. In that respect, I used to look forward to receiving them. A few years later, under a new regime and different Chief Constable, all that stopped. He insisted that all communication from politicians, at all levels, be directed to him and that he would deal with them. He did this by sending on a copy and asking for your response. It was an unnecessary interference in policing at a local level, and all about control. That was a Strathclyde senior officer trait, and – as many have now discovered – years after my service came to an end, it carried on into the Police Service of Scotland.

Being a Local Unit Commander was a special job. It was the first time – certainly in front line policing, since my Hamish Macbeth years in Fearn – that I had control of my own command. It consisted of four shifts, each with a Sergeant and four Constables. There were two Area Constables;

some called them Community Constables. There was a Traffic Warden and a civilian receptionist. She was worth her weight in gold. She was born and raised in Bo'ness, and there was not one person she did not have a handle on. An invaluable resource. Twenty-four staff in total. I nearly lost the Traffic Warden after a couple of years. The Falkirk Command, the largest in the Division, had several Traffic Wardens and it was decided they were overworked and needed ours. A long report was produced that divided the total number of parking tickets issued in Falkirk over the previous year. Divide that by the number of Traffic Wardens. The output of tickets issued by my lone operative came nowhere near the Falkirk figure. The conclusion was that I had no need for a Traffic Warden, and the plan was to transfer him to Falkirk. The plan broke down on so many levels. Firstly, they should have broken the average down from a year to an hour. That was the only comparable figure. My guy did not work overtime, nor did he work six days a week – or on certain evenings – like they did in Falkirk. I reported back with that argument, and added as their main task was road safety and making sure vehicles were not parked illegally – and not acting as tax collectors – then the higher figure indicated a failure of duty and a lower figure indicated a success. They left him in Bo'ness.

# CHAPTER 26

IN taking charge of Bo'ness, I felt it was important to create a vision. Policing is not complicated; in fact, it is simple. Obviously some incidents and situations can be complicated, but overall the principle is not. Part of my philosophy was to be as important to the town as their local junior
football team, Bo'ness Juniors. I do not say that tongue-in-
cheek. I am only too aware that the police could never hope to
achieve that level of 'attachment'. But my vision was to create
a feeling that we were their police and we could be trusted –
not worshipped like their beloved football team, but at least
respected. So as I give this account of my Bo'ness days as their
top police officer, I will try to give a flavour of my role. It was
not the same as my front line officers; it could never rise to
their level, because they were working cheek by jowl, twenty-
four hours a day, every day – dealing with tragedy, loss,
trauma, and more. They were, by far, more important than I
could ever be. I was their support behind the scenes; adjust-
ing, tuning the strings, overseeing, and trying to create a team
with vision.

I will, however, give examples of some of the things I
did get up to – mostly meetings and the like, but not all meetings. No, sometimes I got involved in interventions. In my
view, the philosophy of leadership is about taking responsibility. It has nothing to do with taking the glory, but it does

have a lot to do with taking the blame. The popular Command and Control model, pretty much the police way and certainly the new Single Scottish Police way, is not the best way to motivate staff – and, by definition, it is not the best way to get the best from them. One must find a way to lead that allows each officer in your command to develop, in order to allow them to use their own knowledge and skills. Trust them, and let them take risks; it is the only way they will grow in confidence and flourish.

Do not fear your staff. Your legacy has to be to help and encourage them to develop till they achieve their maximum potential. If that means they are better at it than you, is that not what you want? Like the old successful curling skip said, when asked why he had won so much: 'I just make sure I pick players that are better than me'. Your main aim is that your Command, your unit, is successful. That takes precedence over your ego, which should be left in the house. To achieve all that is easy. Well, it can be, as long as you take heed of the ego advice. It is not about you. There is no lexicon for this. It has to be common sense decisions; letting go of power, sharing the tiller. How did I do it, assuming I did? I supported my officers. I spoke to them, and I listened. No, I really listened. I took advice from front line Constables. I included them in decisions, and let them come up with the plan.

Importantly, I also took risks. One example was when legislation emerged that gave the police power to confiscate alcohol from a person under eighteen years of age in a public place. That was in addition to the legislation about buying it and drinking it. I took the legislation to the muster room, and talked about what we should do about it. A Constable suggested we should keep a record of all confiscations and report on the findings in due course. They gave that reporting job to me. Two designed the recording form. I was impressed; it was like a Crime Pattern Analysis form. Names, ages, location of find, where purchased, exact description of the alcohol and amount. They also wanted a letter to be sent to the respective parents. So we had a plan, and it had not been imposed from on high. We were the only Command who did that. It was very successful, and after six months I reported the findings to the Central Scotland Drug and Alcohol Group that met in the Health Board. I took one of the Constables with me. While the group was impressed and waxed lyrically about the report and the conclusions, they did nothing and said more research was required. I should not have taken the young officer, as it just depressed him. He wondered what the point of our work was. I assured him it was our duty to be the best we could be, and that we could not be responsible for others. I said that 'you do it because it is the right thing to do, and you do it for your self-respect'. That reminded me about a common plea, not only in the police service: 'We must be seen to do something'. I have always regarded that as a weak response, and based on internalised decision-making. Would it not be better to respond: 'We will do the right thing'. Not just anything. In fact, to be honest, in some circumstances the right thing is to do nothing. Be brave and explain.

The unit supervisor's six-weekly strategic meeting arrived. The meeting that covered the 'where are we, where are we going, what do we need to tackle, and who will do it' kind of stuff. It was not as democratic as that. In any team, one has to work out strengths and weaknesses and, while one works to address weaknesses with members of staff through training or supported exposure to the experience, on occasion you need to pick the correct horse for the correct course. Sometimes we would encounter a directive from on high to do something or change something, or even to introduce a new way of working – whatever. It was often pretty straightforward, and we just got down to understanding it and doing it. However, it was not always like that. Once we had a brand new process landed on us. We discussed it for a while, and I fielded various suggestions and objections. Once I was happy we had a handle on what was required, I vacated the chair with the comment: 'You are going to have deliver this, so work out how and let me know. I will get the coffee.' I headed out, got the bacon rolls and cups of coffee, and returned about twenty minutes later with the scran. Ten minutes to devour it, and then back to our deliberations and a way forward. I was not passing the buck: far from it. The buck would always finish up with me. No, I was giving officers space to think through things without feeling like I was watching, assessing them. We were a team.

Another ploy was to get them looking at the monthly crime detection rates, in particular ours, and to get performing better. The monthly force detection rates were circulated down to local unit level. They showed the detection rate for each individual local unit. In that way, one could chart your performance against your opposition, all the other units and commands. It was a print-out and, while read by the boss and pinned up on the muster room notice board, it really did not get universal attention. I decided to use it as a motivational tool for the troops. I represented the information in a different way. I had one of my computer wizards reproduce the information in pictorial form. Every unit was represented by a different coloured horse. Each had the monthly detection rate for the unit they represented as a number on the saddle. They were all in the correct order, racing to the 100% winning post. That simple tactic energised the troops, and each month they checked out where their horse was and worked on strategies to get into the lead next time. They were motivated, and it was working. The actual crime rate was not circulated.

Despite all that involvement and encouragement, I was clear about what kind of service I wanted delivered in our community: 'better than good' was how I described it. All of the above, and more, helped to get that message over and get it delivered. I had another technique. Every call we got was logged. It used to be written in a log book; however, we were slowly moving with the times and it was now on a computer. Once every month I would stay on for a few hours and access the Bo'ness computer logs and examine three full days' worth at random. Either I was happy with the way they had been closed down, or I was not happy. Every one in the latter category I printed off. I then wrote on the printout my comments, along with why and what I wanted to see happen. They were then issued to the Sergeants responsible and then, over the next few days, I met with every Sergeant and we talked through every 'comment' I had made. Oh, I also printed off a selection of good work and gave positive comments. I did that every month. It was not too long until we were all singing from the same hymn sheet, and my message was being understood.

Many years before I was in the police, I had been on management training and learned of GOYA management. It referred to a dynamic, 'get involved' management style. I fear that much management over the years has become more about memos and telephone. Today that will be e-mail and text. The counter to that is GOYA style of management – the 'Get Off Your Arse' method – where the manager spends time on the shop floor and communicates and interacts with the workforce. A systems manager will know all about the rope ladder and how to commission it. A leader will know where and when to position it and how to climb it. I used to be frustrated by some officers who constantly asked for my permission to do certain things. It is not their fault, and it may well hark back to previous experiences. I did encourage free thinking and decision-making. Part of that message was a notice I had in the office. It read: 'Is it Legal? Is it Ethical? Is it part of our mission? Then don't ask me – just do it!' I had another saying, and that was 'better to seek forgiveness than to seek permission'.

The two tales I relate are true. Sad, but true. In my opinion, they both expose misuses of power and an inability, certainly in the first example, to admit to having got it wrong and do the decent thing: apologise. I received a force-wide instruction. It indicated that an unidentified officer had been using his 'ghost' number to log onto the force computer and submit his reports. That was not allowed. Each officer is issued a unique number to log onto and access the computer system, and of course to identify the officer. A few had an extra log-in number. It was because they had a particular duty that required access to dual screens. That was called a 'ghost' number. I brought that to the attention of supervisors for their action. A few days later I received a personal memorandum from the Deputy Chief Constable. The unidentified officer was one of mine. The memorandum was not particularly complimentary. It accused me of having no idea what my officers were doing, and claimed the use of a 'ghost' log-in evidenced that reports were being submitted without being seen or authorised by a supervisory officer. The memorandum went on, and ordered me to check every report that was ever submitted from Bo'ness using the force computer system. That was a lot of work. It meant going back six or seven years. The weakness in the instruction was two-fold. I had only been in Bo'ness about two years. The person who penned the memorandum for the Deputy Chief Constable was the officer I had taken over from, and he had been there for the first four years of the computer system. The second weakness in the instruction was that the accused officer was innocent, and the person working for the Deputy Chief Constable had not thoroughly investigated the situation. Before responding to the instruction I interviewed the officer and his Sergeant. The officer had properly logged in to the system. The system automatically defaulted to his 'ghost' number. Both the officer and his Sergeant were aware of that, and had repeatedly reported the problem to a named person in the IT section at headquarters. I verified that by speaking to that person in IT, who confirmed the dialogue with my staff and added: 'He is not the only officer this is happening to. We know about it, but cannot find why it is happening. It is a big problem.' I then penned a reply, in which I intimated how long I had been in Bo'ness and asked if the instruction meant that I was to check back the years that had nothing to do with me? I then set out the information on the 'ghost' number situation and that in fact it had nothing to do with the maligned officer.

I heard nothing for a few weeks. Then I got a telephone call from the senior police officer in charge of IT for the force. It was not a positive call. He accused my officer of lying, and asked me which member of his staff I had been speaking to. I had not included his identity in my memorandum, because – whilst a bit naïve – I am not that naïve. I said I could not remember. He ordered me to tell him, and told me to call him 'sir' as he held a higher rank than I did. I insisted that I did not know the person's name, and finished by telling him that even if I did remember I would not tell him, as he would

not be able to properly handle the information. He was furious, and said that I had not heard the end of this; he was sure
that my officer was lying, and he would check every keystroke
the officer had ever made and prove that he was lying. I hung
up. Sad, but true.

More weeks passed, and not a whisper. Then, one sun-
ny morning, a telephone call. It was the self-same head of IT,
and he opened with one phrase: 'Ian, big problems'. I said that
as a Local Unit Commander it was my job to deal with problems. He then said: 'No, you don't have the problem; it's us.
The officer is telling the truth.' I responded by saying, 'yes, I
knew that; I assume you are on to apologise to him?' He said
no. I asked if he would write a report explaining the situation
and absolving my staff of any blame? He said he would not.
So I did. It was a long report, and it covered all the bases and
asked for an apology. There was no apology; not verbally, not
in writing, not by carrier pigeon... nothing. The officer concerned did thank me for my efforts to clear his name.

Another day, another problem. Because of long-term
sickness and training issues, I was down from four full shifts in
Bo'ness to three. I had to move my pieces on the chessboard
to fill the gaps. It meant running four depleted shifts for a
month. One such team being an experienced officer with a
young probationary Constable, a non-driver. Just the two of
them. They were run ragged. Not a complaint from either of
them; just decent officers doing what they were good at. I had
some leave and, when I got back, I was informed that the experienced officer in my stop-gap team had been complained
about by a local female. She had been accused of theft by
shoplifting, and in fact was charged as a result. She had tried
to barge out of the shop past the shopkeeper. She claimed his
arm brushed her breast. She said it was deliberate, and re-

ported him for indecently assaulting her. The officers thoroughly investigated both elements of the situation. There was evidence to support the theft by shoplifting. The officers traced two female witnesses who had been in the shop, and they corroborated the shopkeeper's version of events. The female accused of shoplifting would not back down. However, she said that she was willing to drop her accusation if the shopkeeper would drop the theft accusation. The officers closed the indecency accusation down and continued with the theft report. She said the officers had done nothing about her accusation and complained to the Chief Constable. The senior officer of the two was cited for two counts of neglect of duty.

I came back from my leave into this. I checked all the logs and the documents concerned. I was satisfied that the officer had carried out a full and proper enquiry. Reaching a different outcome from that which another officer would have made – senior or not – as a result of having carried out a proper enquiry does not constitute a neglect of duty. The problem is that some think it does. The hearing was looming, and the officer and his Federation representative asked if I would give evidence for the defence. I immediately agreed. Normally the officer in charge of a command of a unit would write a character reference on behalf of the officer. I was a defence witness, and resolved to provide a character reference at the hearing whilst giving my evidence. I was told I could not be a defence witness. I asked why not. There being no reason given, I did appear at the hearing. It was like a scene from an episode of *Perry Mason*. The Inspector presenting the case against the Constable was supported by a Sergeant, who constantly scribbled notes and shuffled them on to him. I nearly laughed. My difficulty was that I did not want to make things worse for the officer. I could tell they were not best pleased at my role, and much of their efforts were to question my motives and my management style. One ridiculous question was whether I thought it was alright for my officers to ignore reports of indecent assault. 'Of course not', was my terse reply; 'This was not an indecent assault – it was a form of blackmail to get the crime of theft dropped. My officer investigated it fully, including interviewing two independent witnesses who refuted the woman's allegations. In fact, I would suggest it was an attempt to pervert the course of justice. He did not neglect his duty'. In the end he was admonished on one count, relating to his recording of the event, and the neglect of duty 'charge' was dismissed. No case to answer. The officer was the self-same 'ghost' log-in innocent. I wondered if they were keen to teach him, or perhaps me, a lesson. Supporting members of your team also comes with the programme.

# CHAPTER 27

THE Complaints and Discipline Department in Central Scotland Police was headed up by a Chief Inspector, answering directly to the Deputy Chief Constable. Internal police discipline involves a multi-pronged approach. If criminal, the allegation would be subject to a regular criminal enquiry, carried out by members of the Force Complaints and Discipline Department or, if very serious, by detectives from the CID under the overall command of the officer in charge of Force Discipline, the Deputy Chief Constable. Some other major enquiries would be 'farmed' out to other forces. The majority, however, did not come into any of these categories and were enquired into by officers from the Complaints and Discipline Department. There were exceptions; there always are, and some enquiries were passed out to senior officers in the force. They were usually discipline issues, and not always at the top level of seriousness. Each would be carried out by an officer from a different unit or division.

In the latter years of my term as a Local Unit Commender, a change in policy allowed for the officer in charge of a unit to carry out enquiries into minor complaints about his or her own officers. I will relate one such complaint, and how I handled it. Some will agree with my decision, some will not. It involved a complaint that one of my officers had banged on a door at about two o'clock one morning and swore at and threatened the householder. No other explanation was offered. I knew that the officer, a very experienced Constable, was perfectly capable of using colourful language. I first read the log of the incident then I spoke to the officer and his colleague. They both agreed that profanities were uttered – not just by my officer. They gave me a run-down of the circumstances and how they left the situation. I then interviewed the person who had complained. I explained what I was doing and asked that he go into detail, as his letter was lacking in substance. I told him that I had the officer's version of events. I said that after our discussion I would be in a better position to make a deliberation on his complaint and explain my reasoning. He said he was happy with that. He could question my decision and take his complaint higher if not satisfied. He agreed that was fair. We discussed his day and the lead-up to the police visit to his house. He had been at the football in the afternoon, and had been drinking all day. When the police called at his house he had a few visitors; they were having a bit of a party, and music was playing. I asked if he understood why neighbours had called the police. He did. However, he was irked at the way they had banged on his window. I explained that the officers got no answer at the door because the music was so loud, and felt that was the only way he would know they were at his door. He agreed it was maybe a bit loud. I said the neighbours thought it was worse than that. He then said: 'Well, that is no excuse to swear at me'. I asked if he might be able to work out why the officer had sworn at him. Silence.

I again jogged his memory. 'What did you say to him?'

'I think I told them to fuck off. You know, I was pretty drunk. I was a bit out of order.'

I agreed the officers did say that. 'In fact, I wondered why they did not just lock you up.'

He again agreed. 'I don't know either,' adding: 'You know, I was angry when I complained about them. I was a bit out of order. I don't want to take this any further.'

He signed my notebook to that effect, and we shook hands. I reported back to the officer and told him the result, then unofficially warned him to 'be careful' with that short fuse. So that is a very minor piece of the day-to-day life of a Local Unit Commander. Something about nothing, and yet still requiring time and 'persuasive' understanding.

Another inquiry involved several thousand pounds of cash found in a holdall, in a storeroom in a police office. One night, after tripping over said holdall that had been lying about for months with nobody taking any interest, an Inspector opened it. Oops. It was full of loose cash, all paper, and it amounted to about £10,000. He reported his discovery, and I was tasked to find out where it came from, whose property it was, who deposited it there, what had that person done to establish the owner, and where was the record of the enquiry? Lastly, why was it not logged through a system? I quickly established the two officers who had dumped it there. I also established, just as quickly, that they had done nothing to record it through any system, nor had they carried out any meaningful enquiry. I further established that the money was found by these officers, some months before, at a disturbance in a house in the area. The house occupier was known to use drugs. She had a boyfriend from outwith the area. He was suspected of dealing in drugs. The flat was on the second floor of a block, and the holdall was found in a grass area near the flats. It was possible it had been thrown out of a window, although no witnesses were found. The suspected dealer was never traced and, when I interviewed the woman who had been the occupier of the flat, she could or would not shed any light on the issue and claimed to know nothing about the money. However, the officers who retrieved it were of the opinion it did belong to her and/or her ex-boyfriend. In terms of contact with the Procurator Fiscal, no trace of any memorandum was found, and the Fiscal denied any knowledge. I even put a request to IT to trace the memorandum in the system. They refused on the grounds that they were too busy. I attempted, without success, to get a higher authority to intervene. I submitted a report in which I concluded that the two officers were culpable on two counts: of failing to properly record an item of found property, and of failing to carry out reasonable enquiry. I recommended that both be subject to disciplinary proceedings for neglect of duty. I was summoned to see a senior officer ,who asked that I change my conclusions as he agreed with the officers that the money was 'drugs' money, as he called it. I opined that this was not the point. It may well have been 'drugs' money, but that did not absolve them of their duty to properly record the item or to carry out proper enquiry. My recommendations were not acted upon, and the issue was dropped. The money eventually was recorded, and the last I heard the woman in the flat – the one I spoke to – contacted the police to claim it was hers. I did not hear the conclusion of her claim.

My main point, however, was about the self-investigation process. I gave four varying types of enquiry. The latter involved two officers who were 'well thought of' and therefore whom, in my opinion, the system was reluctant to pursue in terms of disciplining them. I will add – and of this I am certain – if some other officers I could name had left £10,000 lying about unrecorded, disciplinary proceedings would have been swift. So while I have reservations about the occasional 'unfairness' in the system, on balance – in terms of my thoughts on the police investigating themselves – I think it should continue to be carried out principally in-house, but be subject to regular external inspection. In terms of the very local complaint in a community, as described, I am happy that should be left local, with the proviso that the person complaining has the option to go higher if not satisfied.

To bring us back to the everyday, mundane Bo'ness police office, it was – assuming it still exists, which I doubt – situated near the site of the Bo'ness Railway Preservation Society. The self-same place where dozens of steam engines were mothballed all these years before, when 'I were a lad' living nearby – and when I did not steal bits and pieces from them. As it happened, steam trains regularly passed by the office as they gathered speed out of their depot. The famous Thomas the Tank Engine being amongst them. As they passed the office, they sounded their shrill steam whistle, Box-Car Willie-style. This had nothing to do with entertaining or annoying the police; there was a crossing near the office, and the warning was for pedestrians.

One of my Sergeants and I were working on an issue in my office one summer evening, and the window was open. The Sergeant was on the telephone to an officer from the Met Police in London. We had to get a copy of a document to him, and he asked if we would fax it. We did not have a fax machine. 'Ah. What about another electronic transfer?' he asked. Still no joy at our end. It was just at that precise moment a passing steam engine sounded its whistle. The Met officer asked what it was.

'Oh', quipped the Sergeant, 'that's a steam train passing the office'.

A pregnant pause, and then: 'A what?'

'A steam train', the Sergeant repeated.

Another pause, and then: 'Ah, right. Is it alright to ask if you are wearing a kilt?'

We managed to get through the heather to a fax machine and get the document to London.

Prior to being in this position I had majored in the development of partnership working, based on the principle that causes of anti-social behaviour and criminality lie pretty much outwith the remit or the expertise of the police to greatly influence. The stuff I argued earlier. Well now, as a Local Unit Commander in charge of my own 'patch' – to use a *Dixon of Dock Green* expression – I could get on and try it out for real. I must add that it would have pitfalls and difficulties, as I had previously experienced in my Regional Council secondment. Nevertheless, it still was an exciting challenge. There would be principally three main partners, as I saw it. The community, in which I include political representatives, other services, and my staff. Three groupings with perhaps a myriad of views, opinions and agendas. I had learned from my earlier experiences, and hoped that would help my navigation skills. While getting people from different backgrounds, professional experiences and services around a table might be easy enough, one has to try and quickly establish their agenda. Each might have a different vision and a different outcome in mind. While that is perfectly understandable, it does require to be teased out and discussed in order to find common ground. I had spoken at various locations about just that. To aid understanding of that point, I used 'ambiguous' drawings obtained from the Psychology Department at Stirling University. I would show one, and ask people not to confer and simply write down what they saw. The old woman/young woman sketch was probably the most instructive. There were others. I would select someone and ask them to tell me what they had written down. I would then ask for a show of hands from those who concurred. After that, I would check out the others. It was my experience that the majority immediately saw a young woman in the sketch; the others, the old woman. Some struggled to see both images. The whole point of the exercise was to show that we do not all see the same thing, and this applied to more than 'ambiguous' sketches. The lesson being, be sure those involved agree on the agenda and understand the outcome.

A real difficulty in this arena is when an organisation represents itself at meetings with different people. You can get situations where agreement is reached and a way forward agreed, only for a different person to turn up at a subsequent meeting and totally disagree with the outcome his or her colleague had previously signed up to. It is not about them, their organisation had decided. It can be about egos. However, through all that one can weave a way that reaches agreement. Having briefly unearthed difficulties, I will now go on to describe my approach and how I operated in the community I served. First of all, I made a point of attending just about every public community meeting. The Community Council, the Area Committee, the Bo'ness Fair management meetings, and many more. Some I attended alone, and some I was accompanied by an Area Constable or a Sergeant. Some I attended when I was not invited, and some I called. One cannot police in a vacuum, as I have said before, and working alongside the community – at all levels – was crucial.

I will mention my attitude towards the local press at this point, because they are an important partner in working with communities. I met the local journalist for coffee, and we set out the rules of engagement. They were pretty simple. I was willing to share everything I had. Sometimes, however, there might be an issue or a detail I would not want printed. Perhaps a serious confidentiality or secrecy issue, or a legal issue as a case was still being investigated. We had few such issues. As I said, they got everything – with that caveat. I promised they would always be first to hear. The press were delighted, because in reality they got it all, with little or no restriction. In return, they would give me the 'heads-up' on a brewing story that I might not have been aware of.

On one occasion, a young fifteen year old in Bo'ness received a prison sentence for drug offences. He was the youngest person in the country to have been sentenced to imprisonment for such offences. The media were all over the story, and a reporter from the BBC turned up to record an interview. We did the usual and went over the type of questions I would face. However, a very early question had not been on the agreed list. Nothing new there. She explained the situation and asked me if I was pleased by the sentence. I said nothing for a moment then explained I was far from pleased. What was pleasing about a young teenager, fifteen years old, being imprisoned. No, I am anything but pleased. We have failed him; not just the police – society. I think she realised I was irked. It went out on the air pretty much as I had said it.

I recall two such 'heads-up' warnings. One involved a meeting called by two local councillors about anti-social problems in an area. They had not seen fit to invite me; political intrigue. I attended in any case, in uniform and deliberately a minute or two late. I took my seat at the back of the hall, just in time to hear the politicians explaining how they would go about dealing with the problem. I short, they were going to petition me. A member of the public sitting next to me shouted that I was present. Silence from the floor. Another shouted that it would be better if I was at the front. He was correct. I waited and did not move. After a moment, one politician asked me if I would join him at the front, which I did. I did not sit down, and stood in front of the assembly. I then took many questions, and we agreed a plan of action. These included involving a few in the meeting working with the Area Constable to ease the situation they faced. Why had I not been invited? As I indicated: party politics.

Another situation was not so easy. A call from the local reporter warned that a convicted paedophile had been housed back with his mother in the family house, in the same street his victim lived. A meeting had been called by the mother of the victim, and the word 'vigilante' hung heavy in the air. Along with one of my Sergeants we visited her, unannounced and uninvited. She was angry at first, and wondered how I knew what she planned. I suggested meeting with one or two people from Falkirk Council, the housing department and the criminal justice social work team, as well as her local councillor. She agreed. I warned her that she had better make sure that no public protests took place. If so, I would arrest her first. The meeting took place a few days later, and she was there along with another two people from the street. The officer from police headquarters who carried that portfolio was also in attendance. I chaired the meeting. It was a bit hot for a while. It calmed, and the Councillor agreed to take the issue forward and reach an amicable solution. Things went back to normal, and we heard no more.

Another was about a regular complaint: young people causing 'trouble' in a community. I listened carefully to the details of the complaints. I did not need to encourage dialogue; they were well-motivated and angry. After their outpourings,

I asked if they would let me know what their solutions might be. Again I listened and took notes. When I was sure they had run out of ideas, I spoke. I went over their 'solutions' and pointed out those that were simply illegal, slowly homing in on the possible. One example of a community solution involved taking them away in a 'Black Maria' and dropping them off at the other side of Bo'ness. I think I used the word 'abduction' in my comments. We talked about evidence, and agreed that most of the young people actually lived nearby and had a right to be in their community. We got into staffing numbers and other issues, and slowly a plan emerged. Again, like other areas, it involved the Area Constable linking with them and attending on a more planned schedule. It also involved calling at some of their houses on patrol to see how they were. It was one of the areas we eventually engaged in the Cross Talk initiative that I was involved in designing during my Regional Council days, and referred to earlier. Again, while it was not always a total success, it was a great improvement and something to work on, assuming an open mind.

These meetings were many and varied. Another two were more general, and related to community concerns about drug traffickers in the town and about some retail outlets selling alcohol to persons underage. It terms of the latter, we had done a bit of work and I was able to inform them of half a dozen cases we had reported. I was also able to explain why it made little difference what we did. The Procurator Fiscal in Falkirk said it was a licensing issue, and he would not prosecute. Meanwhile, discussion with the Clerk to the Licensing Court in Falkirk revealed the never-ending circle: they would only take action in such cases if there was a conviction. *Catch-22* remake. Having listened to my information, the community group wrote to both organisations expressing their disgust towards what they regarded as stupidity and a total lack of care for the community. Taking decisions that were patently not in the public interest (though probably using more refined terminology).

The drug trafficking, and our relative lack of success, was also explained. The local trafficker gets in the dealer package and, within two to three hours, it was cut, divided into £10 bags and out the door. A better marketing scheme than most big stores. Hitherto we would get a call, get a Justice of the Peace warrant locally, turn the house as quickly as possible, and certainly within an hour of getting the tip off. We were quite successful and made a few arrests. Then the use of a JP warrant was outlawed. That was because it was misused on an industrial scale by one or two of the bigger forces. The new system was to get a Sheriff's warrant. That involved a written report to the Procurator Fiscal. There was often an inquisition about the request, and often it was refused. If it was accepted then it had to go to a Sheriff to be considered at that level, and – if the grounds were accepted – a warrant was issued. As many such cases were last minute calls to the police, informing them that 'so and so' has the drugs there now, waiting for hours or even a day or two to get a warrant did not help our chances of a successful drug find. It also led to some members of the public losing faith and thinking we were, in fact, doing nothing. I am sure in the bigger 'main dealers' world it worked fine, but at a community level it was less than successful. It was as a result of that public meeting that the Procurator Fiscal got a difficult time in the 'do you walk on water' meeting some months later, which I have made mention of.

The mother of a drug-using son and daughter called at the office, desperate for help. She was in tears. We spoke for a while, and I handed her two of the 'stock' help leaflets issued by the Scottish Office and the local Health Service. She threw them on the floor and said she would not use them as toilet paper. She was a bit more graphic. I asked her what she saw as the problem. We spoke for a while, and hatched a simple plan. One problem, as she saw it, was the lack of services for young people. There were services for young pregnant women, but – if not pregnant or if male – there was nothing. I agreed to assist her in setting up a help group for parents, and they could meet as often as they wanted in my conference room. That is exactly what they did. At the first meeting there were six or seven, and then it grew. As an aside, we were a no smoking organisation; however, they smoked. The issue being addressed was bigger than a non-smoking policy. Eventually they moved out to a bigger venue, free of charge, and I kept up with them. I arranged for other professionals and community support from the Council, and soon they started a project and brought in other members of the community who had different skills and who could help them grow and develop. The health service also worked with them, and they were able to attract community grants and employ a co-ordinator.

Some years later, when I had moved on from Bo'ness to a promoted role at headquarters, I was able to participate with other services and – with the Bo'ness group's help – in designing and developing a drug service to work in communities the length and breadth of NHS Forth Valley and to address the gap identified at that very first meeting in my office all these years before. A service that included young men and women. That service was Signpost Forth Valley. As I write today, in 2017, that service – drawing nearly one million pounds of grants a year – is a crucial part of drug and alcohol services in communities and has in excess of twenty full-time employees. It is now called Signpost Recovery, and it is a successful merge of services and communities. It started with an awkward meeting in my office, and it took a risk on my part and the inspiration of a committed community activist. It has to be a lesson to us all; despite the difficulties I have mentioned, working in partnership can work and must work.

# CHAPTER 28

SOMETIMES I could not help bumping into street issues; it must be my nature. I was heading back into Bo'ness about one o'clock on a Saturday morning. I had been covering the whole of the Division, and was heading back to my office to sort out some paperwork. I reached a part of Bo'ness town centre that was called – locally – the 'East Partings', right at the old Co-operative Footwear Department Shop. My dad had been the manager there years before. It was not that now. There was a crowd of a dozen or more men – varying ages, but older than teenagers – standing in a rather menacing group in the middle of the highway. As I was passing them, I saw why they were there. One of our police cars was parked outside a local hostelry, about twenty yards from the grinning throng. It was unattended, and it had been used as target practice. The windscreen was smashed, as was the passenger side window. There were dents all over the bonnet. I assumed my officers were hiding nearby.

I swung my car around and got out beside the group. As I got out, there was a low murmur. I walked up to them and congratulated them on a good night. I asked if they had enjoyed themselves and suggested there was no point in asking how the car was damaged. There was a collective grin. (I don't think there is a noun for a collective grin.) It was then that I noticed most were drinking out of beer cans and beer bottles. It was against the local bye-laws to drink alcohol in that bit of Bo'ness. As I announced that, I pushed in amongst them and – one by one – grabbed a can or a bottle and carefully poured the contents over the feet of the lawbreaker. I think there were six or seven. They protested and, though I am not sure, I might have been called a couple of unprintable names. I had started, so I was going to finish. No one resisted, and they took their punishment well. I then told them to fuck off or I would call the real police and anyone left about would get arrested. They wandered off, and 'daft bastard' was the worst I heard. My feet, shoes, socks, and the bottom of my trousers were all soaked in beer. Or was it lager?

I then dealt with my officers, neither of whom lasted much longer in my Unit. I was taken aside by two or three of my other Constables on the Monday. They had heard what I had done; it seems that it was all over the town. They were sincere in warning me about my behaviour; they did not want to see me hurt. I thanked them, and conceded it was a bit risky. However, occasionally one has to make some kind of statement or the wrong people would think they were in charge.

Sometimes opportunities presented themselves in different ways. I will relate another situation. In working on this book, I made contact with the young man I will write about. In his thirties now, he lives out the area, has a good job and a family. He is a credit to himself. He was adamant I should not identify him, because these days were behind him and he did not want to go back. I respect that wish, so I will amend the facts and the details accordingly, but the essence of the story remains.

Whilst in charge of policing in Bo'ness, we had suffered a repeat offender over a few months. He was detected and charged with several crimes – more than once. Our interventions were proving to be a waste of our time. Such was his desire to do what he was doing, being arrested and charged time and again was no deterrent. After another wild weekend, and as the CID had finished interviewing him for the umpteenth time, I intervened. I told the CID to leave, and I would speak to the young man on my own. We talked, and what stood out was that he was a very articulate, personable fifteen year old. Some are not so, and almost grunt at you. I had done my homework before my intervention and was able to suggest an alternative, legal activity that offered a similar experience to his illegal activity. The only caveat was that he had to stop what he had been doing. He asked me if I could really do that. I said that I could; it would be up to him after I had taken him to the threshold of the opportunity. 'I cannot do it for you.' He agreed, stood up, and stretched out his hand. We, the Local Unit Commander and a fifteen year old 'juvenile offender' shook hands on the deal. He was fifteen; he was not a criminal.

So that is what happened. About six months after that handshake, I got a telephone call to go to Falkirk Sheriff Court. I was met by a lawyer who said he was representing the young lad. He had been arrested that weekend after going back on his word. I asked him, what did he want from me? He wondered if I would write a report in support of his client, who wanted to see me. I went to the cell and he was crying. He apologised for letting me down. I told him I was not let down – I was a police officer; he could only let himself down. I duly wrote a report, and it was presented by his lawyer to the court. It seems that it kept him from being sent to prison. He never offended again, and went on to be a serious international success in the activity he had been pointed at. He has now retired and, as I said, lives a good life out of the area. I will not identify him, but I will congratulate him on being brave and breaking free from what would have destined him to a non-life. It is possible, you see. It takes courage, and he showed that. I was spoken to by a senior officer during the early days of that arrangement; the agreement between a senior police officer and a lost wee boy. The officer told me I had a dangerous management style and, in terms of the young person, I would finish up with egg on my face. I responded by saying that egg on your face is a concept: an illusion, if you will. If you see egg on my face, then that is what you see. I actually will not have egg on my face. He shook his head, and I headed back to my style of policing. The style I was weaned on when serving in Ross and Sutherland Constabulary.

Missing persons when they are reported can be long, soul-destroying enquiries. Children are a particular challenge, and immediately treated in the top tariff of importance. Sometimes the person reported missing is in fact not missing, but have deliberately gone away. It is not unknown to locate such a person, sometimes only in their late teens, to be told: 'I am not missing, and I do not want you to tell my parents where I am'. That is difficult. You have a duty to keep that confidence; they are adult. However, you still have a duty to the parents – at least to let them know their offspring is alive and well. No matter how much they may plead, you are bound not to divulge the location. It is not a good place, but worse for the parents.

I had been away for a few days on a mountain expedition in the north of Scotland. I got back to work on Monday morning to face the issue of two missing women that weekend. Both on the Friday. They had not been found. I took over the investigation from a colleague who had been standing in for me. I went over all the notes and decided to start from the beginning. I laid out a map of the town and wrote down all that had been done, then all the assets I could call on. Helicopter, underwater search unit, police dogs, specialised search unit, and – because we were on the banks of the River Forth – why not ask the MOD at Rosyth to head along our side and have a look? We would search the two houses again. Another team would handle checking out bank transactions, telephone messages and friends, friends' houses, etc. I also, probably because of my mountain rescue experience, called out the Scottish Search and Rescue Dogs (SARDA). I indicated to the underwater unit where I wanted searched, then briefed the boss on what my plans were. Basically, apart from the boat on the river – a long shot – and the underwater guys, all other searches would start at the houses and systematically work outward. We had no real plan for a helicopter, so we held that one back. Four SARDA dogs and handlers turned out and – after a briefing – they started at one of the houses, the one nearest the shore. That house was adjacent to a huge area of foreshore, trees and bushes. They had not been out for twenty minutes when I was called to join them near one of the missing person's homes. Out the back was an area of seriously dense and prickly bushes; they were about five feet high and about fifty yards by thirty yards. A dog had picked up a scent from the centre. I lay on the ground and saw the lady, lying right under the bushes and right in the middle. She had obviously crawled right in. We got the council to cut a way in to her. She was dead, and had probably died on the Friday. A bottle of spirits lay beside her, along with a bottle of pills. She had headphones on, and music had been playing. What a tragedy. She was a young woman. There were no suspicious circumstances. From a purely selfish, professional viewpoint, it was a relief to find her so quickly. We continued searching for the other lady, who was older than the first one. We finally found her on Wednesday morning, in one of the areas of water we were searching. She was also dead, and there were no suspicious circumstances. We expend a lot of hours on such searches and many – like the two described – do not end well.

Many years before, when a Constable in Tullibody, we found an old man in the River Devon. He had not been reported missing, and someone had come across his body. He was considerate, we think, and had tied himself to a fencepost on the banking. By the looks of it, he had walked into the river to drown. We assumed he had tethered himself to the fencepost to prevent being washed away and causing people too much bother. I don't really know, but why else would he do that?

Policing, like many public service organisations, seems not to regard the person's time as important. They are at their work, they get paid anyway, so what does it matter what they are actually doing? I think it is flawed budgeting, false economy, leading to serious inefficiencies. One issue I came across when in charge in Bo'ness involved the towels in the shower block. Headquarters had a contract with a laundry. Dirty towels were removed weekly and replaced with clean towels. All very efficient. Then we had none. Clean towels, I mean. In fact, towels of any kind – clean or dirty. A call to headquarters revealed the new master plan. The contract with the laundry was too expensive. Solution: install a washing machine and tumble dryer in headquarters, then give two cleaners a couple of hours' overtime to wash and dry towels. I am sure they did it well. The obvious question: how do we actually get the towels? You drive to headquarters. So all over the police area, officers are delivering and picking up towels.

How is that cheaper? It is all about hidden budgets and lack of accountability. It did not stop with the single police service. I wrote a memorandum questioning the new arrangement, but to no avail. A week or two later, I was in headquarters and a Superintendent asked about my 'towels memorandum'. I did not engage. There was a Chief Superintendent there, and he asked what it was about. I did not elaborate, but did mention the new arrangement. He responded by saying the following: 'Hot air. The way forward is hot air.' The perfect foil, really. I replied: 'Yes, but all the hot air is in headquarters'. I walked out before he caught on.

The Deputy Chief Constable and a Chief Superintendent called at my office completely unannounced on a day in early June in the year 2000. I got tea and scones rustled up, and over the refreshments we indulged in small talk – nothing world shattering. I was puzzled as to the reason for the call. Then, almost off the cuff, the Deputy asked if I would be interested in being promoted to Chief Inspector and take on running the Community Safety Department at headquarters. It had been divorced from the CID by then. Crime Management Services was no more. I entered into a discussion about the position, and was cut short by the Deputy asking: 'Do you want the job or not?' I said yes. I was getting promoted again, outwith the promotion system. I think the Army would call that a 'field promotion'. He explained that leading up to and during my time within Central Regional Council, we – Central Scotland Police – had been at the forefront of Community Safety in Scotland. We were noticed: the Scottish Office sought our advice and involved us. However, we had lost our way; we now led nothing. Promoting me was to get me into a position to get us back where we once were. I resisted the desire to ask about my reception on my return from the Regional Council, where my time there was not regarded as real policing and crucially would not count towards my 'career'. If my work was so important then why was it not recognised? Why was it another nail in my career coffin? To highlight that as the reason I was being offered promotion I found insulting. However, for once I took the cowardly path and said nothing. I took the job. Had I abandoned my values? Time would tell. While I was sure I would relish the challenge, I had been out of the picture for a while and in reality had no idea about the practical support I was likely to get. I was soon to find out.

I had one last, important function to perform for Bo'ness. I had the Fair to negotiate. Then it was Friday 30<sup>th</sup> June 2000. It was Bo'ness Children's Fair day; my last Fair, and my last day in Bo'ness before taking up the promoted post in Stirling on the Monday. I have already made mention of the Children's Fair, during my term in Bo'ness as Sergeant. To coincide with the emancipation of miners, a Miner's Fair started in the town in 1779. In 1879 that day was changed, and out of it emerged the world famous Bo'ness Children's Fair Day. The date changed about a bit in the early days, but is now firmly in the Bo'ness consciousness as the last Friday in June – hail, rain or shine.

There is a story of two Hamebiders, marooned on a desert island having survived a shipwreck. It is over 100°C, and they are down to their last half-cup of water. Things are looking bleak for them.

One wiped his brow and asked 'what day is it?'
'Oh, it's Friday the 29<sup>th</sup> of June', came the reply.
'Brilliant! What a great day they've got for the Fair!'
I notice nowadays the police lead the procession with an officer in a police car. For years we paid the occasion its

true respect, and the Local Unit Commander led the procession on foot – yes, at the very front. It was a privilege, and I regarded it as such. There is not a big list of officers who can claim that honour. I had four years of leading the procession. To work closely with a community of sixteen or so thousand and help them deliver their big day is the core of community policing, and I fear we are losing that important connection. It was never us and them, but it is increasingly thus as an egotistical, controlling government has its misguided way. For the first time I had the added privilege of being invited to the Fair Dinner in the Town Hall on my last Fair Day; my last day in Bo'ness. The Chief Constable, the local MP and other dignitaries were in attendance. After the dinner there were a few speeches and presentations. I heard my name being mentioned, along with a few nice words about my service to the town and wishing me well in my next posting. Then I was asked to come forward and, to my astonishment, I was presented with a gold Bo'ness Children's Fair Day medal. My third medal as a police officer, and the most important. My good conduct medal – handed to me in a corridor, after not being invited to the official ceremony – and my Queen's Jubilee Medal, have no place in my heart, and neither comes anywhere near my cherished Bo'ness and Dunblane mementos. The latter was the handwritten card I previously mentioned, from an unknown Dunblane resident.

That was only a snatch of what working as police boss in a local community was like. It was challenging, energising, often sad, and sometimes hilarious. Standing in the canteen of the Bo'ness office on a winter afternoon was inspirational. The docks and the River Forth opposite were a favourite place for flocking (yes, flocking – stop adding your own words) shore birds. Sometimes they displayed, and huge flocks would speed one way, then – as though by magic – change direction, instantly flick over in flight and dip or rise, creating a complete change from black to white or the other way around. They were waders, murmurating – the same as the more famous murmuration of starlings. It was mesmeric, and they looked like they were being controlled by an electric switch. They somehow created a counterbalance to my thoughts of the issues I dealt with. No matter how communities co-exist, no matter how unfortunate or unpalatable some incidents were, nature – on your very doorstep – just did its thing regardless.

I was interviewed by the local paper about my departure and, when asked if there had been any high spots, without hesitation I recalled the young man who took his chance and moved out of crime and became a success in another field. I also mentioned the development of the parents' support group and community drug initiative that had emerged after the difficult meeting in my office. I was reminded by the reporter of another achievement; well two, actually. In my time in charge, the recorded crime rate had steadily fallen and our detection rates were amongst the highest in Scotland. While they are to be applauded, I was still mindful of the systematic way we had achieved these successes. It was about the community, and it was about teamwork. It was about hard work, and it was about leadership. Then I was off to leave the good people of Bo'ness, because that is what they were. They still are. I had taken the King's Shilling, so to speak, and was to enter the dragon's den on the first Monday of July 2000. I was soon to find out how true that would be.

# CHAPTER 29

I ENTERED my new office on the first floor of Police Headquarters in Stirling on Monday 3rd July 2000. My rank was Chief Inspector, and I had another Bath Star. I was in the heady atmosphere of headquarters, right amongst the Snakes in Suits – not that they all were, but enough to make each step a test. I got no briefing. I had a secretary who introduced me to my computer, explained how to set it up, and told me what my telephone number was. There were a few letters and other documents awaiting my attention. I was underway.

I was going to have to sort out my own agenda and do what I was good at: look, listen, take stock, work it out. I had no other staff. In my absence, the Community Safety department had been disbanded as a unit and the staff had all been dispersed to the divisions, answering to the Divisional Commanders. My HQ role was strategic, with no management responsibility for the Divisional staff. The aim was to get Central Scotland Police Community Safety back to the heights of five or six years ago. I had picked up the gauntlet, but I had no idea just how far we had fallen. People with other interests had been allowed to take over. In fact, I might even suggest that sabotage of the whole concept was their strategy. If I regard that as a bit strong, I might replace the word 'sabotage' with 'disinterest', but I am not so sure.

Whatever the reason, it seemed to have worked. There was no leadership, nothing. It was impossible. I had strategic responsibility for Youth Justice, Intruder Alarm Policy, Support for Victims, the force's Diversity strategy, Drug Awareness, Partnership Working, Community Safety, Crime Prevention, and Design Out Crime issues. Each was a national issue, and before I knew what was happening I was travelling all over Scotland attending meetings, presentations and working groups. Each one generated work.

Most forces had different officers at these meetings, each with a single portfolio. I had them all. I was a font of knowledge, but it was stressful. I was working long hours. It was not just once that I sat in my office in tears. Anyway, that was not going to get anything done. I visited all the officers in division and I met with the Divisional Commanders. I had a grasp on how they worked. I identified and 'tapped' the officers I thought I needed to get into position to stop the slide. I then travelled the force and found a possible office to locate the, as-yet-'virtual', team. My first real move after that was to write a ten page report laying out all the issues, the responsibilities, and crucially what I saw as the answer – including the staff I wanted, and the office I had located for them. In it, I likened my position to a wheel. I was the hub, but there were no spokes. My report was approved, almost without alteration. The only change insisted on by the force strategy group was that I remain in my office at headquarters and not join my unit in Dunblane. I was cooking with gas, although a bit distant from the cooker.

That exercise took some months. In the meantime, I ploughed a lone furrow in attempting to establish stability, trying to find where the management support within HQ lay. It was not plentiful. Not one officer would take responsibility for Community Safety. There were plenty of opinions on different aspects, but no leader. It was down to me. It was not ideal. I was carrying responsibility for some nationwide, important issues, and yet I was not allowed onto the Force Strategic Group. When we did hold our own at a national level, we had a supportive Chief Constable and a dedicated Superintendent. None of that existed when I headed to Headquarters, nor would it change during my tenure. I soldiered on, regardless.

Being so close to the force's senior decision makers was quite eye-opening. One revelation – although why was I surprised? – was that many of these senior officers displayed homophobic tendencies. I am certain each one of them, to a man – as was the case then – would be horrified at my assertion. Why do I say that, and what evidence do I have to back up my claim? As I intimated, I travelled the country representing Central Scotland Police on many working groups and forums. I also attended and represented Central Scotland Police on the Association of Chief Police Officers (Scotland) – or ACPOS, for short. The latter was a Chief Constables' association, and hardly a suitable venue for a Chief Inspector. I do myself a disservice, perhaps, as it was agenda-based and I did have a smattering of knowledge in some areas. While I think the Chief Constables, in the main, were completely at ease and charming, there were a couple of exceptions who gave the impression of being 'rank-conscious'. These excursions of mine often led to a paper on some subject or other being produced and circulated for comment by forces. My way of dealing with these was to add my own comments and suggested recommendations, then forward to the Chief Constable for inclusion in his Strategy meetings within force. Sometime he might ask for a verbal discourse. Most of the papers really met with little, if any, comment, and were pretty much rubber-stamped. That was until I circulated a paper on police handling of complaints by and against members of the LGBT (Lesbian, Gay, Bisexual and Transsexual) community. I sat on a national working group with police officers and members of the wider LGBT community throughout Scotland. That paper rebounded on me as though I had written it on rubber. Most senior officers, who hardly ever commented or took little interest in previous documents, certainly had something to say on that occasion. Not one comment was positive. I was astounded. Or was I? A short time later, I was asked to attend a Force Strategic meeting about another issue. As I entered the room, a Chief Superintendent looked over at me and said: 'Oh, here he is – our gay officer'.

This was the same officer who once said to me, at a partnership meeting: 'If I had a gun, Mr McNeish, I know who I would be using it on'. I had led a review into RAH-MAS: Racist Attacks and Harassment Multi Agency Strategy. It was a key strategy in our attempt to address these issues locally, and was well-supported by all our partners. The review, like many such 'reviews', already had one or two outcomes that 'had' to be reached. In this case, some of the main players wanted to amend an important element. The strategy did not allow the name of a person being investigated for a racist incident to be shared amongst the partners. There wish was to change that, and allow the sharing of the identity of the accused. In the end, and after a few weeks of meetings and some serious differences of opinion, I reported back to the strategic group. The review made twenty-seven recommendations for change, the majority minor and of little consequence. The major item – the sharing of the accused person's name prior to any enquiry or finding of guilt – was not changed.

That was a majority decision; some really had wanted to make the change. My argument, supported by the majority however was simple: it would be a live police enquiry and therefore Sub Judice, which meant the case was not open for public discussion or disclosure at that time. I read out the review recommendations and, as I got to that one – announcing the status quo – the senior police officer in the chair, who was, along with the Chair of the local Racial Equality Group, determined to see that change, was angry that we had not followed his directive. He lost his cool and made the 'gun' remark. Our partners were horrified, and wanted me to make an issue of it. I didn't. Not because of career issues or being frightened; nothing like that. I knew the officer well, and he was always coming away with ridiculous statements. He did not mean any of them. He was more of a bluster than a bully.

Part of my portfolio was diversity, in the widest sense. When I had my new troops cosy in their new office in Dunblane, I divided up the portfolios between them. While I took the lead, the bulk of the legwork was being carried out by my 'Sergeants Three'. An early task was to write the force's Racial Equality Scheme as required by the then-Commission for Racial Equality (CRE), which was later merged into the new Equality and Human Rights Commission. All authorities – police, fire, health boards, and more – had to submit their own scheme. Of all the 'schemes' presented to the CRE, as it turned out, only six – nationally – were acceptable without changes. The Central Scotland Police scheme was in the acceptable half-dozen. Part of our commitment to diversity involved having liaison officers for different groups, not solely minority ethnic. I liaised with the Sikh community in Central, and with the local LGBT community. Both were rewarding in different ways.

In terms of LBGT issues, I confessed to being a little light in my knowledge. Having said that, at my first couple of meetings I was pleased – intrigued, perhaps – to get a call from a female senior lecturer at a University. I duly met her, explained my new role and confessed my ignorance. She was extremely understanding and helpful, and we discussed her situation and more general stuff over the next hour. We discussed female partners having children by artificial insemination and a lot more. We talked about the difficulties that people in lesser positions – not as well off, perhaps, and/or with fewer connections – would face when trying to address the same issues that she had dealt with. 'Artificial insemination?' I asked. She smiled and nodded. It was an eye-opener for me, and I will always be grateful to her. A stranger, who allowed me to into her life just to help me understand. It was a really brave thing to do. I was humbled, not for the first time. We covered a lot of ground, and she finished with one piece of advice that has remained with me till this very day: a simple statement. You know, she said 'we are just people trying to live a life and survive and be normal'. There was a smile on her lips at that last part. Stop making an example of us. Does my sexuality matter? I knew exactly what she meant, and I resolved – as far as I could, in my limited sphere of influence – to work as hard as I could to achieve that for her.

I had come across the same comment from a black doctor working in this area. He said to me: 'Ian, we are just people; all of us. While certain actions and behaviours may cause comment, it must not be because we are black, or gay, or whatever'. Both had an issue about the media highlighting ethnicity or sexuality when referring to a person achieving some feat or other. Common example being: 'First black person to play for [[whoever]]', or 'First gay player to score a goal for [[so and so]]'. That approach, he said, continues to keep the issue alive. He was clear about something else. Please do not use us – black people, he meant – to be the reason to crucify one of your officers if they come away with some remark, even if it is ill-advised.

A while after that I was at an LGBT local authority police liaison meeting in Aberdeen. A particular LGBT group, from Fife, appeared unhappy with my presence. It seemed they were annoyed at the police in my area for creeping up on them in disguise, wearing dresses. I assured them I had no idea what they were talking about and would find out. I duly did, and updated them at the next meeting. Two officers were creeping through trees to an out-of-the-way spot, well-known for gay liaisons. It was a bright summer evening, and the officers were in shirt sleeves – white shirts. To make themselves less conspicuous, they cut holes in black bin bags and wore them over their uniform shirts. Hence the dress reference. We had a laugh at the ridiculousness of it all when I told them.

One sad connection I made was with FLAGS (Falkirk Lesbian and Gay Society), a group from the Falkirk area. It was sad because they felt so outlawed and unsupported; any venue they found to meet in was soon removed from them when people found out they were members of the LBGT community. That was fifteen years or so ago; things move on, and perhaps – if the group still exists – they now have a safe meeting place.

We set up a three layer interpreting process, to be used by front line officers, and to support and guide all our officers through this politically-charged area of work we researched, wrote and produced a comprehensive guidance document on dealing with racist incidents. It was out of a discussion from my liaison with the Sikh community that we came up with a new idea to provide support for minority ethnic victims of crime. We employed a minority ethnic person, a female, to support and develop relations in an area where certain members of some communities felt uneasy when dealing with male officers. She worked with the Falkirk branch of Victim Support and, by the time I retired, it had grown into a very positive development.

We, Central Scotland Police, were to launch our Diversity Strategy at a local hotel. My diversity Sergeant and I worked tirelessly on the detail for the day. We had managed to get Gurbux Singh – Chairman of the Commission for Racial Equality at that time – to attend at the official launch. That was a real coup for us. Again, it had us on the map. The only police service in the country to get it right first time, and the only service in the country to have Mr Singh to our event. It did involve negotiation with his staff and, in the end, we agreed the following. He required to be picked up from his train in Edinburgh and taken back to Waverley Station to catch his train after our event. He was speaking at a dinner in Newcastle that evening and must not miss his train. He also insisted on a quiet sit-down lunch with a few local dignitaries. He would not attend a buffet. The reason given was that a buffet kept him on his feet, meeting and greeting, and as he would have left home very early that morning to travel a seated lunch was preferable. That was exactly what we planned for. Guests at lunch would be the Chief Constable, the three Council Chief Executives, the Health Board Chief Executive, The Chair of the local Racial Equality Group, as well as the local MP and MSP. Probably not as chilled as he would have wanted, but there were some local politics to milk. Two days before the actual big day, I was alerted by the Chief Constable's secretary – I had been in the same class at school as her – that he was having a meeting with two Superintendents and it was about arrangements for the Diversity launch. I had not been invited. So what would you do? I gatecrashed the meeting, to be told I was not invited. I sat down anyway. They continued with their counter arrangements. They had not once asked me anything about the 'actual' arrangements. I had briefed the Chief Constable, but it appeared he wished for an alternative. The new arrangements involved an 'Indian Buffet'. One of the Superintendents had connections in the Indian community, and he had arranged they bring a buffet to the hotel. I stopped the conversation to announce that there will be no buffet, Indian or otherwise. I suggested there might be a modicum of institutional racism involved in thinking the Chairman of the Commission for Racial Equality, a Sikh, would somehow only prefer Indian food. In any case, there were two main flaws in the plan. Mr Singh did not want a buffet. We had already arranged a sit-down lunch with the people I mentioned. And lastly, did they check with the hotel to see if they are in agreement about us bringing an outside caterer into their dining room? Bearing in mind that we have already booked the meal. I was then asked to leave the meeting. There was no buffet.

The day went very well, and Mr Singh made all his train connections. As the event was breaking up, our local MSP and our MP came over and spoke to me. I saw the Chief Constable staring at me. When they left, he called me over and told me not to speak to them. He was the Chief Constable; that was his job. During these days, he stopped me in the corridor to ask how the Diversity Strategy was coming along. I said that it was doing fine, and was in the process of giving him an update when he stopped me in my tracks and said: 'Good, as long as my back is covered'.

That incident probably will give a clue as to my standing with some of the headquarters hierarchy. Not too positive. I kept believing and telling myself that I was not in the police service to please – or displease, for that matter – such people. It was all about communities. Another incident provides additional evidence of my status. I have mentioned representing the Chief Constable at national Association of Chief Police Officers, Scotland (ACPOS) meetings. That is the forum for Chief Constables. At one such meeting, an agreement was reached to set up an all-force working party to develop a particular issue. The issue would affect all forces, hence the requirement that they all be represented. On my return I prepared a report about the issue, and the decision that Central Scotland Police should be represented. The issue was not my area of work, so the Chief Constable would have to get a suitable officer to attend. My report had to go via a Superintendent to the Chief Constable for action at his Force Strategy Group. My report came back with the ubiquitous red-penned 'NO' written across it. I queried that with the Superintendent, who was clear: the Chief Constable is not sending an officer. I informed the secretariat of ACPOS of the decision. A response told me that this was not an option. I carried that forward, and again was rebuffed. By chance – about that same time – Central Scotland Police recruited a new Assistant Chief Constable. She attended the next ACPOS meeting, and when the item on the agenda was the issue I had highlighted she resolved to sort it. How did she go about that? By blaming me for not bothering to get an officer for the working group. The Superintendent, on being asked, said I had not made it clear. My report was crystal clear. Whatever else that little episode shows, you can be sure of one thing: it evidences a top floor management that pays scant regard for the truth when protecting themselves is on the agenda. In these circumstances, throwing a Chief Inspector to the wolves is reasonable in their eyes. People of honour? I have my doubts.

# CHAPTER 30

WE continued to work in the drug education and awareness-raising area, and received a lot of positive feedback. It did not mean I was totally satisfied, but one can only do so much. I had mentioned some drug development ideas that came out of my time in Bo'ness. That experience, which I kept to the forefront of my thinking, eventually came to fruition after the General Manager of the Forth Valley Health Board recognised the problem and found a budget. I was involved with a doctor from the Health Board and a Director of a Stirling Council service to design a new service. That was Signpost Forth Valley. It is now Signpost Recovery, and a well-respected service in the Forth Valley area.

Our work with youth was also being developed, and I will cover only two developments. One involved a computer-based early warning system that highlighted certain activities, to age and to frequency. If a young person got hits on all three criteria, his or her name was flagged as being at risk and brought to the fore for joint work to address the behaviour. It was successful at that time. I have no idea if it survived the transition to Police Scotland. Then we got a grant from the Scottish Office Youth Crime budget and had twenty area officers trained in Restorative Practices. It was a week-long course and was well received by the officers, who agreed it opened their mind to a new way of thinking about criminal activity and speaking to young people. I then set up, with the Reporter to the Children's Panel, a new type of police warning arrangement for low-tariff criminal activity involving juvenile perpetrators. There used to be an option called a senior police officer's warning; however, because one Reporter to the Children's Panel had actually seen it in action, it was dropped as not being a positive way to deal with young offenders. To quote that Reporter: 'I could have shouted at them just like he did'. With officers now trained in Restorative Practices, it was felt that the option could be re-introduced with more confidence. It was, and continued to be an option for the Reporter to the Children's Panel – certainly up until the day I resigned.

I can only think that despite the difficulties, we were showing some signs of life as some memories seemed to be stirring at Scottish Government level. I was asked to write the Scottish Police Service Strategy on our approach to Youth Justice issues. After liaison with the Scottish Office, Young Scot, The Chief Executive of Stirling Council and some local organisations – including one of the Reporters to the Children's Panel, as well as my own Sergeants – I produced the first draft strategy. It had an overall vision, supported by four main pillars. One pillar concentrated on the police crime detection route. It was a strategic document, and therefore left the particular police options open to their own local needs and requirements. While it was received well in many areas, it was slaughtered by the police as being – to quote one source – 'lacking in deterrent and weak'. I explained that it was strategic, and left room for the police to mould their own actions and outcomes. It was not the place of the strategy to dictate weak or strong tactics: it was a strategic document. It fell on deaf ears, and was taken from me and re-written. I did get calls from some of the other partners who were unhappy with that outcome. I had left the police before the final document emerged.

My new team of Sergeants were working hard, and really relishing the challenge. We were not setting any heather fires, but we were addressing some issues and making progress. Without a really senior officer, backed by the Chief Constable to drive the agenda, it was always going to be a slow road. However, despite that, we at least had a road and were travelling.

It was during that final phase of my service I attended a week-long conference at the National Policing Improvement Agency at Bramshill, Hampshire. Two announcements from the stage made me sit up and take notice. An Assistant Chief Constable and a senior civil servant from the Home Office announced that budgets were to be made available to encourage work with young people to reduce crime. They said we, the police service, had been aiming at the wrong age group – teenagers – where it was too late in their development to make much difference. The new money and activity would be towards a lower age, under ten years of age down to eight years of age. I was in despair. I asked if they had considered the pre-school programmes being positively reported on from the USA. No, was the answer – we will be doing what we announced; these schemes are expensive. I agree with that comment; at the front end they are intensive and expensive. However, that is paid back in spades. I have to conclude now, as I did then, that with a politician having a five year span between elections, the success has to be achieved within that span. Long-term sustainability, even if it is proved to be successful, is not even in their agenda. One has to conclude –

harshly, some may argue – that many of our politicians are career politicians and surviving from election to election is their main aim. Long-term solutions that may benefit the communities they serve comes second.

The second announcement I found more shocking. Again, a very senior police officer and a civil servant came on stage to announce that after an extensive activity analysis in one of the big police services in the south – not the Metropolitan Police – they had made an interesting discovery. Slightly more than a third of a front line police officer's time is spent 'simply' patrolling. That, they concluded, was a waste of public money. We do not train officers to the level we do and pay them what we do for them to spend as much time patrolling. We must find ways to get the patrolling element carried out by other agencies and cheaper. The police officer can then be freed up to get on with investigating and the other things they are trained to do. There was more said. However, I and others just looked at each other. Had they any idea what policing is about? It is a complete package, and patrolling – for a lot of reasons – is a crucial element in that package of service delivery. What do we do in a single station in a rural area? Who patrols that? That announcement has gone on to take shape over the years and has, certainly in some areas, seen a decline in service and an ever-growing gap between the public and police officers. One has to assume it is all about money. Be honest and tell us the true financial situation; do not avoid the issue by introducing unsustainable processes that damage police credibility and diminish the service where it is most needed, coupled to laughable performance indicator figures.

* * *

It was early in 2004, and my thirty years under the black and white checks – and, for a time, the dazzling Bath Stars – was fast approaching. 'Who knows where the time goes?' as Sandy Denny once sung. Well, I heartily agree. Where exactly had it gone? I had intended staying on until my sixtieth birthday – until fate intervened, that is. I applied for a promoted post. Yes, you would think I should have known by then. I was quite well qualified for the role, and honestly thought my application might reach the 'hmm, worth a second look' pile. What I was not prepared for was what actually happened.

The first contact asked why I had submitted the application. 'I am not going to support you. Anyway, why did you send it to me?' Not sounding too positive, I thought. Next day I was summoned to a Chief Superintendent, who was not quite so unsure. I am not supporting you. On asking why, he told me I was not strategic. I reminded him that I wrote the Forces Drug Strategy and their Diversity Strategy, not to mention the nationally and internationally-recognised Community Safety Strategy, and – to finish – the National Youth Strategy, as well as the Design Out Crime Strategy. He was not impressed, and reiterated his refusal to consider my application. I was wasting my time. To finish, I asked that he put his refusal in writing as he was obliged to. He refused. This was going nowhere, and he said he had no more to say. However, he did ask if I had anything I wanted to add. I was at the end of my tether, and I told him he was a fucking idiot. My service was effectively over at that point. I left his room.

I reported for work the next day and was working on an important report in support of one of my new Sergeants when the Assistant Chief Constable came into my office. It was not the most positive visit. After that brief meeting I finished the report I was writing, packed my briefcase, and headed to see my General Practitioner. He signed me off work for two full weeks. Stress-related. That was a Friday. I called at the office on the Monday to hand in my Sickness Certificate. The Superintendent who had not supported my application asked if he could borrow my office for a few days – no longer than the coming weekend, he said. Seems the new Press Officer needed a place for a few days. A full two weeks later, I revisited my General Practitioner. He said it would adversely affect my health if I were to return too quickly, and issued me a certificate for seven full weeks. That would give me time to take stock and consider my future. It also coincided with the completion of my thirty years of police service.

I went in on the Sunday to hand in the certificate and to take some things from my office. I need not have bothered; there were none of my belongings in my office. On the corridor floor lay a pile of black plastic bags. My possessions. The lock on the office door had been changed, and my name replaced with someone else's. I was quite emotional; it had all come down to this. There was not a soul about to witness the ending of a career. So it really was over. I sadly removed the black bags, containing uniforms and my other belongings, and carried them out to my car. A few trips, in silence. They had made one error; something that I took to a lawyer. He advised me to move on. I took his advice. The error? I kept a float of about five pounds in loose change in one of my desk drawers – coffee money, no more. It was not in my possessions, and I never saw it again.

One cannot beat the system. A system is nebulous. It does not have spine or a heart; it is an all-enveloping, creeping, faceless thing. Your only real choice is to be true to yourself.

I soon tendered my resignation and it was accepted. I never went back into the building. To be honest, I could not;

it was too sore, too raw. The seven weeks soon passed, and it really was over. I felt the loss. I think part of that loss was that my own officers did not think I was worthy of a farewell. I had lived and worked through a particular phase of the Scottish Police Service. I had posed a question at the beginning, if only to myself, about whether I was joining a service or a force. I was clear it was a service. I am not so clear now. While I have to agree that any officer through police history could claim to have lived through a particular phase and witnessed change, I am not so sure if it would have been quite so dramatic as the last forty years or so. The significant change I worked through – and in some small way, helped happen – was a definite move to partnership working and involving communities. I say that in the knowledge that, like most change, it was not taken seriously by many and resisted by some. However, as King Cnut discovered, the turning tide was relentlessly moving and change was unstoppable. The partnerships grew and we saw – amongst others – the emergence of joint police, social work child protection and investigation teams, racist attacks and harassment joint strategies, drug and alcohol partnerships, and more. Yes, the face of the service has changed dramatically over the years of my service, and it was good to be part of that.

In terms of my own understanding of my service, I have no regrets. I loved every bit of it, from working on my own in the single officer beat of Fearn in Ross-shire through to the hard shifts in Tullibody, to running my own Command and all the other bits. I worked with so many decent honest men and women who would do anything for you, including risking their life. In my book you will detect a fair amount of what some of my senior officers called 'belligerence' on my part. In fact, on reading it you may agree. I will be unhappy if that is your judgement, however. In every case I have recounted, I have supported my stance with reasoning and evidence. I can offer no more. There were a few instances when I was bullied. Let me put these headings into some perspective. The bullying was a miniscule, hardly measurable part of my thirty years of service. In terms of belligerence, I dispute that. I prefer the heading 'contrary'. Belligerence implies aggressive behaviour. That was not my style. I was sometimes challenging. If I can quote Dr Israel Shahak: 'Only an open conflict of ideas and principles can produce any clarity. Conflict may be painful, but the painless solution does not exist, in any case the pursuit of it leads to the painful outcome of mindlessness and point-lessness, the apotheosis of the ostrich'. I am clear in my own mind that there are situations when it not only reasonable to ask the 'why' question; it is imperative. One may then suggest that if I were contrary, then perhaps I was a dissident. I reject that on the grounds that such a title has to be earned and comes with an element of risk. Was I a maverick, or perhaps radical? Perhaps, in some ways, I was both. However, I will stick with contrarian. To me, that implies reasoned counter argument and, whilst conducted within the civilised realm of a police service, it did come with a level of risk – if not to the person, certainly to one's career prospects. It was sometimes a lonely and a hard road. I will finish my discourse on my per-sonality within the police service with these words from Christopher Hitchens: 'For the dissenter, the sceptical mental-ity is at least as important as any armour of principle'.

The titles 'contrarian' or 'dissident', however, pale into insignificance when one considers my question at the start. 'Was I a fit and proper person to hold a dying young man?' Because if I was not, it was all for nothing.

My dad had been correct all along. I was not hard enough. To be really hard, one must have no conscience; one must not care. I had both, and that made me vulnerable. It is the Achilles heel of all honourable folk. That is what he meant; he knew me, and I had misunderstood him all these years.

# Illustrations

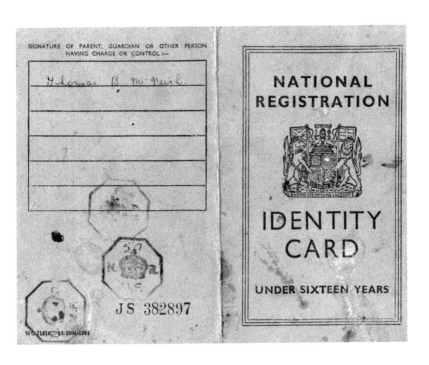

The author's post-War Identity Card

(Image from author's personal collection)

The author's mother and father:
Catherine O'Hara or McNeish (died 1973 –
51 years) and Thomas Barbour McNeish (died
1974 – 54 years).

(Image from author's personal collection)

An X craft submarine on the Forth and Clyde
Canal in the early 1950s.

View of the 'steamy' (near lower-right), outside
house in Balloch, circa 1956.

(Image from author's personal collection.)

The author as a teenager in the early 1960s.

(Image from author's personal collection.)

John McNeish
Structural
Department

The author's pass image for his first job
at Carron Ironworks, 1961.

A Scottish pillar box door, innocent of the
EIIR insignia.

The author's Constable's warrant card
Photograph for Ross and Sutherland
Constabulary, 1974.

(Image from author's personal collection.)

First family police house (the closest cottage)
near Muir of Ord, in 1974.

(Image from author's personal collection.)

The *Hermes* and *Highland Queen*,
accommodation ships at Nigg Yard in 1974.

Oil rig jacket BP1 being towed from Highland
Fabricators yard at Nigg to Fortes Field in 1974.

Police House and office (extension) at Fearn,
taken by the author some years later when it
was a private dwelling.

(Image from author's personal collection.)

Northern Constabulary Officers and British
Army personnel setting out in search for
Renee MacRae and her three year old son
Andrew in 1976.

A 'Green Goddess', the Bedford RLHZ Self-
Propelled Pump used during the fire-fighters'
strike of 1977 by the British Armed Forces.

The rescue of a young boy following his bad fall
in an Ochils gorge.

The author, while a Sergeant at Bo'ness in 1987, in a PR picture prior to setting out on charity mountaineering event.

Launch of Zero Tolerance Campaign in the early
1990s, involving Central Regional, Falkirk,
Clackmannanshire and Stirling Councils,
in partnership with Central Scotland Police,
Rape Crisis, Women's Aid, Victims Support,
and other partners.

A collection of documents publicising
Community Safety, produced while the author
was seconded to Central Regional Council,
circa 1996.

(Image from author's personal collection.)

Det. Insp. McNeish & The Team (Dunblane.)

Thank you all Very Much for
What you are doing!
We appreciate your Work & Support
for the Public.

May '96,

The words on a card sent to the author during police work in the aftermath of the Dunblane tragedy in 1996.

(Image from author's personal collection.)

A PR photograph showing alcohol confiscated
from under-age young adults.

The Search and Rescue Dogs Association
at Bo'ness to assist with a vulnerable missing
person search in the late 1990s.

(Image from author's personal collection.)

An ambiguous sketch, used by author as part of
lecture to partnership groups in order to
illustrate that not everyone sees the same thing,
and therefore that partners might not be
addressing the same problem.

(Image from author's personal collection.)

The author with Lieutenant Craig Watson of
the City of Sandy Police Department in Utah,
who is pictured trying out a Scottish police
truncheon for the first time.

A mishap with a Microlight aircraft
near Blackness, circa 1998.

(Image from author's personal collection.)

The author on his last duty as Inspector, leading Bo'ness Children's Fair Parade as Local Unit Commander in June 2000 and enjoying every minute of it.

The author in June 2000 on promotion to the
rank of Chief Inspector.

(Image from author's personal collection.)

# Acknowledgements

'By the time I was acutely conscious of the gap
between law and justice, I knew the letter of the
law was not as important as who held the power in
any real life situation.'
**Howard Zinn**

There are several people without whom this book would never have seen the light of day. I take this opportunity to thank them. If my failing memory has omitted anyone, forgive me and I will try to make it up to you one day.

Anne, for her patience;

Allan Meek and David Conner, for their knowledge of police history and snippets of interest;

Wendy Morrison and Cliff Wedgbury, for being brave enough to read sections and comment;

Angus Mackay, George Mackay, Donnie Beaton, Henry MacMillan and Hugh Mackay, for their collective understanding of policing and communities and for trusting me enough to let me into that rich seam of knowledge;

John Bellshaw, for sticking with me through our early policing years;

Bill Shannon, for his insights to Highland Fabricators;

Frances Watson, for making me believe;

Gordon Addison and Keith Yates, for support with my thought process at sections of the book;

Brian Watters, for guidance at the start;

Andrew Young, Chairman of the Letter Box Study Group;

John McLean and John Anderson, two retired coal miners and decent men, who gave of their time to speak about their experiences as striking miners;

Doctor Allister McNeish, for being my brother;

Lest I forget, the staff of the Burgh Coffee House in Stirling for allowing me to spend endless hours with one cup of coffee,

And to all the people in all the communities I served; thank you for making my service special and a pleasure. I hope I did not let too many of you down.

Thank you.

# About the Author

Ian McNeish was born in 1946, in Falkirk. That not only made him a Bairn, but also a Bulge Baby. His formative years in the post-War period were spent in Bonnybridge then Balloch. His early employment was with Carron Ironworks in Falkirk and then Ferranti Limited in Edinburgh, before heading south for a time to Cosser Electronics where he worked as an Organisation and Methods Officer in the electronic manufacturing sector. He then came back home to a job with Aberdeenshire County Council where, in addition to examining work methods and producing detailed project management reports, he also liaised with staff, unions and management.

In 1974 Ian joined Ross and Sutherland Constabulary, and in seven months was trusted to police in a single station officer role within a rural area of Scotland with a population of six thousand people. In 1978 Ian transferred to Central Scotland Police where he rose to the rank of Chief Inspector, before retiring in 2004.

In the police service Ian gained a Higher National Certificate in police studies, as well as a certificate on Strategic Investigation and a certificate on Structured Debriefing. He is a trained Emergencies Planning officer and successfully completed his Strategic Chief Inspector's course at the Scottish Police College. He trained at the Home Office Crime Prevention Centre, and gained certificates in Crime Prevention and Community Safety as well as Architectural Liaison and Designing Out Crime.

In 1992 Ian was seconded to work within the Policy Unit of Central Regional Council to develop a strategy on community safety, the first officer to take on that role within a Regional Council in Scotland. The strategy, entitled 'Switched on to Safety', was successful and recognised by the Secretary of State for Scotland's Advisory Group on Sustainable Development. It was highlighted in the white paper 'This Common Inheritance, 1996'. The strategy was further recognised by the UK National Council for the United Nations Conference on Human Settlements as one of the top Best Practice examples in the UK and presented at the Habitat ll, United Nations City Summit Conference in Istanbul in June 1996.

On returning to the force, Ian continued his career in Falkirk and then as Local Unit Commander based in Bo'ness. He was promoted to Officer in Charge of Community Safety at Police Headquarters, and took charge of the force's Safety in Communities strategy with particular responsibility for Youth Crime, Safety in Communities, Diversity, Drug Education and liaison with partner agencies, Victims of Crime, and general Crime Prevention issues.

In that role, Ian acted as senior police advisor to the Scottish Office Environment Department when they put together and published their Planning Advice Note 46, entitled 'Planning For Crime Prevention'. He was also responsible for planning and writing the booklet on women's safety entitled *Talking Sense/Seeing Sense*, and advising the Scottish Office on production of the video of the same name. 300,000 copies of the booklet were printed, as well as scores of the video, for use throughout Scotland.

On leaving the police service, Ian set up his own company advising small businesses on policy issues as well as carrying out investigations on employment disputes and preparing reports. Ian has also chaired several internal discipline hearings and produced written judgements. He also was Chairman of the board of Signpost Recovery, and for about eighteen months managed the project.

As a consequence of the foregoing he has amassed a wealth of experience carrying out investigations and producing reports for the criminal justice system and the internal police discipline system, as well as strategic reports and latterly reports and judgements of disputes in the employment arena. Ian has also carried several indepth investigations involving employment disputes and reported his findings to an employment lawyer.

His spare time is taken up with mountaineering, for a time being in Mountain Rescue. He has found time to ascend Mont Blanc and climb all the Munros. He also cycles and has some long distance treks to his name, including cycling from Edinburgh to Paris. He plays competitive curling and also coaches beginners. He did play golf, but cut back on that as he could not spare the time. He has a family: three boys and six grandchildren. When he is not employed with any or all of the above, he writes.

# An Innocent Abroad

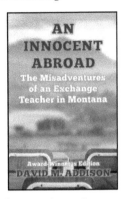

## The Misadventures of an Exchange Teacher in Montana

### By David M. Addison

When, in 1978, taking a bold step into the unknown, the author, accompanied by his wife and young family, swapped his boring existence in Grangemouth in central Scotland for life in Missoula, Montana, in the western United States, he could never have foreseen just how much of a life-changing experience it would turn out to be.

As an exchange teacher, he was prepared for a less formal atmosphere in the classroom, while, for their part, his students had been warned that he would be "Mr Strict". It was not long before this clash of cultures reared its ugly head and the author found life far more "exciting" than he had bargained for. Within a matter of days of taking up his post, he found himself harangued in public by an irate parent, while another reported him to the principal for "corrupting" young minds.

Outwith the classroom, he found daily life just as shocking. Lulled by a common language into a false sense of a "lack of foreignness", he was totally unprepared for the series of culture shocks that awaited him from the moment he stepped into his home for the year – the house from *Psycho*.

There were times when he wished he had stayed at home in his boring but safe existence in Scotland, but mainly this is a heart-warming and humorous tale of how this Innocent abroad, reeling from one surprising event to the next, gradually begins to adapt to his new life. And thanks to a whole array of colourful personalities and kind people (hostile parents not withstanding), he finally comes to realise that this exchange was the best thing he had ever done.

Also Available from Extremis Publishing

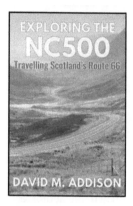

# Exploring the NC500

## Travelling Scotland's Route 66

### By David M. Addison

Travelling anti-clockwise, David M. Addison seeks his kicks on Scotland's equivalent of Route 66. Otherwise known as NC500, the route takes you through five hundred miles of some of Scotland's most spectacular scenery. No wonder it has been voted as one of the world's five most scenic road journeys.

There are many ways of exploring the NC500. You can drive it, cycle it, motorbike it or even walk it, even if you are not one of The Proclaimers! And there are as many activities, places of interest and sights to be seen along the way as there are miles.

This is a personal account of the author's exploration of the NC500 as well as some detours from it, such as to the Black Isle, Strathpeffer and Dingwall. Whatever your reason or reasons for exploring the NC500 may be, you should read this book before you go, or take it with you as a *vade mecum*. It will enhance your appreciation of the NC500 as you learn about the history behind the turbulent past of the many castles; hear folk tales, myths and legends connected with the area; become acquainted with the ancient peoples who once lived in this timeless landscape, and read about the lives of more recent heroes such as the good Hugh Miller who met a tragic end and villains such as the notorious Duke of Sutherland, who died in his bed (and may not be quite as bad as he is painted). There are a good number of other characters too of whom you may have never heard: some colourful, some eccentric, some *very* eccentric.

You may not necessarily wish to follow in the author's footsteps in all that he did, but if you read this book you will certainly see the landscape through more informed eyes as you do whatever you want to do *en route* NC500.

Sit in your car and enjoy the scenery for its own sake (and remember you get a different perspective from a different direction, so you may want to come back and do it again to get an alternative point of view!), or get out and explore it at closer quarters – the choice is yours, but this book will complement your experience, whatever you decide.

# Planes on Film
## Ten Favourite Aviation Films

### By Colin M. Barron

One of the most durable genres in cinema, the aviation film has captivated audiences for decades with tales of heroism, bravery and overcoming seemingly insurmountable odds. Some of these movies have become national icons, achieving critical and commercial success when first released in cinemas and still attracting new audiences today.

In *Planes on Film: Ten Favourite Aviation Films*, Colin M. Barron reveals many little-known facts about the making of several aviation epics. Every movie is discussed in comprehensive detail, including a thorough analysis of the action and a complete listing of all the aircraft involved. With information about where the various planes were obtained from and their current location, the book also explores the subject of aviation films which were proposed but ultimately never saw the light of day.

With illustrations and meticulous factual commentary, *Planes on Film* is a book which will appeal to aviation enthusiasts, military historians and anyone who has an interest in cinema. Written by an author with a lifelong passion for aircraft and their depiction on the silver screen, *Planes on Film* presents a lively and thought-provoking discourse on a carefully-chosen selection of movies which have been drawn from right across the history of this fascinating cinematic genre.

# Battles on Screen
## World War II Action Movies

### By Colin M. Barron

The Second World War was one of the defining historical events of the Twentieth Century. This global conflict was responsible for enormous trials and great heroism, and the horrors and gallantry that it inspired has formed the basis of some of the most striking movies ever committed to celluloid.

From the author of *Planes on Film*, *Battles on Screen* offers both an analysis and celebration of cinema's engagement with World War II, discussing the actors, the locations, the vehicles and the production teams responsible for bringing these epics to life. Reaching across the decades, the impact and effectiveness of many classic war films are examined in detail, complete with full listings of their cast and crew.

Ranging from the real–life figures and historical events which lay behind many of these features to the behind-the-scenes challenges which confronted the film crews at the time of their production, *Battles on Screen* contains facts, statistics and critical commentary to satisfy even the most stalwart fan of the war movie genre.

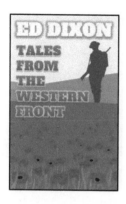

# Tales from the Western Front

### By Ed Dixon

Tales from the Western Front is a collection of stories about the people and places encountered by the author during more than three decades of visiting the battlefields, graveyards, towns and villages of France and Belgium.

Characters tragic and comic, famous and humble live within these pages, each connected by the common thread of the Great War. Meet Harry Lauder, the great Scottish entertainer and first international superstar; Tommy Armour, golf champion and war hero; "Hoodoo" Kinross, VC, the Pride of Lougheed; the Winslow Boy; Albert Ball, and Jackie the Soldier Baboon among many others.

Each chapter is a story in itself and fully illustrated with photos past and present.

For details of new and forthcoming books
from Extremis Publishing,
please visit our official website at:

# www.extremispublishing.com

or follow us on social media at:

www.facebook.com/extremispublishing

www.linkedin.com/company/extremis-publishing-ltd-/